Walking with God
through
Pain and Suffering

REDEEMER

TIMOTHY KELLER

Walking with God through Pain and Suffering

DUTTON

DUTTON

Published by the Penguin Group
Penguin Group (USA) LLC
375 Hudson Street
New York, New York 10014

USA | Canada | UK | Ireland | Australia | New Zealand | India | South Africa | China
penguin.com
A Penguin Random House Company

 REGISTERED TRADEMARK—MARCA REGISTRADA

LIBRARY OF CONGRESS CATALOGING-IN-PUBLICATION DATA
has been applied for.

ISBN 978-0-525-95245-9

Printed in the United States of America
1   3   5   7   9   10   8   6   4   2

Set in ITC Galliard Std
Designed by Leonard Telesca

While the author has made every effort to provide accurate telephone numbers, Internet addresses, and other
contact information at the time of publication, neither the publisher nor the author assumes any responsibility
for errors or for changes that occur after publication. Further, the publisher does not have any control over
and does not assume any responsibility for author or third-party websites or their content.

To my sister Sharon Johnson,
one of the most patient and joyful people I know,
who has taught me much about bearing burdens,
facing grief, and trusting God.

Contents

Contents

Introduction

The Rumble of Panic beneath Everything

I think that taking life seriously means something like this: that whatever man does on this planet has to be done in the lived truth of the terror of creation . . . of the rumble of panic underneath everything. Otherwise it is false.

—Ernest Becker, *The Denial of Death*[1]

I will bless the LORD at all times; his praise shall continually be in my mouth. My soul makes its boast in the LORD; let the afflicted hear and be glad. O magnify the LORD with me, and let us exalt his name together! (Psalm 34:1–3)[2]

Suffering is everywhere, unavoidable, and its scope often overwhelms. If you spend one hour reading this book, more than five children throughout the world will have died from abuse and violence during that time.[3] If you give the entire day to reading, more than one hundred children will have died violently. But this is, of course, only one of innumerable forms and modes of suffering. Thousands die from traffic accidents or cancer every hour, and hundreds of thousands learn that their loved ones are suddenly gone. That is comparable to the population of a small city being swept away every day, leaving families and friends devastated in the wake.

When enormous numbers of deaths happen in one massive event—such as the 1970 Bhola cyclone in Bangladesh, the 2004 Indian Ocean tsunami, or the 2010 Haiti earthquake—each of which killed 300,000 or more at once—it makes headlines around the world and everyone reels from the devastation. But statistics are misleading. Such historic disasters do not really change the suffering rate. Tens of thousands of people die every day in unexpected tragedies, and hundreds of thousands around them are crushed by grief and shock. The majority of them trigger no headlines because pain and misery is the norm in this world.

Shakespeare understood this when he wrote:

> Each new morn
> New widows howl, new orphans cry,
> New sorrows strike heaven on the face.[4]

Evil and suffering are so pervasive that the statistics I just recounted hardly make us blink. Yet we must blink. Author Ernest Becker spoke about the danger of denying the misery of life and the randomness of suffering. When we hear of a tragedy, there is a deep-seated psychological defense mechanism that goes to work. We think to ourselves that such things happen to other people, to poor people, or to people who do not take precautions. Or we tell ourselves that if only we get the right people into office and get our social systems right, nothing like this will happen again.

But Becker believed such thinking fails to "take life seriously" or to admit the "lived truth of the terror of creation . . . of the rumble of panic underneath everything."[5] That panic comes from death. Death is irreducibly unpredictable and inexorable.

The same message comes through in an article written in *The New York Times Magazine* during the time of the "Beltway Sniper," who was shooting people in the Washington, DC, area in what appeared to be a completely random way, without concern for race or age. Ann Patchett wrote:

> We are always looking to make some sort of sense out of murder in order to keep it safely at bay: I do not fit the description; I do not live in that town; I would never have gone to that place, known that person. But what happens when

there is no description, no place, nobody? Where do we go to find our peace of mind? . . .

The fact is, staving off our own death is one of our favorite national pastimes. Whether it's exercise, checking our cholesterol or having a mammogram, we are always hedging against mortality. Find out what the profile is, and identify the ways in which you do not fit it. But a sniper taking a single clean shot, not into a crowd but through the sight, reminds us horribly of death itself. Despite our best intentions, it is still, for the most part, random.

And it is absolutely coming.[6]

Patchett and Becker expose the common ways we seek to deny the rumble of panic. This book is an effort to do what they urge—to take life seriously. I want to help readers live life well and even joyfully against the background of these terrible realities. The loss of loved ones, debilitating and fatal illnesses, personal betrayals, financial reversals, and moral failures—all of these will eventually come upon you if you live out a normal life span. No one is immune.

Therefore, no matter what precautions we take, no matter how well we have put together a good life, no matter how hard we have worked to be healthy, wealthy, comfortable with friends and family, and successful with our career—something will inevitably ruin it. No amount of money, power, and planning can prevent bereavement, dire illness, relationship betrayal, financial disaster, or a host of other troubles from entering your life. Human life is fatally fragile and subject to forces beyond our power to manage. Life is tragic.

We all know this intuitively, and those who face the challenge of suffering and pain learn all too well that it is impossible to do so using only our own resources. We all need support if we are not to succumb to despair. In this book we will argue that inevitably this support must be spiritual.

"Let the Afflicted Hear and Be Glad"

On our wedding day, Kathy and I spoke our vows to each other in front of our friends and families. To the traditional words of commitment we added a passage of Scripture—Psalm 34:1–3—which is engraved on the inside of our wedding rings.

> I will bless the Lord at all times; his praise shall continually be in my mouth.
>
> My soul makes its boast in the Lord; let the afflicted hear and be glad.
>
> O magnify the Lord with me, and let us exalt his name together!

Saying our vows was a heady moment, and the lofty words of the text enhanced it. We were embarking on a lifetime of Christian ministry together, and we anticipated boldly presenting the God we knew to the world. At the time, however, we almost completely ignored the words at the center of the passage. The text's definition of ministry success is that "the afflicted hear and be glad." One of the reasons that phrase was lost on us then was because, as Kathy said later, "at that age neither of us had suffered so much as an ingrown toenail." We were young, and the hubris of youth does not imagine pain and suffering. Little did we understand how crucial it would be to help people understand and face affliction, and to face it well ourselves.

As I took up life as a minister, I tried to understand why so many people resisted and rejected God. I soon realized that perhaps the main reason was affliction and suffering. How could a good God, a just God, a loving God, allow such misery, depravity, pain, and anguish? Doubts in the mind can grow along with pain in the heart. When I sat with sufferers, I often found myself fielding white-hot objections to God's existence and to Christian faith. Some years ago, a Hollywood actress was interviewed after her lover had died suddenly in an accident. She had been living without thought or reference to God for a long time, but once this happened she said, "How could a loving God let this happen?" In an instant she went from indifference to God to anger toward him.[7] It is this kind of experience that has led a host of thinkers to argue, as the writer Stendhal (Marie-Henri Beyle) did, that "the only excuse for God is that he doesn't exist."[8]

But at the same time, I learned that just as many people *find* God through affliction and suffering. They find that adversity moves them toward God rather than away. Troubled times awaken them out of their haunted sleep of spiritual self-sufficiency into a serious search for the divine. Suffering "plants the flag of truth within the fortress of a rebel soul."[9] It is an exaggeration to say that no one finds God unless suffering comes into their lives—but it is not a big one. When pain and suffering come upon us, we finally see not only that we are not in control of our lives but that we never were.

Over the years, I also came to realize that adversity did not merely lead people to believe in God's existence. It pulled those who already believed into a deeper experience of God's reality, love, and grace. One of the main ways we move from abstract knowledge about God to a personal encounter with him as a living reality is through the furnace of affliction. As C. S. Lewis famously put it, "God whispers to us in our pleasures, speaks in our conscience, but shouts in our pain."[10] Believers understand many doctrinal truths in the mind, but those truths seldom make the journey down into the heart except through disappointment, failure, and loss. As a man who seemed about to lose both his career and his family once said to me, "I always knew, in principle, that 'Jesus is all you need' to get through. But you don't really know Jesus is all you need until Jesus is all you have."

Finally, as I grew in my understanding of the Bible itself, I came to see that the reality of suffering was one of its main themes. The book of Genesis begins with an account of how evil and death came into the world. The book of Exodus recounts Israel's forty years in the wilderness, a time of intense testing and trial. The wisdom literature of the Old Testament is largely dedicated to the problem of suffering. The book of Psalms provides a prayer for every possible situation in life, and so it is striking how filled it is with cries of pain and with blunt questions to

God about the seeming randomness and injustice of suffering. In Psalm 44, the writer looks at the devastation of his country and calls, "Awake, O Lord! Why do you sleep? . . . . Why do you hide your face and forget our misery and oppression?" (Ps 44:23–24) The books of Job and Ecclesiastes are almost wholly dedicated to deep reflection on unjust suffering and on the frustrating pointlessness that characterizes so much of life. The prophets Jeremiah and Habakkuk give searing expression to the human complaint that evil seems to rule history. New Testament books such as Hebrews and 1 Peter are almost entirely devoted to helping people face relentless sorrows and troubles. And towering over all, the central figure of the whole of Scripture, Jesus Christ, is a man of sorrows. The Bible, therefore, is about suffering as much as it is about anything.

Inevitably, Kathy and I found ourselves facing our own griefs. In 2002, I was diagnosed with thyroid cancer and went through surgery and treatment. Around the same time, Kathy's Crohn's disease became acute and she had to undergo numerous surgeries over the next few years, once enduring seven in one year. At one point, I found myself facing the agonizing possibility that I should leave the pastoral ministry because of my wife's chronic illness. It was the darkest time of our lives so far. And we know for certain, from Scripture and experience, that there are more dark times to come. And yet also more joy than we can now imagine.

Looking back on our lives, Kathy and I came to realize that at the heart of why people disbelieve *and* believe in God, of why people decline *and* grow in character, of how God becomes less real *and* more real to us—is suffering. And when we looked to the Bible to understand this deep pattern, we came to see that the great theme of the Bible itself is how God brings fullness of joy not just despite but *through* suffering, just as Jesus saved us not in spite of but *because* of what he endured on the cross. And so there is a peculiar, rich, and poignant joy that seems to come to us only through and in suffering.

What we have learned from these years of ministry to "the afflicted" is in this volume. Simone Weil writes that suffering makes God "appear to be absent." She is right. But in Psalm 34, David counters that though

God feels absent, it does not mean he actually is. Looking back at a time when his life had been in grave danger and all seemed lost, David concludes, "The Lord is close to the brokenhearted and saves those who are crushed in spirit" (v. 18).

I'm writing this book because we have found in our own lives that this is true.

The Fiery Furnace and the Plan for This Book

So is this a book for sufferers? Yes, but we must make some distinctions. We are all sufferers, or we will be. But not all of us are currently in an experience of deep pain and grief. Those who are not feeling it, but are seeing it in others, will have a host of philosophical, social, psychological, and moral questions about it. On the other hand, those who are in the grip of pain and difficulty *now* cannot treat it as a philosophical issue. Speaking to the questions of the nonsufferer as well as to the struggles of the sufferer in one book is a not a simple task. While the afflicted person may cry out using philosophical questions—"Why do you allow such things, God?"—the real concern is personal survival. How can you survive it? How can you get through it without losing the best parts of yourself? To speak in a detached philosophical manner to an actual sufferer is cruel. And yet the experience of pain leads almost inevitably to "big questions" about God and the nature of things that cannot be ignored.

As I read books on evil and suffering, it became clear that most volumes treated the subject mainly from just one perspective. Many books used the philosophical perspective, weighing the "problem of evil" and whether it made the existence of God more or less likely or Christianity more or less plausible. Others took a theological approach, distilling and assembling all the biblical themes and teachings about pain and suffering. Finally, many books took a devotional approach, writing a series of meditations designed to help actual sufferers in the midst of their grief. There was also a smaller number of articles and books that took both a historical and an anthropological approach, examining how different cultures have helped its members face troubles and trials. The more I read, the clearer it became that these various perspectives informed one another, and that any treatment that confined itself to only one vantage point left far too many unanswered questions.

And so I have divided the book into three parts, each part looking at the issue using somewhat different tools. What unites them is the central image of suffering as a fiery furnace. This biblical metaphor is a rich one. Fire is, of course, a well-known image for torment and pain. The Bible calls trials and troubles "walking through fire" (Isa 43:2) or a "fiery ordeal" (1 Pet 4:12). But it also likens suffering to a fiery *furnace* (1 Pet 1:6–7). The biblical understanding of a furnace is more what we would call a "forge." Anything with that degree of heat is, of course, a very dangerous and powerful thing. However, if used properly, it does not destroy. Things put into the furnace properly can be shaped, refined, purified, and even beautified. This is a remarkable view of suffering, that if faced and endured with faith, it can in the end only make us better, stronger, and more filled with greatness and joy. Suffering, then, actually can use evil against itself. It can thwart the destructive purposes of evil and bring light and life out of darkness and death.

In the first part of the book, we will look at the "furnace" from the outside—the phenomenon of human suffering, as well as the various ways that different cultures, religions, and eras in history have sought to help people face and get through it. We also will look at the classic philosophical "problem of evil" and what responses we can give to it. Because this first part of the book surveys a great deal of scholarship, it inevitably will be a more theoretical discussion. It is crucial for seeing the entire picture but, frankly, may feel too abstract for a person in the midst of adversity.

The second part of the book moves away from more theoretical issues and begins to digest all that the Bible says about the character of suffering. This section begins a journey from the philosophical toward the personal. We could almost say that, like a parent with a toddler, the Bible is teaching us to walk, step by step. The Bible calls us to walk steadily through afflictions, and to do so requires that we understand its wonderfully balanced and comprehensive teaching on this subject—

both profoundly realistic and yet astonishingly hopeful. This keeps us from thinking we can run from the furnace (avoid it) or quickly run through it (deny it) or just lie down hopelessly (despair in it).

Finally, the third part of the book provides the most practical material. The Bible does not perceive going through the "furnace of affliction" as a matter of technique. Suffering can refine us rather than destroy us because God himself walks with us in the fire. But how do we actually walk with God in such times? How do we orient ourselves toward him so that suffering changes us for the better rather than for the worse? Each chapter is based on one main strategy for connecting with God in the furnace of pain and suffering. They should not be read as discrete "steps" to be followed in strict order but as various facets or aspects of a single action—to know the God who says "when you pass through the waters . . . when you walk through the fire . . . I will be with you" (Isa 43:2).

If you are in the very midst of adversity, you may wish to read parts two and three of the book first. There you will find a surprising range of ways to face suffering, and they vary widely—at times almost seeming to contradict each other. Part of the genius of the Bible as a resource for sufferers is its rich, multidimensional approach. It recognizes a great diversity of forms, reasons for, and right responses to suffering. To show the many possible human responses to suffering, I have included at the end of many chapters a first-person story from someone who has encountered suffering and walked with God through it. These stories are both inspirational and realistic. The Bible does not promise that suffering will issue in full resolution or a "happy ending" in this life. But these stories show how people of faith have dealt with the varieties of suffering and walked through the furnace with God's help. These stories are a reminder to recognize God's presence even in the worst of times. Especially in the worst of times.

In perhaps the most vivid depiction of suffering in the Bible, in the third chapter of the book of Daniel, three faithful men are thrown into a furnace that is supposed to kill them. But a mysterious figure appears beside them. The astonished observers discern not three but four persons in the furnace, and one who appears to be "the son of the gods."

And so they walk through the furnace of suffering and are not consumed. From the vantage of the New Testament, Christians know that this was the Son of God himself, one who faced his own, infinitely greater furnace of affliction centuries later when he went to the cross. This raises the concept of God "walking with us" to a whole new level. In Jesus Christ we see that God actually experiences the pain of the fire as we do. He truly is God *with* us, in love and understanding, in our anguish.

He plunged himself into our furnace so that, when we find ourselves in the fire, we can turn to him and know we will not be consumed but will be made into people great and beautiful. "I will be with you, your troubles to bless, and sanctify to you your deepest distress."[11]

PART ONE

Understanding the Furnace

ONE

The Cultures of Suffering

"What's the point?" my father asked as he lay dying.

Training for Suffering

Suffering seems to destroy so many things that give life meaning that it may feel impossible to even go on. In the last weeks of his life, my father faced a great range of life-ending, painful illnesses all at once. He had congestive heart failure and three kinds of cancer, even as he was dealing with a gall bladder attack, emphysema, and acute sciatica. At one time he said to a friend, "What's the point?" He was too sick to do the things that made his life meaningful—so why go on? At my father's funeral, his friend related to us how he gently reminded my father of some basic themes in the Bible. If God had kept him in this world, then there were still some things for him to do for those around him. Jesus was patient under even greater suffering for us, so we can be patient under lesser suffering for him. And heaven will make amends for everything. These brief words, which were expressed in the most compassionate spirit, reconnected my father to Christian beliefs he had known for years. It restored his spirit to face his final days.

We will look at length at those Christian resources later, but at this point, it is necessary only to understand this: Nothing is more important than to learn how to maintain a life of purpose in the midst of painful adversity.

One of the main ways a culture serves its members is by helping them face terrible evil and adversity. Social theorist Max Scheler wrote: "An essential part of the teachings and directives of the great religious and philosophical thinkers the world over has been on *the meaning of pain and suffering.*" Scheler went on to argue that every society has chosen some version of these teachings so as to give its members "instructions . . . to encounter suffering correctly—to suffer properly (or to move suffering to another plane.)"[12] Sociologists and anthropologists have analyzed and compared the various ways that cultures train its members for grief, pain, and loss. And when this comparison is done, it is often noted that our own contemporary secular, Western culture is one of the weakest and worst in history at doing so.

All human beings are driven by "an inner compulsion to understand the world as a meaningful cosmos and to take a position toward it."[13] And that goes for suffering, too. Anthropologist Richard Shweder writes: "Human beings apparently want to be edified by their miseries."[14] Sociologist Peter Berger writes, every culture has provided an "explanation of human events that bestows meaning upon the experiences of suffering and evil."[15] Notice Berger did not say people are taught that suffering itself is good or meaningful. (This has been attempted at various times, but observers have rightly called those approaches forms of philosophical masochism.) What Berger means rather is that it is important for people to see how the *experience* of suffering does not have to be a waste, and could be a meaningful though painful way to live life well.

Because of this deep human "inner compulsion," every culture either must help its people face suffering or risk a loss of its credibility. When no explanation at all is given—when suffering is perceived as simply senseless, a complete waste, and inescapable—victims can develop a deep, undying anger and poisonous hate that was called *ressentiment* by Friedrich Nietzsche, Max Weber, and others.[16] This *ressentiment* can lead to serious social instability. And so, to use sociological language, every society must provide a "discourse" through which its people can make sense of suffering. That discourse includes some understanding of the causes of pain as well as the proper responses to it. And with that discourse, a society equips its people for the battles of living in this world.

However, not every society does this equally well. Our own contemporary Western society gives its members no explanation for suffering and very little guidance as to how to deal with it. Just days after the Newtown school shootings in December 2012, Maureen Dowd entitled her December 25 *New York Times* column "Why, God?" and printed a Catholic priest's response to the massacre.[17]

Almost immediately, there were hundreds of comments in response to the column's counsel. Most disagreed with it but, tellingly, disagreed in wildly divergent ways. Some held instead to the idea of karma, that suffering in the present pays for sins in past lives. Others referred to the illusory nature of the material world, which comes from Buddhism. Still others accepted the traditional Christian view that heaven is a place of reunion with loved ones and will serve as consolation for suffering on earth. Some alluded to how suffering makes you stronger, implicitly drawing on the thought of Stoic and pagan thinkers from the classical Greek and Roman era. Others added that since this world is all we have, any recourse to "spiritual" consolation weakens the proper response to suffering—namely, action toward eradicating the factors that caused it. The only proper response to suffering, in this view, was to make the world a better place.

The responses to the column were evidence that our own culture gives people almost no tools for dealing with tragedy. Commenters had to look to many other cultures and religions—Hindu, Buddhist, Confucianist, classical Greek, and Christian—to address the darkness of the moment. People were left to fend for themselves.

The end result is that today we are more shocked and undone by suffering than were our ancestors. In medieval Europe approximately one of every five infants died before their first birthday, and only half of all children survived to the age of ten.[18] The average family buried half of their children when they were still little, and the children died at home, not sheltered away from eyes and hearts. Life for our ancestors was filled with far more suffering than ours is. And yet we have innumerable diaries, journals, and historical documents that reveal how they took that hardship and grief in far better stride than do we. One scholar of ancient northern European history observed how unnerving it is for modern readers to see how much more unafraid people fifteen hundred years ago were in the face of loss, violence, suffering, and death.[19] Another said that while we are taken aback by the cruelty we see in our ancestors, they would, if they could see us, be equally shocked by our "softness, worldliness, and timidity."[20]

We are not just worse than past generations in this regard, but we are also weaker than are many people in other parts of the world today. Dr. Paul Brand, a pioneering orthopedic surgeon in the treatment of leprosy patients, spent the first part of his medical career in India and the last part of his career in the United States. He wrote: "In the United States . . . I encountered a society that seeks to avoid pain at all costs. Patients lived at a greater comfort level than any I had previously treated, but they seemed far less equipped to handle suffering and far more traumatized by it."[21] Why?

The short response is that other cultures have provided its members with various answers to the question "What is the purpose of human life?" Some cultures have said it is to live a good life and so eventually escape the cycle of karma and reincarnation and be liberated into eternal bliss. Some have said it is enlightenment—the recognition of the oneness of all things and the attainment of tranquility. Others have said it is to live a life of virtue, of nobility and honor. There are those who teach that the ultimate purpose in life is to go to heaven to be with your loved ones and with God forever. The crucial commonality is this: In every one of these worldviews, suffering can, despite its painfulness, be an important means of actually *achieving* your purpose in life. It can play a pivotal role in propelling you toward all the most important goals. One could say that in each of these other cultures' grand narratives—what human life is all about—suffering can be an important chapter or part of that story.

But modern Western culture is different. In the secular view, this material world is all there is. And so the meaning of life is to have the freedom to choose the life that makes you most happy. However, in that view of things, suffering can have no meaningful part. It is a complete interruption of your life story—it cannot be a meaningful part of the story. In this approach to life, suffering should be avoided at almost any cost, or minimized to the greatest degree possible. This means that when facing unavoidable and irreducible suffering, secular people must smuggle in resources from other views of life, having recourse to ideas of karma, or Buddhism, or Greek Stoicism, or Christianity, even though their beliefs about the nature of the universe do not line up with those resources.

It is this weakness of modern secularism—in comparison to other religions and cultures—that we explore in these first few chapters.

Edified by Our Miseries

Richard Shweder provides a good survey about how non-Western cultures today help their people to be "edified by misery." Traditional cultures perceive the causes of suffering in highly spiritual, communal, and moral terms. Here are four ways such societies have helped victims of suffering and evil respond.

There is what some anthropologists call (not pejoratively) the moralistic view. Some cultures have taught that pain and suffering stem from the failure of people to live rightly. There are many versions of this view. Many societies believe that if you honor the moral order and God or the gods, your life will go well. Bad circumstances are a "wake-up call" that you need to repent and change your ways. The doctrine of karma is perhaps the purest form of the moralistic view. It holds that every soul is reincarnated over and over. Into each life, the soul brings its past deeds and their latent effects, including suffering. If you are suffering now, it is likely your desserts from former lives. If you live now with decency, courage, and love—then your future lives will be better. In short, no one gets away with anything—everything must be paid for. Your soul is released into the divine bliss of eternity only when you have atoned for all your sins.

There is also what has been called the self-transcendent view.[22] Buddhism teaches that suffering comes not from past deeds but from unfulfilled desires, and those desires are the result of the illusion that we are individual selves. Like the ancient Greek Stoics, Buddha taught that the solution to suffering is the extinguishing of desire through a change of consciousness. We must detach our hearts from transitory, material things and persons. Buddhism's goal is "to achieve a calmness of the soul in which all desire, individuality, and suffering are dissolved."[23] Other cultures achieve this self-transcendence by being communal in a way almost impossible for contemporary Western people to comprehend. In such societies, there is no such thing as an identity or sense of well-being apart from the advancement and prosperity of one's family and people. In this worldview, suffering is mitigated because it can't harm the real "you." You live on in your children, in your people.[24]

Some societies address suffering with a high view of fate and destiny. Life circumstances are seen as set by the stars or by supernatural forces, or by the doom of the gods, or, as in Islam, simply by the inscrutable will of Allah. In this view, people of wisdom and character reconcile their souls with this reality. The older pagan cultures of northern Europe believed that at the end of time, the gods and heroes would all be killed by the giants and monsters in the tragic battle of Ragnarok. In those societies, it was considered the highest virtue to stand one's ground honorably in the face of hopeless odds. That was the most lasting glory possible, and through such behavior one lived on in song and legend. The greatest heroes of these cultures were strong and beautiful but sad, with high doom upon them. In Islam too, surrender to God's mysterious will without question has been one of the central requirements of righteousness. In all these cultures, submission to a difficult divine fate without compromise or complaint was the highest virtue and therefore a way to find great meaning in suffering.[25]

Finally, there are those cultures with a "dualistic" view of the world. These religions and societies do not see the world under the full control of fate or God but rather as a battleground between the forces of darkness and light. Injustice, sin, and pain are present in the world because of evil, satanic powers. Sufferers are seen as casualties in this war. Max Weber describes it like this: "The world process although full of inevitable suffering is a continuous purification of the light from the contamination of darkness." Weber adds that this conception "produces a very powerful . . . emotional dynamic."[26] Sufferers see themselves as victims in this battle with evil and are given hope because, they are told, good will eventually triumph. Some more explicit forms of dualism, like ancient Persian Zoroastrianism, believed a savior would come at the end of time to bring about a final renovation. Less explicit forms of dualism, such as some Marxist theories, also see a future time in which forces of good overcome evil.

At first glance, these four approaches seem to be at odds with one another. The self-transcendent cultures call sufferers to think differently, the moralistic cultures to live differently, the fatalistic cultures to embrace one's destiny nobly, and the dualistic cultures to put one's hope in the future. But they are also much alike. First, each one tells its members that suffering should not be a surprise—that it is a necessary part of the warp and woof of human existence. Second, sufferers are told that suffering can help them rise up and move toward the main purpose of life, whether it is spiritual growth, or the mastery of oneself, or the achievement of honor, or the promotion of the forces of good. And third, they are told that the key to rising and achieving in suffering is something they must take the responsibility to do. They must put themselves into a right relationship to spiritual reality.

So the communal culture tells sufferers to say, "I must die—but my children and children's children will live on forever."[27] Buddhist cultures direct its members to say, "I must die—but death is an illusion—I will still be as much a part of the universe as I am now." Karmic sufferers may say, "I must suffer and die—but if I do it well and nobly, I will have a better life in the future and can be freed from suffering someday altogether." But in every case, suffering poses a responsibility and presents an opportunity. You must not waste your sorrows. All of these ancient and diverse approaches, though they take suffering very seriously, see it as a way toward some greater good. As Rosalind's father, Duke Senior, says in Shakespeare's *As You Like It*:

> Sweet are the uses of adversity,
>   Which like the toad, ugly and venomous,
>   Wears yet a precious jewel in his head. (Act 2, Scene 1, 12–17)

These traditional cultures see life as inevitably filled with suffering, and their prescriptions to their members have to do mainly with *internal* work. They call for varied forms of confession and purification, of spiritual growth and strengthening, of faithfulness to the truth, and of the establishment of right relationships to self, others, and the divine. Suffering is a challenge which, if met rightly, can bring great good, wisdom, glory, and even sweetness into one's life now, and fit one well for eternal comfort hereafter. Sufferers are pointed to hope in a good future on earth, or eternal spiritual bliss and unity with the divine, or enlightenment and eternal peace, or the favor of God and unity with one's loved ones in paradise.

Here's a schematic of the various views:

	Moralistic	Self-transcendent	Fatalistic	Dualistic
Cause	Wrongdoing	Illusion	Destiny	Cosmic conflict
Response	Do good	Detachment	Endurance	Purified faithfulness
Resolution	Eternal bliss	Enlightenment	Glory and honor	Triumph of the light

Interrupted by Our Miseries

After surveying these other, more traditional cultures, Shweder points out that Western culture's approach to suffering stands very much apart. Western science sees the universe as "naturalistic." While other cultures see the world as consisting of both matter and spirit, Western thought understands it as consisting of material forces only, all of which operate devoid of anything that could be called "purpose." It is not the result of sin, or any cosmic battle, or any high forces determining our destinies. Western societies, therefore, see suffering as simply an accident. "[In this view] while suffering is real it is outside the domain of good and evil."[28] An unusually clear statement of the secular view of evil and suffering is made by Richard Dawkins in his book *River Out of Eden: A Darwinian View of Life*. He writes:

The total amount of suffering per year in the natural world is beyond all decent contemplation. . . . In a universe of blind physical forces and genetic replication, some people are going to get hurt, other people are going to get lucky, and you won't find any rhyme or reason in it, nor any justice. The universe that we observe has precisely the properties we should expect if there is, at bottom, no design, no purpose, no evil, no good, nothing but pitiless indifference.[29]

This is a complete departure from every other cultural view of suffering. Each one sees evil as having some purpose as a punishment, or a test, or an opportunity. But in Dawkins's view, the reason people struggle so mightily in the face of suffering is because they will not accept that it *never* has any purpose. It is senseless, neither bad nor good—because categories such as good and evil are meaningless in the universe we live in. "We humans have purpose on the brain," he argues. "Show us almost any object or process, and it is hard for us to resist the 'Why' question. . . . It is an almost universal delusion. . . . The old temptation comes back with a vengeance when tragedy strikes . . . 'Why oh why, did the cancer/earthquake/hurricane have to strike *my* child?'" But he argues that this agony happens because "we cannot admit that things might be neither good nor evil, neither cruel nor kind, but simply callous—indifferent to all suffering, lacking purpose. . . . As that unhappy poet A. E. Housman put it: 'For Nature, heartless, witless Nature, will neither care nor know.' DNA neither knows nor cares. DNA just is. And we dance to its music."[30]

In short, suffering does not mean anything at all. It is an evil hiccup. Dawkins insists that to deny that life is "empty, pointless, futile, a desert of meaninglessness and insignificance" is right, and to look to any spiritual resources to find purpose or meaning in the face of suffering is "infantile."[31]

Shweder counters, however, that exhortations like Dawkins's are both wrong and impossible to achieve. "The desire to make suffering intelligible," he writes, "is one of those *dignifying* peculiarities of our species. . . ."[32] That is, one of the things that distinguishes us from animals is that we do not simply squeal under suffering and seek to flee it. We search to find some point in the pain and thereby to transcend it, rather than seeing ourselves as helpless cogs in a cruel machine. And this drive to find meaning in suffering is not only dignifying, it is indelible. Peter Berger and the whole field of students of human culture insist that Dawkins is asking for the impossible. Without meaning, we die.

Of course, Dawkins goes on to say, "The truly adult view . . . is that our life is as meaningful, as full and wonderful as we choose to make it."[33] In other words, you must create your own meaning. *You* decide the kind of life that you find most valuable and worth living and then you must seek to create that kind of life.[34]

But any self-manufactured meaning must be found within the confines of this world and life. And that is where this view of reality and its understanding of suffering represent such a departure from all others. If you accept the strictly secular assumption that this is a solely materialistic universe, then that which gives your life purpose would have to be some material good or this-world condition—some kind of comfort, safety, and pleasure. But suffering inevitably blocks achievement of these kinds of life goods. Suffering either destroys them or puts them in deep jeopardy. As Dr. Paul Brand argues in the last chapter of his book *The Gift of Pain,* it is because the meaning of life in the United States is the pursuit of pleasure and personal freedom that suffering is so traumatic for Americans.

All other cultures make the highest purpose of life something besides individual happiness and comfort. It might be moral virtue, or enlightenment, or honor, or faithfulness to the truth. Life's ultimate meaning might be being an honorable person, or being someone whom your children and community look up to, or about furthering a great cause or movement, or of seeking heaven or enlightenment. In all these cultural narratives, suffering is an important way to come to a good end to the story. All of these "life meanings" can be achieved not only in spite of suffering but *through* it. In all these worldviews, then, suffering and evil do not have to triumph. If patiently, wisely, and heroically faced, suffering can actually accelerate the journey to our desired destination. It can be an important chapter in our life story and crucial stage in achieving what we most want in life. But in the strictly secular view, suffering cannot be a good chapter in your life story—only an interruption of it. It can't take you home; it can only keep you from the things you most want in life. In short, in the secular view, suffering always wins.

Shweder puts it this way. When it comes to suffering, the "reigning metaphor of this contemporary secular [view] is chance misfortune. The sufferer is a victim, under attack from natural forces devoid of intentionality." And that means that "suffering is . . . separated from the narrative structure of human life. . . . a kind of 'noise,' an accidental interference into the life drama of the sufferer. . . . Suffering has no intelligible relation to any plot, except as a chaotic interruption."[35] In older cultures (and non-Western cultures today) suffering has been seen as an expected part of a coherent life story, a crucial way to live life well and to grow as a person and a soul. But the meaning of life in our Western society is individual freedom. There is no higher good than the right and freedom to decide for yourself what *you* think is good. Cultural institutions are supposed to be neutral and "value free"—not telling people what to live for, but only ensuring the freedom of every person to live as he or she finds most satisfying and fulfilling. But if the meaning of life is individual freedom and happiness, then suffering is of no possible "use." In this worldview, the only thing to do with suffering is to avoid it at all costs, or, if it is unavoidable, manage and minimize the emotions of pain and discomfort as much as possible.

Victims of Our Miseries

One of the implications of this view is that the responsibility for responding to suffering is taken away from the sufferer. Shweder says that under the metaphor of accident or chance, "suffering is to be treated by the intervention of . . . agents who possess expert skills of some kind, relevant to treating the problem."[36] Traditional cultures believe that the main responsibility in dark times belongs to the sufferers themselves. The things that need to be done are forms of internal "soul work"—learning patience, wisdom, and faithfulness. Contemporary culture, however, does not see suffering as an opportunity or test—and certainly never as a punishment. Because sufferers are victims of the impersonal universe, sufferers are referred to experts—whether medical, psychological, social, or civil—whose job is the alleviation of the pain by the removal of as many stressors as possible.

But this move—making suffering the domain of experts—has led to great confusion in our society, because different guilds of experts differ markedly on what they think sufferers should do. As both a trained psychotherapist and an anthropologist, James Davies is in a good position to see this. He writes, "During the twentieth century most people living in contemporary society have become increasingly confused about why they suffer emotionally." He then lists "biomedical psychiatry, academic psychiatry, genetics, modern economics" and says, "As each tradition was based on its own distinctive assumptions and pursued its own goals via its own methods, each largely favored reducing human suffering to one predominant cause (e.g., biology, faulty cognition, unsatisfied self-interest)."[37] As the saying goes, if you are an expert in hammers, every problem looks like a nail. This has led to understandable perplexity. The secular model puts sufferers in the hands of experts, but the specialization and reductionism of the different kinds of experts leaves people bewildered.

Davies's findings support Shweder's analysis. He explains how the secular model encourages psychotherapists to "decontextualize" suffering, not seeing it, as older cultures have, as an integral part of a person's life story. Davies refers to a BBC interview with Dr. Robert Spitzer in 2007. Spitzer is a psychiatrist who headed the taskforce that in 1980 wrote the DSM-III (third edition of the *Diagnostic and Statistical Manual of Mental Disorders*) of the American Psychiatric Association. The DSM-III sought to develop more uniformity of psychiatric diagnoses. When interviewed twenty-five years later by the BBC, Spitzer admitted that, in hindsight, he believed they had wrongly labeled many normal human experiences of grief, sorrow, and anxiety as mental disorders. When the interviewer asked: "So you have effectively medicalized much ordinary human sadness?" Spitzer responded, "I think we have to some extent. . . . How serious a problem it is, is not known . . . twenty percent, thirty percent . . . but that is a considerable amount."[38]

Davies goes on to say that the DSM focused almost completely on the symptoms:

> They were not interested in understanding the patient's life, or why they were suffering from these symptoms. If the patient was very sad, anxious, or unhappy, then it was simply assumed that he or she was suffering from a disorder that needed to be cured, rather than from a natural and normal human reaction to certain life conditions that needed to be changed.[39]

The older view of suffering was that the pain is a symptom of a conflict between a person's internal and external world. It meant the sufferer's behavior and thinking may need to be changed, or some significant circumstance in the environment had to be changed, or both. The focus was not on the painful and uncomfortable feeling—it was on what the feelings told you about your life, and what should be done about it. Of course, to make such an analysis takes moral and spiritual standards. It requires value judgments. And this was a discussion that the experts trained in secular cultural institutions are ill-equipped to facilitate. So the emphasis was instead not on the person's life story but on the symptom of emotional pain and discontent. Through various scientific techniques, the job of the experts was to lessen the pain. The life story was not addressed.

Davies concludes:

> The growing influence of the DSM was one among many other social factors spreading the harmful cultural belief that much of our everyday suffering is a damaging encumbrance best swiftly removed—a belief increasingly trapping us within a worldview that regards all suffering as a purely negative force in our lives.[40]

Outraged by Our Miseries

In the secular view, suffering is never seen as a meaningful part of life but only as an interruption. With that understanding, there are only two things to do when pain and suffering occur. The first is to manage and lessen the pain. And so over the past two generations, most professional services and resources offered to sufferers have moved from talking about affliction to discussing stress. They no longer give people ways to endure adversity with patience but instead use a vocabulary drawn from business, psychology, and medicine to enable them to manage, reduce, and cope with stress, strain, or trauma. Sufferers are counseled to avoid negative thoughts and to buffer themselves with time off, exercise, and supportive relationships. All the focus is on controlling your responses.

The second way to handle suffering in this framework is to look for the cause of the pain and eliminate it. Other cultures see suffering as an inevitable part of the fabric of life because of unseen forces, such as the illusory nature of life or the conflict between good and evil. But our modern culture does not believe in unseen spiritual forces. Suffering always has a material cause and therefore it can in theory be "fixed." Suffering is often caused by unjust economic and social conditions, bad public policies, broken family patterns, or simply villainous evil parties. The proper response to this is outrage, confrontation of the offending parties, and action to change the conditions. (This is not uncalled for, by the way. The Bible has a good deal to say about rendering justice to the oppressed.)

Older cultures sought ways to be edified by their sufferings by looking inside, but Western people are often simply outraged by their suffering—and they seek to change things outside so that the suffering never happens again. No one has put the difference between traditional and modern culture more succinctly than C. S. Lewis, who wrote: "For the wise men of old the cardinal problem had been how to conform the soul to reality, and the solution had been knowledge, self-discipline, and virtue. For . . . [modernity] the problem is how to subdue reality to the wishes of men: the solution is a technique. . . ."[41] Philosopher Charles

Taylor, in his magisterial book *A Secular Age*, recounts how Western society made what he calls "the anthropocentric turn," the rise in the secular view. After this turn, Taylor says the "sense of God's ordering presence begins to fade. The sense begins to arise that we can sustain the order [of the world] on our own." As a result, Western society's "highest goal is to . . . prevent suffering."[42]

In Western culture, then, sufferers are not told that their primary work is any internal adjustment, learning, or growth. As Shweder points out, not only is moral responsibility virtually never assigned to sufferers but to even hint at it is considered "blaming the victim," one of the main heresies within our Western society. The responses to suffering, then, are always provided by experts, whether pain management, psychological or medical treatment, or changes in law or public policy.

In the *Boston Review*, Larissa MacFarquhar was interviewed on her writing and research on very "saintly" people who make great sacrifices for the good of others. Many of them were religious, of course, and MacFarquhar, a staff writer for *The New Yorker*, had no religious faith, nor was she raised in one. At one point, the interviewer asked how she viewed these people. She spoke with insight and candor, speaking about "a difference between religious . . . and secular people that was very enlightening." She said:

> I . . . think that, within many religious traditions, there is much more of an acceptance of suffering as a part of life and not necessarily always a terrible thing, because it can help you become a fuller person. Whereas, at least in my limited experience, secular utilitarians hate suffering. They see nothing good in it, they want to eliminate it, and they see themselves as responsible for doing so.

She said that secular people also have no belief in a God who will someday put things right. For people of faith, "God is in control, and God's love will see the world through. Whereas for secular people, it's all up to us. We're alone here. That's why I think that, for secular people, there can be an additional layer of urgency and despair."[43]

Christianity among the Cultures

Here, then, is a schematic way to understand secularism as a fifth culture of suffering:

	Moralistic	Self-transcendent	Fatalistic	Dualistic	Secular
Cause	Wrongdoing	Illusion	Destiny	Cosmic conflict	Accident
Response	Do good	Detachment	Endurance	Purified faithfulness	Technique
Resolution	Eternal bliss	Enlightenment	Glory and honor	Triumph of the light	Better society

How does Christianity compare to all of these? German philosopher Max Scheler, in his famous article "The Meaning of Suffering," pointed out the uniqueness of the Christian approach. Scheler writes that in some ways, "Christian teaching on suffering seems a complete reversal of attitude" when compared to the interpretations of other cultures and religious systems.[44]

Unlike the more fatalistic view so prevalent in the shame and honor cultures, "in Christianity there is none of the ancient arrogance . . . none of the self-praise of the sufferer who measures the degree of his suffering against his own power to which others bear witness." Instead of stoic endurance of high doom, "the cry of the suffering creature resounds everywhere in Christianity freely and harshly," including from the cross itself.[45] Christians are permitted—even encouraged—to express their grief with cries and questions.

Unlike Buddhists, Christians believe that suffering is real, not an illusion. "There are not reinterpretations: pain is pain, it is misery; pleasure is pleasure, positive bliss, not mere 'tranquility' . . . which Buddha considered the good of goods. In Christianity there is no diminution of sensitivity, but a mellowing of the soul in totally enduring suffering."[46] Again, we see this in Jesus himself. In the Garden of Gethsemane, he said, "My soul is overwhelmed with sorrow even to the point of death" (Mark 14:34) and his anguish was such that his bloody sweat fell to the ground as he prayed (Luke 22:44). He was the opposite of tranquility. He did not detach his heart from the good things of life to achieve inner calm but instead said to his Father, "Not my will but thine be done" (Mark 14:36).

Unlike believers in karma, Christians believe that suffering is often unjust and disproportionate. Life is simply not fair. People who live well often do not do well. Scheler writes that Christianity succeeded in doing justice to the full gravity and misery of suffering by acknowledging this, as the doctrine of karma does not, which insists that all an individual's suffering is fully deserved. The book of Job is of course the first place this is clearly stated, when God condemns Job's friends for their insistence that Job's pain and suffering had to be caused by a life of moral inferiority.

We see this most of all in Jesus. If anyone ever deserved a good life on the basis of character and behavior, Jesus did, but he did not get it. As Scheler writes, the entire Christian faith is centered on "the paragon of the innocent man who freely receives suffering for others' debts. . . . Suffering . . . acquires, through the divine quality of the suffering person, a wonderful, new nobility." In the light of the cross, suffering becomes "purification, not punishment."[47]

Unlike the dualistic (and to some degree, the moralistic) view, Christianity does not see suffering as a means of working off your sinful debts by virtue of the quality of your endurance of pain. Christianity does not teach "that an ascetic, voluntary self-affliction . . . makes one more spiritual and brings one closer to God. . . . The interpretation that suffering *in itself* brings men nearer to God is far more Greek and Neoplatonic than Christian."[48] Also, dualism divides the world into the good people and the evil people, with suffering as a badge of virtue and the mark of moral superiority that warrants the demonization of groups that have mistreated you. In stark contrast, Christians believe, as Aleksandr Solzhenitsyn wrote famously, "The line dividing good and evil cuts through the heart of every human being."[49]

No, the Christian understanding of suffering is dominated by the idea of grace. In Christ we have received forgiveness, love, and adoption into the family of God. These goods are undeserved, and that frees us from the temptation to feel proud of our suffering. But also it is the present enjoyment of those inestimable goods that makes suffering bearable. Scheler writes: "It is not the glowing prospect of a happy afterlife, but the experienced happiness of being in a state of grace of God while in throes of agony that released the wonderful powers in the martyrs." Indeed, suffering not only is made bearable by these joys, but suffering can even enhance these joys, in the midst of sorrow. "The Christian doctrine of suffering asks for more than a patient tolerance of suffering. . . . The pain and suffering of life fix our spiritual vision on the central, spiritual goods of . . . the redemption of Christ."[50]

Finally, how does the Christian prescription for sufferers compare to that of the secular culture? We will devote more time to this important question later, but we can summarize it like this. Christianity teaches that, contra fatalism, suffering is overwhelming; contra Buddhism, suffering is real; contra karma, suffering is often unfair; but contra secularism, suffering is meaningful. There is a purpose to it, and if faced rightly, it can drive us like a nail deep into the love of God and into more stability and spiritual power than you can imagine. Suffering—Buddhism says accept it, karma says pay it, fatalism says heroically endure it, secularism says avoid or fix it. From the Christian perspective, all of these cultures of suffering have an element of truth. Sufferers do indeed need to stop loving material goods too much. And yes, the Bible says that, in general, the suffering filling the world is the result of the human race turning from God. And we do indeed need to endure suffering and not let it overthrow us. Secularism is also right to warn us about being too accepting of conditions and factors that harm people and should be changed. Pre-secular cultures often permitted too much passivity in the face of changeable circumstances and injustices.

But, as we have seen, from the Christian view of things, all of these approaches are too simple and reductionist and therefore are half-truths. The example and redemptive work of Jesus Christ incorporates all these insights into a coherent whole and yet transcends them. Scheler ends his great essay by returning to his claim that Christianity is ultimately a reversal of all the other views.

> For the man of antiquity . . . the external world was happy and joyous, but the world's *core* was deeply sad and dark. Behind the cheerful surface of the world of so-called merry antiquity there loomed "chance" and "fate." For the Christian, the external world is dark and full of suffering, but its core is nothing other than pure bliss and delight.[51]

He is right about most of the ancient cultures, but what he says especially fits the secular worldview. Secularism, as Richard Dawkins says, sees ultimate reality as cold and indifferent and extinction as inevitable. The other cultures also have seen day-to-day life as being filled with pleasures, but behind it all is darkness or illusion. Christianity sees things differently. While other worldviews lead us to sit in the midst of life's joys, foreseeing the coming sorrows, Christianity empowers its people to sit in the midst of this world's sorrows, tasting the coming joy.

Life Story: The Fairy-Tale Ending

by Emily

If you had asked me what I was thankful for before September, I would have said that I am thankful for my family, my home, my job, and for God—for a husband who loves and cares for me, for four children (ages fourteen, eleven, nine, five) who are healthy and happy, for a home I never dreamed I could have, for a career that allows me to work from home, use my brain, and make a difference for my company and my clients, and for a God that has provided me those things—regardless of my worthiness.

In September, completely out of the blue, my husband left me and our four children for someone else (who left her husband and two children as well). This other family were friends of ours; we'd vacationed with them on three separate occasions during the summer. I thought they were our friends.

My heart died within me. This could not be happening. My Christian husband—the one who with me sat down with our kids and explained that while divorce does happen, it would never happen to us—we made a covenant, a promise to God and to each other—no matter what—we will always be here for each other and for them. I sobbed and begged him not to go, that we would figure this out. No, he was leaving.

I asked what he was going to tell the kids; he said he didn't know. I told him, "You can't just leave without telling the kids something." Surely, this would hit him—he would not be able to look at these precious children and tell them that he was leaving . . . but he did. He called them back downstairs from bed and told them he was leaving. They didn't understand. . . . Is this for work? When will he be back? No, kids, I'm moving out—not to come back. He left. We were crushed.

After eight weeks, my heart was still crushed. God, is this really your plan? How could this be your plan? I know that you will heal my heart, I know that something good will come from this—but how and why THIS? I feel you—I feel people praying . . . but what is going to become of us? I have never been so angry. Our poor children are suffering terribly; their father's "wants" come before their "needs." "I still love my kids," he says. Really? How can you love them and cause them such pain?

After four months, God is beginning to heal me in a way I'm not sure I want to be healed. I want to see justice, but it is not mine to inflict. I am beginning to try to pray for him . . . not about him. I am beginning to pray for his heart to be healed. For him to come back, not to me but back to God. I need to move on without him, for now and maybe forever, but I have to forgive him to get through the bitterness. I will not be bitter for the rest of my life.

But how am I going to make it? God says pray, so I do.

I love my family, and I will always love the man I married. I'm praying for a miracle—for him to snap out of this and find his way back home—but I am also moving forward without him. I'm planning and trying to continue with my life, with everything that needs to be done from a practical, spiritual, emotional, and financial perspective.

I am going to pray for him on a regular basis, I am going to love him (but I will not be a doormat). I am going to support my family and I am going to seek God's plan for our life. I am going to forgive him, but I won't forget—because if I forget, I won't be able to use what I learn to help others who may go through this nightmare. I need to feel the pain, allow God to heal that pain and transform me into someone that he had intended for me to become all along. Somehow, I feel excited. It feels wrong in so many ways—to be excited to be going through this nightmare.

It has now been six months, my situation has gotten worse, and yet I feel truly blessed.

My husband is still gone, still with his girlfriend. He has told me that they will be a part of our kids' lives and I need to get used to that and not hate her. He told me that if she was my enemy, then I was his.

My kids are still dealing with the impact that their dad left; they are depressed, angry, confused, and frustrated. My oldest has started questioning his faith; he is rebelling against all authority, and lashing out at his family. My house is up for sale—a short sale, which could turn into being a foreclosure. We have no idea where we will move.

And yet, in the midst of all this—I have come to know God on a different level, to see him work in a way I had only heard about. To experience this is quite amazing.

I've never had a big tragedy in my life—never really had to depend on God. I mean, sure, I prayed and I saw God work—but not like this. I never had the need to rely on God, truly just fall and rest on him. When I needed God's comfort, the image in my head was me clinging to Jesus and him hugging me. My image now is me just completely collapsed, and him carrying me—and it is awesome.

In the midst of this horrible situation, where my whole identity and where my family has been attacked, I see glimpses of what God is doing and how my life and our lives will be changed—and I get excited to see who I get to be at the end of all this. Like being in a race, where it starts to rain and you hit a mud pit. You can't go around it, you have to go through it—and the rain and the mud are weighing you down—you can't go through it fast; you must concentrate on each painful step . . . but at the same time, something is keeping you upright and compelling you to continue. In the distance, you see what appears to be a sheet of rain (almost like a car wash rinse) and then you see it—the sun; it is perfectly clear . . . The person you will be there will be stronger, with more understanding of how to run this race, and with satisfaction/peace. Yes, that person is tired—but they are also energized by the experience. I can't wait to use what God has taught me; I can't wait to learn more. I have explained it to my children like this: In every fairy tale, there is always a tragedy, and the protagonist faces that adversity, overcomes it, and thrives because of it. God is giving us our fairy tale—what do you see at the end?

TWO

The Victory of Christianity

When Heaven is going to give a great responsibility to someone, it first makes his mind endure suffering. It makes his sinews and bones experience toil, and his body to suffer hunger. It inflicts him with poverty and knocks down everything he tries to build. In this way Heaven stimulates his mind, stabilizes his temper, and develops his weak points.

—The Book of Mencius (Chinese, 300 BC)

We have seen how different societies equip their members to face suffering. Having looked at how different cultures have done this, we will now examine how this has played out in different centuries, particularly in the West.[52]

Philosophy to "Save One's Skin"

The classical author Cicero famously argued that the main task of philosophy is to teach us how to face death. The fact of mortality and death, says Cicero, necessarily creates fears, unfulfilled desires, and sadness. It is the purpose of philosophy to give people relief from these things, to provide some way to care for the soul that is weighed down by them. And so "philosophy both allows and requires one to become one's own spiritual physician."[53] Contemporary French philosopher Luc Ferry does not think Cicero's definition of philosophy can be bettered. "One does not philosophize to amuse oneself, nor even to better understand the world . . . but sometimes literally to 'save one's skin.' "⁵⁴ Living life well depends on learning to conquer our fears of "the various faces of death" as well as of "boredom, the sense of time slipping by." Perhaps the most terrible truth we must face is that we will inevitably be separated from all those we love. Ferry asks, What do we desire above everything else? It is to be understood and loved rather than be alone, and therefore above all *"not to die and not to have [our loved ones] die on us."*⁵⁵

Ferry knows that many secular people today (as did Epicurus and other thinkers of ancient times) argue that death should not be given a second thought. It is merely the "end of life," they say. When you die, you simply don't exist—you don't know anything, you are not around to worry about it—"Why [then] . . . would you bother yourself with such a pointless problem?" But Ferry replies that this line of reasoning is "too brutal to be honest."⁵⁶ What is it that primarily gives your life meaning? Isn't it relationships with people you love? Can you really honestly say that you have no dread of a future state that will strip you of everything you hold dear now? Do your loved ones mean so little to you that you don't care about being separated from them forever? But this loss of what gives life meaning begins even before we die ourselves. "The irreversibility of things is a kind of death at the heart of life."⁵⁷ It is this that we rightly call evil and suffering. And Ferry concludes that honest people must admit that death and all its consequences is an enormous human problem—perhaps *the* problem. To live well and freely, capable of joy and love, we must learn how to conquer the inevitable terrible fear of these irreversible losses.⁵⁸

The ancient Greek philosophers believed that the very purpose of philosophy was to discover how to face evil, suffering, and death well. In fact, Ferry argues that *only* philosophy or religion can possibly help us deal with pain and death. Why? Suffering takes away the loves, joys, and comforts that we rely on to give life meaning. How can we maintain our poise, or even our peace and joy, when that happens? The answer is that we can do that only if we locate our meaning in things that can't be touched by death. But that means locating the answers to the questions "What is human life for?" and "What should I be spending my time doing here?" in things that suffering cannot destroy. That can be done only by philosophy or religion. "It is an error," he concludes, "to believe that modern psychology, for example, can substitute for this [process]."[59] Ferry (who is not a religious man) knows he is bucking the secular worldview at this point, but he insists that science cannot help us with suffering, because it cannot help us find purpose. Science can tell us what is but never what ought to be—that entails philosophy and faith. Yet without determining these issues, we cannot handle the hardness of life.

And so each stage in history has offered sufferers its own "consolation" literature to train and aid them in their trials and losses. We will look at three eras of Western history—the ancient, the medieval, and the modern—and how each one sought to do this.

Salvation through Reason

Perhaps the most influential school of Greek philosophy was that of the Stoics.[60] The Stoics believed that the universe has a divine rational structure to it called the Logos. They did not believe the universe is made up strictly of physical matter, but neither did they believe the universe had a God in the sense of a personal God who created and transcended it. Rather, the universe was divine, beautiful, well structured, and had an orderliness to it that was rational and capable of being perceived by our reason. They believed, therefore, that there were moral "absolutes"— right ways of behavior that were in accord with the order of the universe—as well as wrong ways of living that went against its grain. These could be deduced and inferred from what we could see of the world. Despite apparently chaotic times and disorderly places, the universe was at essence harmonious, with all things taking their rightful place and fulfilling their rightful role or task.

To the Stoics, then, the task of our human minds and reason was to perceive and align with the orderliness of the world. And this meant facing death and suffering in three ways. The first way meant "accepting the unexpected twists and turns of fate as the providential and beneficent workings of God."[61] If the universe itself is divine, rational, and perfectly ordered, then living "in accord with the universe" meant to fully embrace whatever the world sent you. For the Stoics, "the good life is a life stripped of both hopes and fears. In other words, a life reconciled to what is the case, a life that accepts the world as it is."[62]

The second way was to give reason preeminence over emotion, and to learn to avoid too much attachment to anything in life, for that is where the overwhelming pain of suffering comes from. One scholar summarizes this principle well. It meant, "through the exercise of reason, becoming indifferent to all things that exceeded one's reach. . . . The soul had to expel or suppress strong emotions."[63] For example, in the *Discourses* of Epictetus, the philosopher tells his students:

> The principal and highest form of training, and one that stands at the very entrance to happiness, is, that when you become attached to something, let it not be as something which cannot be taken away. . . . When you kiss your child, or your brother, or your friend, never give way entirely to your affections, nor free rein to your imagination; but curb it, restrain it.[64]

Epictetus went on to tell his students to "remind yourself likewise that what you love is mortal, that what you love is not your own. . . . What harm is there while you are kissing your child to murmur softly, 'Tomorrow you will die'?"[65]

Luc Ferry agrees this sounds enormously cold, but he defends Epictetus. He argues that the philosopher is not saying to be cruel to your children but "to love the present to the point of desiring nothing else and of regretting nothing whatsoever."[66] If you do that, then you can say to yourself, "When catastrophe strikes, I will be ready." In fact, Ferry says, if you could achieve the Stoic goal, then you touch on something resembling salvation, in the sense that nothing further can trouble a serenity which comes from the extinguishing of fears concerning the dimensions of time. When he achieves this degree of enlightenment, the sage does indeed live "like a god," in the eternity of an instant that nothing can diminish.[67]

The third thing Stoics offered to sufferers had to do with their own death. When we die, they taught, we don't cease to exist. Death is a transformation from one state into another. The universe had need of you, as it were, in your form as a human person. But when you die, your substance—both soul and body—continues to be part of the universe in another form. Marcus Aurelius said, "You came into this world as a part: you will vanish into the whole which gave you birth, or rather you will be gathered up into its generative principle by the process of change."[68]

Submitting to Fate, Detaching from the World

The two most influential writers on suffering in classical antiquity were the Roman thinkers Cicero and Seneca, both of whom were strongly influenced by the Greek Stoics. The central theme of Cicero's *Tusculan Disputations* is that death is not an evil and should not be regarded with fear and loathing. Your life is a loan from nature that can be recalled at any time. It is wisdom to recognize and agree to the terms of the loan, for there is no other choice after all. Cicero believed sorrow over the death of loved ones was unavoidable and right, provided it is kept moderate. Having granted this, Cicero maintained that grief is still a useless thing, with no positive function. It arises from false beliefs about the nature of things and therefore must be controlled.[69] The other most influential Roman work of consolation was Seneca's *To Marcia on Consolation*. Marcia was a woman who had lost a son and was still grieving three years later. Using arguments similar to Cicero's, Seneca calls her to overcome her grief and "move on." Nature gives us no promise that we are allowed to keep our loved ones forever or even for long. Though he died young, he avoided many evils in life—indeed, this may have been a way for him to escape some suffering that would have been far worse. All this points to one key to living life well—Marcia should submit to fate, and not protest or struggle against it.

Even as the Greek and Roman philosophers were formulating their understanding of fate and suffering, a somewhat similar view was already thriving in another part of the world. For centuries, Eastern cultures and religions held that this material world, and the perception that human beings exist as separate entities within it, is all an illusion. The Vedas, the oldest Scriptures of Hinduism and Indian thought, taught that all differences are ultimately unreal. The ultimate truth is *Tat tvam asi*— "Thou art That." In other words, the physical world appears to contain many discrete individual objects. This object A is not that object B. That's what our senses (and science and logic) tell us. While one person suffers losses, another person has plenty. But this is a deceptive appearance called *maya*. There is not only no evil but no good, no individuals, no material world. Everything is actually part of the One, the All-Soul, the Absolute Spirit. Nothing is outside of it.[70] Ultimately we cannot lose anything. We are part of everything.

The most pure and influential form of this thought today is Buddhism.[71] According to tradition, Prince Siddhartha Gautama was living a secure and secluded life of wealth and luxury, but when he went outside his palace, he was confronted with the "Four Distressing Sights"—a sick man, an old man, a dead man, and a poor man. In response, he determined to give his life to discovering how to live a life of serenity in the presence of human suffering. After a number of years, he achieved enlightenment under a tree. In his first sermon, he outlined for his followers the Four Noble Truths, namely that (1) all life is suffering, (2) the cause of suffering is desire or craving, (3) suffering ends only when craving is extinguished, and (4) this can be achieved by following the Eightfold Path to enlightenment. The Eightfold path is a comprehensive approach to all areas of life—right views, intentions, speech, conduct, livelihood, effort, mindfulness, and meditation. It is an extremely balanced life, not demanding asceticism and deprivation but demanding a life of simplicity, service to others, and many disciplines of self-control.

The way to overcome suffering is to detach your heart, to not love anything in this world too much. The core problem of a sufferer, it is believed, is an unsatisfactory state of consciousness. Our craving and therefore our pain in suffering is based on the illusion that we are individual selves or persons. Put in simple language, if we see that everything is impermanent, we won't be attached to it. If we see that everything is really part of us, we will not cling to it or mourn it as if it has been lost.

You can't in the end really lose anything, because each thing is part of the Absolute, the One that we all will return to eventually.

By now it may be evident that there are strong similarities between this and the approaches of the Greeks and particularly of the Stoics.[72] The Stoics taught that the underlying reality of the world is an impersonal, universal Logos that is the heart of the cosmos and determines all things. And so the most practical way to live life well is, as we saw, to "never give in to your affections" but to restrain your love or joy in anything. French philosopher André Comte-Sponville points out the close connection between Stoicism and Buddhism. Both deny that it is a good thing to "live in hope." On the contrary, they both say hope is a killer. If we live hoping that our plans will succeed, and if we tell ourselves our happiness depends on their fulfillment, we will be suffering anxiety during the interim and then devastation when the goals are not accomplished. And it will be our fault.[73] As the Greek essayist Plutarch once wrote, we must submit "uncomplainingly and obediently to the dispensation of things."[74]

A Greater Hope

When Christianity began to grow, its writers quickly began to bring many new ideas into the world of human thought, differing markedly not only from Western pagan beliefs, but also Eastern thought, especially on the topic of pain and grief.[75] It is almost impossible to overestimate the importance of the Christian approach to suffering for its success in the Roman Empire and for its impact on human thinking.

Early Christian speakers and writers not only argued vigorously that Christianity's teaching made more sense of suffering, they insisted that the actual lives of Christians proved it. Cyprian recounted how, during the terrible plagues, Christians did not abandon sick loved ones nor flee the cities, as most of the pagan residents did. Instead they stayed to tend the sick and faced their death with calmness.[76] Other early Christian writings, like Ignatius of Antioch's *To the Romans* and Polycarp's *Letter to the Philippians,* pointed to the poise with which Christians faced torture and death for their faith. "Christians used suffering to argue for the superiority of their creed . . . [because] they suffered better than pagans."[77] The Greeks had taught that the very purpose of philosophy was to help us face suffering and death. On this basis, writers such as Cyprian, Ambrose, and later Augustine made the case that Christians *suffered and died better*—and this was empirical, visible evidence that Christianity was "the supreme philosophy." The differences between the pagan and Christian population in this regard were significant enough to give real credibility to Christian claims. Unlike the current moment, in which the existence of suffering and evil makes Christian faith vulnerable to criticism and doubt, early Christians pointed to the pain and adversity of life as one of the main reasons for embracing the faith.

Why were Christians so different? It was not because of some distinction in their natural temperament—they were not simply tougher people. It had to do with what they believed about the world. Classics scholar Judith Perkins argues that the Greek philosophical tradition's account of suffering was neither practical nor satisfying for the average person. The Christian approach to pain and evil, with both greater room for sorrow and greater basis for hope, was a major factor in its appeal.[78]

First, Christianity offered a greater basis for hope. Luc Ferry, in his chapter "The Victory of Christianity,"[79] agrees that the Christian approach to suffering was a major reason that Christianity so thoroughly defeated Greek philosophy and became the dominant worldview in the Roman Empire. To Ferry, one of the main differences had to do with Christian teaching about the love and meaning of persons. The most obvious difference was the Christian doctrine of the future bodily resurrection and restored material world. The Stoic philosophers had taught that, after death, we continue as part of the universe, yet not in an individual form. As Ferry summarizes, "The Stoic doctrine of salvation is resolutely *anonymous* and *impersonal*. It promises us eternity, certainly, but of a non-personal kind, as an oblivious fragment of the *cosmos*."[80] But Christians believed in the resurrection—through its confirmation by hundreds of eyewitnesses of the risen Christ. *That* is our future, and that meant we are saved as our individual selves—our personalities will be sustained, beautified, and perfected after death. And so our ultimate future is one of perfect, unhindered love—love with God and others. Ambrose wrote:

> Let there be this difference between the servants of Christ and the worshippers of idols, that the latter weep for their friends, whom they suppose to have perished forever. . . . But from us, for whom death is the end not of our nature but of this life only, since our nature itself is restored to a better state, let the advent of death wipe away all tears.[81]

The Greek philosophers and especially the Stoics had tried "valiantly to relieve us of the fears linked to death, but at the cost of obliterating our individual identity."[82] But Christianity offered something radically more satisfying. Ferry says that what human beings want "above all is to be reunited with our loved ones, and, if possible, with their voices, their faces—not in the form of undifferentiated fragments, such as pebbles or vegetables."[83]

There is no more striking statement of this difference between Christianity and ancient paganism than that found in the first chapter of the New Testament gospel of John. There, John brilliantly co-opts one of Greek philosophy's main themes when he begins his account saying that "in the beginning [of time] was *the Logos*" (John 1:1). But then he goes on to say, "The *Logos* became flesh, and made his dwelling among us, and we have seen his glory" (John 1:14). This was an electrifying claim. John was saying, "We agree that there is an ordering structure behind the universe, and that the meaning of life is to be found in aligning oneself with it." But John was also saying that the *Logos* behind the universe was not an abstract, rational principle that could be known only through high contemplation by the educated elite. Rather, the *Logos* of the universe is a person—Jesus Christ—who can be loved and known in a personal relationship by anyone at all. Ferry summarizes John's message to the culture like this: "The divine . . . was no longer an impersonal structure, but an extraordinary individual."[84] This, Ferry said, was an "unfathomable shift" which had an "incalculable effect on the history of ideas."

And Greater Room for Sorrow

The other major difference between the Greek philosophers and Christianity was seen in how Christian consolation gave far more scope to expressions of sorrow and grief. Tears and cries are not to be stifled or even kept under strict limits—they are natural and good. Cyprian cites St. Paul, saying that Christians *are* to really grieve—but to do so bathed in hope (1 Thess 4:13).[85] Christians did not see grief as a useless thing to be suppressed at all costs. Ambrose did not apologize for his tears and grief over the death of his brother. Pointing to Jesus' tears at the tomb of Lazarus, he wrote: "We have not incurred any grievous sin by our tears. Not all weeping proceeds from unbelief or weakness. . . . The Lord also wept. He wept for one not related to Him, I for my brother. He wept for all in weeping for one, I will weep for the all, in my brother."[86]

For Christians, suffering was not to be dealt with primarily through the control and suppression of negative emotions with the use of reason or willpower. Ultimate reality was known not primarily through reason and contemplation but through relationship. Salvation was through humility, faith, and love rather than reason and control of emotions. And therefore, Christians don't face adversity by stoically decreasing our love for the people and things of this world so much as by increasing our love and joy in God. Ferry says, "Augustine, having conducted a radical critique of love-as-attachment in general, does not banish it when its object is divine."[87] What he means is that, while Christianity was able to agree with pagan writers that inordinate attachment to earthly goods can lead to unnecessary pain and grief, it also taught that the answer to this was not to love things less but to love God more than anything else. Only when our greatest love is God, a love that we cannot lose even in death, can we face all things with peace. Grief was not to be eliminated but seasoned and buoyed up with love and hope.

Besides using love and hope to season our sorrow, Christians were also called to use the comfort of knowing God's fatherly care. Ancient consolers had counseled sufferers to accept the inevitability of heartless fate. Fate was random, they said, a turning wheel of chance, without rationale or purpose. Therefore we should reconcile ourselves to it and not engage in self-pity or complaint.[88] Christianity rejected this view strongly. Instead of multiple gods and power centers struggling against each other, and impersonal fate ruling over it all, Christianity presented Greco-Roman culture with an entirely new view. Historian Ronald Rittgers writes that Christians asserted a single Creator who sustained the world in personal wisdom and love, "in direct opposition to pagan polytheism and pagan notions of fate."[89] He summarizes it like this: "This God had created humankind for fellowship with himself" and imposed death and suffering only when the human race broke away from this fellowship to be their own masters—"mortality and hardship were not simply part of the original nature of things." After the Fall of the human race and the coming of pain and evil, God began a process of salvation to restore human fellowship through Christ. During this time, "trials, tribulations, and adversities" were used by God "for the proving of human souls," and along with them, he provided "hope of deliverance from them. . . . It was he who removed the sting of death."[90] In short, while God's ways are often just as opaque to us as a parent's are to an infant, still we trust that our heavenly Father is caring for us and present with us to guide and protect in all the circumstances of life.

The Victory of Christianity

Slowly but surely, Christian views supplanted the older pagan ones and became the dominant cultural ideas. One of the most important shifts had to do, again, with the doctrine of the resurrection. Christians taught that Jesus came in a physical body and will redeem and resurrect our physical bodies. In contrast to Greek teaching, this implied that *this* material life is good and worth enjoying fully. We are not to loathe or detach ourselves from the pleasures and comforts of ordinary life and relationships. "Though atheists would have us believe otherwise, the Christian religion is not entirely given over to waging war against the body, the flesh, the senses," writes Ferry.[91]

But the resurrection means even more than this. Ferry poignantly describes the sense of irretrievable loss that characterizes our existence, with reference to Edgar Allan Poe's poem "The Raven." The sinister bird can repeat only the word *nevermore*. With frightening pithiness, this conveys the irreversibility of life. Once our youth, our childhood home, our loved ones are gone, there is no going back. Irreversibility is a kind of death in the midst of life. But here is where the doctrine of the resurrection of the body comes in. Even religions that teach heavenly bliss for the eternal soul can offer only a consolation for the life we lost, but Christianity offers a *restoration* of life. We get our bodies back—indeed, we get the bodies we never had but wished we had, and one beyond our greatest imaginings. We get our lives back—indeed, we get the life we longed for but never had. It's all because the Christian hope is not just an ethereal disembodied existence but one in which the soul and the body are finally perfectly integrated, one in which we dance, sing, hug, work, and play. The Christian doctrine of the resurrection is, then, a reversal of death's seeming irreversibility. It is the end of "nevermore."

Ferry comes to a remarkable conclusion, but one that is historically hard to refute:

> Exploiting what it saw as a weakness in Greek wisdom, Christianity created a new doctrine of salvation so effective it opened a chasm in the philosophies of Antiquity and dominated the [Western] world for nearly fifteen hundred years. . . . [Christianity] would seem to be the only version of salvation that enables us to not only transcend the fear of death, but also to beat death itself.[92]

Having established these basic foundations for a groundbreaking new way to face suffering, Christian preachers and writers began to search the Bible and develop more detailed and practical resources for the consolation of sufferers. The result was an increasingly nuanced and sophisticated body of work on the consolation and "cure" of suffering souls. One of the most striking innovations was how Christian consolers began to recognize the great diversity of forms of suffering in a way that earlier thinkers did not.

St. (or Pope) Gregory the Great (c. 540–604) was perhaps the most influential author on the cure of souls at the end of the early history of Christianity. His most important works were his *Book of Pastoral Rule* and *Moralia,* a series of addresses on the book of Job.[93] On the one hand, Gregory rejected the idea that suffering was an illusion or the result of capricious fate—suffering always had a purpose. Rather than being helpless victims of inexorable fate, people were in the hands of a wise God, and, as Gregory argued strenuously, we should not rail against cruel, blind fate but bear our suffering patiently, like Job.

And yet he also rejected the opposite error, that of moralism—as in the Hindu idea of karma, the belief that the proportion of our suffering is due to the proportion of our sins. Gregory taught that while suffering in general is caused by human sin, that does not mean particular forms of suffering are always the result of specific sins. He warned against making too direct a connection between sin and suffering, since that, after all, is one of the main lessons of the book of Job. In *Moralia,* Gregory shows that Job's friends insisted that his great suffering had to be punishment for some equally great wickedness. But they failed to see that suffering in the world is of many different kinds and serves "a number of purposes in the divine economy."[94] Some suffering is given in order to chastise and correct a person for wrongful patterns of life (as in the case of Jonah imperiled by the storm), some suffering is given "not to correct past wrongs but to prevent future ones" (as in the case of Joseph sold into slavery), and some suffering has no purpose other than to lead a person to love God more ardently for himself alone and so discover the ultimate peace and freedom. The suffering of Job, in Gregory's view, belonged to this last category.[95]

A personal God is a purposeful God, and in the Bible, it is possible to recognize different ways that suffering operates in lives. Early Christian pastors did not believe there was a "one size fits all" way to comfort or equip a person to handle adversity.

Luther's Reformation of Suffering

After the time of Pope Gregory, a gradual but significant shift occurred within the church toward the belief that "the appropriate response to [suffering] was to endure it patiently and thus, with the help of divine grace, to merit heaven. . . ."[96] In other words, suffering became a way to work off your sins, with echoes of the Eastern karmic religions. If you accept suffering with patience, it eliminates some of your sin debt and helps you earn God's favor and admission into eternal bliss.

As an example of this, late medieval theologian Johannes von Paltz wrote *Supplement to the Heavenly Mine* in 1504. There he argued that patience under suffering was so morally valuable that even if you had lived your entire life in unrelenting sinfulness, you could merit complete remission for it all if you only accepted your death with calm faith at the very end. Ronald Rittgers points out that this emphasis on meriting salvation through suffering actually pointed away from early Christian teaching back into a more pagan prohibition of any expressions of sorrow. It resulted, in Rittgers's words, in a virtual "Christianized Stoicism."[97] Demonstrations of grief or cries of pain could be interpreted by heaven as a lack of submissive faith, and therefore such outbursts would be less efficacious in procuring a remit from the debt of one's moral failures. Therefore all that mattered was that you suppressed emotion and took your suffering calmly and without questioning. The eruptions of Job or the laments of the Psalms had no place in this understanding of things. The rich, multidimensional teaching of the Bible on how to understand and walk through pain and suffering was flattened out into a tight-lipped endurance.

But the coming of the European Reformation, and particularly Martin Luther's biblical theology, brought not only a renewal of the Church in general but also a deepening of the Christian understanding of suffering in particular. Luther rejected the medieval view of salvation as a gradual process of growth in virtue that eventually merited eternal life. Instead, he saw salvation as coming through faith, and faith not primarily as an inner quality of purity but as "an essentially receptive capacity."

Faith is trust in the promise of God, the means by which we take hold of salvation as a free gift through Christ's saving work, not our own. This had "revolutionary implications" for the Christian view of suffering.[98]

Luther preached that there was nothing more important for a person than to see that he or she could contribute nothing whatsoever to one's own salvation. We can be fully accepted and counted legally righteous in God's sight through faith in Christ, solely by free grace. To understand and grasp this is to finally know freedom from the crushing burden of proving yourself—to society, family, other people, or even to yourself. It means freedom from fear of the future, from any anxiety about your eternal destiny. It is the most liberating idea possible and it ultimately enables you to face all suffering, knowing that because of the cross, God is absolutely for you and that because of the resurrection, everything will be all right in the end.

The belief that we are saved by our virtue, the state of our hearts, or our good works injects a heavy layer of uncertainty and insecurity into our lives. If God's treatment of us is conditioned by the quality of our lives, and the quality of our lives is always far from perfect, then we can never be sure he is completely for us, loving us. To escape this uncertainty requires that you dispel any illusion that through your wisdom and strength you can either create a safe and good life for yourself or put God in the position of owing you such a life.

In Luther's view, suffering plays a dual role. Before we get the joy and love that help us to face and overcome suffering, suffering must first empty us of our pride and lead us to find our true joy and only security in Christ. Luther declares, "For since God takes away all our goods and our life through many tribulations, it is impossible for the heart to be calm and to bear this unless it clings to better goods, that is, united with God through faith."[99] Suffering dispels the illusion that we have the strength and competence to rule our own lives and save ourselves. People "become nothing through suffering" so that they can be filled with God and his grace.[100] "It is God's nature," wrote Luther, "to make something out of nothing; hence one who is not yet nothing, out of him God cannot make anything," and therefore God accepts only the forsaken, cures only the sick, gives sight only to the blind, restores life only to the dead, sanctifies only the sinners, gives wisdom only to the unwise. In short, He has mercy only on those who are wretched.[101]

The Theology of the Cross

But suffering was much more than some preparatory spiritual process for Luther. It was he who coined the phrase "the theology of the cross" in contrast with a "theology of glory." The world expects a God who is strong and whose followers are blessed and successful only if they summon up all their strength and follow his laws without fail. That was the view of Job's friends, of the Pharisees in Jesus' day, and, according to Luther, the mind-set of most of the leaders of the medieval church in his day. It was a "theology of glory," but it was not the theology of the Bible. The Scripture's startling message is rather that the deepest revelation of the character of God is in the weakness, suffering, and death of the cross. This is "the exact opposite of where humanity expected to find God."[102] In his *Explanations of the Ninety-Five Theses,* Luther includes the following:

> That person does not deserve to be called a theologian who looks upon the invisible things of God as though they were clearly perceptible in those things that have been made.
> He deserves to be called a theologian, however, who comprehends the visible and manifest things of God seen through suffering and the cross.[103]

Theologians of "glory," says Luther, think that God's ways are "clearly perceptible." Thus Job's friends were sure that if things are going well for you, you are living rightly and God is pleased with you, but if things are going badly for you, you are living wrongly and God has abandoned you. They thought it was easy to discern God's purposes and plans. But Job's sufferings were actually quite mysterious, and God's purposes were hidden from Job and most of them even from the book's readers. And yet out of Job's agony and suffering came one of the most profound revelations of God's nature in the Bible and indeed in all of literature—as well as a transformed character for Job.

In the same way, the religious leaders of Jesus' day expected a nice, easy-to-understand Messiah who would defeat the Roman power and lead Israel to political independence. A weak, suffering, and crucified Messiah made no sense to them. Those looking at Jesus as he was dying on the cross had no idea that they were looking at the greatest act of salvation in history. Could the observers of the crucifixion "clearly perceive" the ways of God? No—even though they were looking right at a wonder of grace. They saw only darkness and pain, and the categories of human reason are sure God cannot be working in and through *that*. So they called Jesus to "come down now from the cross," sneering, "He saved others . . . but he can't save himself." (Matt 27:42 NIV). But they did not realize he could save others only because he did *not* save himself.

Only through weakness and pain did God save us and show us, in the deepest way possible, the infinite depths of his grace and love for us. For indeed, here was infinite wisdom—in one stroke, the just requirement of the law was fulfilled *and* the forgiveness of lawbreakers secured. In one moment, God's love and justice were fully satisfied. This Messiah came to die in order to put an end to death itself. Only through weakness and suffering could sin be atoned—it was the only way to end evil without ending us.

Luther regarded Jesus' cry from the cross, "My God, my God—why have you forsaken me?" (Matt 27:46) as "the greatest words in all of Scripture."[104] Luther knew personally about what he called *Anfectungen*, a word that means the "assaults" that the world, the flesh, and the devil make on human beings through the evils and suffering of life. For Luther "*Anfectung* is . . . a state of hopelessness and helplessness having strong affinities with the concept of *Angst* [or dread]."[105] But in these words of dereliction from the cross, Luther saw a deep paradox. Christ suffered Godforsakenness in his human nature; he knew *Anfectungen* in infinite degrees, beyond anything any other human being will ever experience. Here, then, is what the New Testament letter to the Hebrews means when it exhorts us to approach Jesus for mercy and grace "in our time of need" because he is able "to sympathize with our weaknesses . . . having been in every respect tested as we are, yet without sin" (Heb 4:14–15 NRSV). Indeed, Luther saw that "in Christ, the God-forsaken sinner has a Savior who has taken on himself the full depths of human estrangement from God—and overcome it."[106]

Why should we be surprised, then, asked Luther, that our lives are often filled with darkness and pain? Even God himself in Christ did not avoid that. But though God's purposes are often every bit as hidden and obscure as they were to Job and to the observers at the foot of the cross, we—who have the teaching of the Bible and have grasped the message of the Bible—know that the way up is down. The way to power, freedom, and joy is through suffering, loss, and sorrow.

Not that these bad things produce these good things automatically, or in some neat *quid quo pro* way. Suffering produces growth in us only when we understand Christ's suffering and work on our behalf. Luther taught, "Christians cannot suffer with Christ"—that is, they cannot imitate his patience and love under pressure—"before they have embraced the full benefits of Christ's suffering *for* them" in their place.[107] Luther had known in his own experience how much suffering tears us apart if we are uncertain of God's love for us. The medieval teaching that we can earn God's favor by the quality of our patience under suffering simply did not work. That could never give peace to the conscience, because we could never know whether we were suffering with a sufficient degree of submission and purity of heart.

And Luther rightly believed that this peace of conscience was perhaps the single most important prerequisite if suffering is to be faced well. We must not try to use patience to earn our peace with Christ—we need the peace with Christ already if we are going to be patient. We must rest in the sufficiency of Christ's sufferings for us before we can even begin to suffer like him. If we know he loves us unconditionally, despite our flaws, then we know he is present with us and working in our lives in times of pain and sorrow. And we can know that he is not merely close to us, but he is indwelling, and that since we are members of his body, he senses our sufferings as his own (cf. Acts 9:4; Col 1:24.)

The Rise of the "Immanent Frame"

In the early modern era, Christianity was ascendant in Europe and in the New World colonies as well. But over the next five hundred years, things changed. As philosopher Charles Taylor asked, "Why was it virtually impossible not to believe in God in, say, 1500 in our Western society, while in 2000 many of us find this not only easy, but even inescapable?"[108] Over the past five centuries, the originally faith-filled and religious societies of the West have slowly become more secular. Religion and faith have decreasing influence in public institutions. Belief in God is allowed but regularly challenged as problematic and seen as just one option for life among many others.

Taylor coins a number of unique terms to describe contemporary secularity. He says that today we live inside an "immanent frame," the view that the world is a completely natural order without any supernatural. It is a completely " 'immanent' world, over against a possible 'transcendent' one."[109] Another phrase he uses is the "buffered self." In older times, the concept of the self was "open and porous." It included a soul, for example, which connected us to God and the spiritual world, and therefore much of our inner nature, feelings, intuitions, and attitudes were under the influence of forces outside of us, forces that we could not control. It was often assumed that one was required to look outside of the self—to nature and to God—to learn the right way to live. Modern people, however, have a "buffered self," a self that is bounded and self-contained. Because there is no transcendent, supernatural order outside of me, it is I who determine what I am and who I will be.[110] I do not need to look at anything outside myself in order to know how to live. Today the self is "master of the meanings of things for it"; indeed, now "we stake our claim as legislators of meaning."[111]

The shift to this new sense of self, Taylor argued, required an enormous new growth in "confidence in our own powers of moral ordering."[112] In older times, there was a much greater humility about our ability to understand the universe. The reason was that it was a bigger universe. There was infinite mystery to it—depths that human reason could never plumb or know. There were "more things in heaven and earth" than could be "dreamt of" in our human philosophies. It was not a universe framed solely by immanence; it was shot through with the spiritual as well. But the immanent frame developed and grew alongside the buffered, self-sufficient self. While Taylor speaks in academic language, more popular and vivid expressions prove his points every day. Recently, a *New York Times* article observed a trend in people—particularly women—naming themselves. One woman who renamed herself after a divorce explained: "Naming myself was symbolic in many ways. It signified to me how I had to take full responsibility for my life. I had to create my own happiness, to build my strength, to be the engine of my momentum."[113]

The shift to the immanent frame did not immediately remove all belief in God, but it altered it. The frame, as it were, was not solid on all four sides but had a small opening at the top. Taylor explains how Deism came in among the elites of the eighteenth century. The idea of Deism is that God created the world for our benefit and now it operates on its own, without his constant or direct involvement. This world works like a clock and can be understood scientifically, without any need for divine revelation. In this understanding of things, God exists but becomes someone or something more distant, not someone we can know. Our main responsibility is *not* to love, worship, and obey him, seeking his forgiveness when we fail to do so. Instead, human beings' main purpose is to use our reason and free will to support human flourishing. In short, the older Christian idea that we exist for God's glory receded and was replaced by the belief that God exists to nurture and sustain us.

Natural Evil and the Lisbon Earthquake

One of the first places that the new, modern self came up against evil and suffering was in the great Lisbon earthquake of 1755, a famous example of what has been called "natural evil"—suffering caused not by human agents but just as part of the natural world. On All Saints Day, November 1, a massive earthquake almost completely destroyed the chief city of Portugal and killed tens of thousands of people. Many philosophers and thinkers of Europe, notably Voltaire, saw this as evidence against the existence of the loving God of the Bible. Looking back on this event from deep within a secular culture, we might think that the "problem of evil"—questioning God in the face of disaster—was completely normal. Today, every new major tragedy evokes the same kind of public questions and challenges to faith in the divine.

But Taylor points out that the "problem of evil" discourse about the Lisbon earthquake was actually a new thing. Of course people have questioned the ways and justice of God in human affairs since the book of Job and earlier. But virtually no one on record had previously argued that evil made the existence of God impossible. The assertion that evil disproves God's existence was something that could arise only if immanent frame assumptions about God were already in place. Taylor writes that when Western society believed in a world that was mysterious and unknowable by reason—and in a God who was glorious and ineffable— the problem of evil was "less acute." In that view, inexplicable evil was to be expected. But the secularity of Deism made the problem of evil much worse, for two reasons.

In earlier times, when suffering occurred, just because we couldn't think within our own mind of good reasons for it didn't mean there couldn't be any. We were humbler about our ability to understand the world. But by the eighteenth century, we believed that with our minds and reason, we could eventually understand everything. We became confident in our powers of exhaustive observation, and this conviction changed the way human beings regarded suffering. Evil now became a much bigger problem.

> The certainty that we have all the elements we need to carry out a trial of God . . . can only come in the age of the World-picture. . . . Earlier, in dire straits in the world [God] made, we can more easily be inclined to appeal to him as helper and

savior, while accepting that we can't understand how his creation got into this fix, and whose fault it is (presumably ours). Now that we think we see how it all works . . . people in the coffee-houses and salons begin to express their disaffection in reflections on divine justice, and the theologians begin to feel that this is the challenge they must meet.[114]

Second, people now believed we were not created primarily to serve God for his benefit. Rather, God had made the world for our benefit. But, Taylor goes on, it was this deistic concept of God—not so much the traditional Christian view—that the Lisbon earthquake threw into crisis. He wrote:

Once we claim to understand the universe and how it works; once we even try to explain how it works by invoking its being created for our benefit, then this explanation is open to clear challenge. . . . In Lisbon, 1755, it seems clearly not to have [worked for our benefit]. So the immanent order ups the ante.[115]

If you believe that the world was made for our benefit by God, then horrendous suffering and evil will shake your understanding of life. Horrendous evil is now a much bigger problem for those with a residue of Christianity—with a belief in a distant God who exists for our benefit—than it was for a full-blown orthodox faith not weakened by the immanent frame. In other words, suffering and evil disprove God's existence only if you have a particular view of God that is already a departure from the more traditional, orthodox view. The skeptical conclusion is largely inherent in the premises. You could argue that, within the immanent frame, the game is rigged against the God of the Bible when we come to evil and suffering.

Residual Christianity and the Problem of Evil

It is often noted that the United States became secularized more slowly than Europe and Canada, but secularization has nevertheless moved forward. Despite the Deism of American founders such as Thomas Jefferson, several powerful spiritual awakenings kept American public culture characterized by Christian beliefs. In particular, those beliefs included the universality of human sin, that every person has a nature prone to and capable of great evil. This meant that "moral evil"—terrible suffering and pain inflicted by human beings on other human beings—was easy to explain. It was seen as part and parcel of living within the sinful human race. In addition, the doctrine of inherent human sinfulness also explained natural evil. Because we had turned from God, it was understandable that our world would be a dark and broken place, since it was under the judgment of a just God. And so earthquakes as well as invasions were occasions for public calls for widespread prayer and repentance.

But America began moving away from older beliefs in human sinfulness and in spiritual blindness and helplessness apart from the assistance of God. Andrew Delbanco wrote *The Death of Satan,* in which he traces how, during the early nineteenth century, American culture began losing its grip on the Christian doctrines of the evil of human nature and the reality of Satan. "Pride of self," he wrote, "once the mark of the devil, was now not just a legitimate emotion but America's uncontested god. . . . Liberal individualism assumed its modern form in these years."[116]

And so we have come to our present day. All of Western societies live within the secular frame, and even though many people still profess fairly traditional beliefs in God, most are affected by this frame. We see ourselves as able to control our own destiny, able to discern for ourselves what is right and wrong, and we see God as obligated to arrange things for our benefit, especially if we live a good enough life according to our own chosen standards. Sociologist Christian Smith calls this mind-set "moralistic, therapeutic deism."[117] Many of the people within this mind-set would identify as believers in God and others would go beyond that and call themselves Christians. But secularization thins out traditional beliefs, as we have seen. And this secularized belief in God, or this residue of Christianity, may be the worst possible preexisting condition in which to encounter suffering.

In ancient times, Christianity was widely recognized as having superior resources for facing evil, suffering, and death. In modern times—though it is not as publicly discussed—it continues to have assets for sufferers arguably far more powerful than anything secular culture can offer. Those assets, however, reside in robust, distinctive Christian beliefs.

The first relevant Christian belief is in a personal, wise, infinite, and therefore inscrutable God who controls the affairs of the world—and that is far more comforting than the belief that our lives are in the hands of fickle fate or random chance. The second crucial tenet is that, in Jesus Christ, God came to earth and suffered with and for us sacrificially—and that is far more comforting than the idea that God is remote and uninvolved. The cross also proves that, despite all the inscrutability, God is for us. The third doctrine is that through faith in Christ's work on the cross, we can have assurance of our salvation—that is far more comforting than the karmic systems of thought. We are assured that the difficulties of life are not payment for our past sins, since Jesus has paid for them. As Luther taught, suffering is unbearable if you aren't certain that God is for you and with you. Secularity cannot give you that, and religions that provide salvation through virtue and good works cannot give it, either.

The fourth great doctrine is that of the bodily resurrection from the dead for all who believe. This completes the spectrum of our joys and consolations. One of the deepest desires of the human heart is for love without parting. Needless to say, the prospect of the resurrection is far more comforting than the beliefs that death takes you into nothingness or into an impersonal spiritual substance. The resurrection goes beyond the promise of an ethereal, disembodied afterlife. We get our bodies back, in a state of beauty and power that we cannot today imagine. Jesus' resurrection body was corporeal—it could be touched and embraced, and he ate food. And yet he passed through closed doors and could disappear. This is a material existence, but one beyond the bounds of our imagination. The idea of heaven can be a consolation for suffering, a compensation for the life we have lost. But resurrection is not just consolation—it is restoration. We get it all back—the love, the loved ones, the goods, the beauties of this life—but in new, unimaginable degrees of glory and joy and strength. It is a *reversal* of the seeming irreversibility of loss that Luc Ferry speaks of.[118]

If one does not find consolation in these Christian doctrines, then I think total disbelief in God is better preparation for tragedy than the thinned-out, secularized belief in God that is so common in our Western world. Many people today believe in God, and may go to church, but if you ask them whether they are certain of their salvation and acceptance with God, or whether the idea of Jesus' sacrificial death on the cross is real and profoundly moving to them, or whether they are convinced of the bodily resurrection of Jesus and believers—you are likely to get a negative answer, or just a stare. Western culture's immanent frame weakens intellectual belief in God, and it makes heart certainty even more difficult to come by. But this partial Christianity or theism is far more difficult to hold in the face of horrendous suffering than is atheism. As Taylor has shown us, natural evil offends those who believe in a God who exists for us, and confounds those who don't believe we are all sinners needing salvation by sheer grace.

Atheist writer Susan Jacoby wrote in *The New York Times* that "when I see homeless people shivering in the wake of a deadly storm, when the news media bring me almost obscenely close to the raw grief of bereft parents, I do not have to ask, as all people of faith must, why an all-powerful, all-good God allows such things to happen."[119] She is right, of course, at one level. If you don't believe in God at all, you don't struggle with the question of why life is so unjust. It just is—deal with it. But you also have none of the powerful comforts and joys that Christian belief can give you, either. Jacoby says that atheism makes you "free of what is known as the theodicy problem" not needing to "square [terrible] things" in this life "with an unseen overlord in the next."

But as we have seen in philosopher Charles Taylor's writing, the "theodicy problem" is largely the product not of a strong belief in God and sin, but of a weaker form of belief. It is as we get larger in our own eyes, less dependent on God's grace and revelation, and surer that we understand how the universe works and how history should go that the problem of evil becomes so intolerable. And it is only as God becomes more remote—a God who is all-loving only in the abstract, not in the sense of having suffered and died for us to rescue us from evil—that he seems unbearably callous in the face of pain. In short, theism without certainty of salvation or resurrection is far more disillusioning in the midst of pain than is atheism. When suffering, believing in God thinly or in the abstract is worse than not believing in God at all.

The End Has Not Been Written

by Tess

My crisis of faith occurred early in adulthood, detached from any significant personal suffering. In my training to be a physician, I had participated in the care of untold numbers of tragedies: seven-year-olds being thrown from pickup trucks, fatal automobile accidents, twenty-five-year-olds diagnosed with breast cancer, heart attacks on Christmas Day, etc. I had seen a lot. I had treated a lot. And as I wrestled with these challenging circumstances, working through them with my husband, Barry, our faith had been tested. God increased our faith such that we trusted Him, even if we didn't understand Him. And over the next several years, as my understanding of the complexities of human physiology grew, I began to develop more and more amazement that anything in the human body ever went right. How any baby was born without birth defects was a miracle. How we could continue to breathe and digest and fight cancer while sleeping was a marvel.

The idea of nature being in a very delicate, very tenuous balance, all by the *sheer grace* of God was driven home to me almost on a daily basis. So the idea of pain and suffering occurring and people asking the question "Why me?" was not part of our narrative. More, the question became, "Why not me? What did I do to deserve this unmerited string of unbroken blessing?"

In early 2012, my mother was diagnosed with metastatic and recurrent ovarian cancer, with a terminal prognosis. We displaced our family of four, pregnant with our third boy, to my parents' house in Arizona to be with her until the end. Three weeks after our arrival, she died and was reunited with our Lord. In the last days of her physical illness, she became increasingly delirious, but remarkably, what she was quoting was Scripture. It was so embedded in her heart, that when disease had ravaged her mind, and reduced her to incoherent ramblings, what was left was the Word of God. As we buried her, my prayer was that the Lord would place His Word so deep in my heart, so that when my mind was *in extremis*, I would only be able to speak His words back to Him.

In August 2012, we welcomed our third boy in three years; our oldest child turned age three six weeks later. Life was near perfect again. Fourteen weeks later, on a beautiful and mild November afternoon, I returned from work into the blissful chaos of our home, just when our nanny was waking our baby from his nap. Her screams of terror took several seconds to penetrate my consciousness. I walked into our bedroom, knowing exactly what had happened. I knew he had died before I laid eyes on him. My very first thought was Job 1:21, "The Lord gives, and the Lord takes away, blessed be the name of the Lord" followed closely by 1 Thessalonians 5:18, "Give thanks in all circumstances; for this is the will of God in Christ Jesus for you." All the years of training, combined with the incredible power of the Holy Spirit to equip you with exactly what you need when you need it, came over me. I was on the phone with my husband at the time. I told him Wyatt had died and he needed to come home immediately. I performed CPR while on speakerphone with 911, but I knew it was just a formality. Policemen and detectives came and went, ruled out a homicide, then the medical examiner's office arrived to take my baby's body. I refused. I was not giving up my baby without a fight, or at least an argument, with God. I knew what He said about asking and receiving, and not receiving because we don't ask, and the widow who annoys the judge enough to wear him down and grant her request, and faith the size of a mustard seed. For one hour, my husband and I, along with our nanny, prayed for resurrection over our son. Actual, physical resurrection, like Lazarus. We went to the throne of God boldly, completely lucid, not grief-stricken, and asked as forthrightly as we could to give us back our baby. Not my will, but Yours be done. God heard our prayer. And He said no. And I told Him, okay, but You're going to have to get us through this, because we cannot do this ourselves. In the end, the cause of death was positional asphyxia, or SIDS (sudden infant death syndrome). He wasn't even sick.

But the end hasn't been written. The Lord has shown us over and over again how He never intended for us to go through this alone. He gave us Himself, and He gave us the Body of Christ. The morning after Wyatt died, two of our friends showed up without calling to look after our other two children. Our Redeemer Church community mobilized an army of prayer warriors and help warriors. Meals were sent, our families flown in from Nicaragua, Arkansas, Texas, and Arizona, people gave up their apartments for our families, rented an apartment down the block, delivered meals to our nanny in Brooklyn, planned and executed the memorial service, printed bulletins, etc. Every single last detail was taken care of, in typical Type-A New Yorker style, with precision and excellence, and all without our knowledge or consent. And so we were allowed to descend to the very depths of our grief, experience it in all its agony, and emerge on the other side. When we emerged, our community had been transformed in unity through suffering, and we were pregnant. "The Lord gives, and the Lord takes away, blessed be the name of the Lord."

Tim Keller once said that God gives us what we would have asked for if we knew everything that He knows. The idea that the prince of Heaven would empty himself and become poor, to live and dwell among us is humbling. The idea that there is nothing in the human experience that God himself has not suffered, even losing a child, is sustaining. And the idea that in His resurrection, Jesus' scars became His glory is empowering. God will use these scars for His glory, as they become our glory. Indeed, the end hasn't been written.

THREE

The Challenge to the Secular

You desire to know the art of living, my friend? It is contained in one phrase: make use of suffering.

Henri Frederic Amiel[120]

In the first two chapters, we have seen the challenges that the secular view has in equipping sufferers. Though classical Greek philosophers insisted that their frameworks helped people face grief and death, they did not work for many, perhaps most, people. Something similar may be happening today. Atheist writers like Richard Dawkins and Susan Jacoby make similar claims that a fully secular view of life eliminates the "problem of evil" and frees people to concentrate on making the world a better place. Yet does this really work for most people?

As Richard Shweder points out, while this framework dominates the elite institutions of Western societies, it is largely ignored by actual sufferers. Shweder argues that the older, more spiritual and traditional approaches persist at a popular level underneath the dominant secular discourse. They exist "as personal or communal 'counter-discourses' to the official discourse of scientific explanation."[121]

Where Were the Humanists?

Not long after the December 2012 Newtown shootings, and all the speeches by civic leaders, memorial services, and funerals were over,

Samuel G. Freedman wrote a column in *The New York Times* titled "In a Crisis, Humanists Seem Absent." Freedman observed the heavy use of explicit religious vocabulary and symbolism in all public ceremonies and by both political leaders and sufferers. Connecticut is hardly the center of the U.S. Bible Belt, yet every single family in Newtown who lost a child chose to hold religious services, which took place in Catholic, Congregational, Mormon, and Methodist churches, as well as in a Protestant mega-church and a Jewish cemetery. A black Christian youth group journeyed from the Deep South to sing "Amazing Grace."[122] President Obama delivered a eulogy that was essentially a sermon, speaking of God "calling the children home." He quoted extensively from 2 Corinthians 4 and 5 and used its hope for a world and life beyond this one to console and make bearable the losses we experience here and now.

Freedman was one of many who found it startling that in an increasingly secular society, where now some twenty percent of the population told pollsters they had "no religious preference," our society turned so visibly to God and faith to communally face the tragedy. Freedman said that it all "has left behind one prickly question: where were the humanists? At a time when the percentage of Americans without religious affiliation is growing rapidly, why did the 'nones,' as they are colloquially known, seem so absent?" (These are Freedman's terms for secular people who do not believe in a personal deity or the supernatural.)

Freedman quoted Greg M. Epstein, humanist chaplain at Harvard, who said, "What religion has to offer people at moments like this—more than theology, more than divine presence—is community. And we need to provide an alternative form of community . . . for the increasing number of people who say they are not believers." In short, Epstein was saying that religion doesn't offer sufferers much more than loving, supportive relationships, and that is what secular people must be able to offer as well.

But our survey of cultures and history has shown that this is not true. Richard Shweder, Peter Berger, and other sociologists and anthropologists certainly would not agree that religious cultures offer primarily supportive community rather than "theology." Above all, religions give sufferers larger explanations of life that make sense of suffering and help them find meaning in their pain. These explanations are profoundly theological and it is at this very point that modern secularism cannot help.

For good measure, Freedman added that not only is secular humanism unable to provide theology, but it is hard even to see how it can offer community. Religions create communities around shared worship, annual observances and festivals, and with calls for deep relationship grounded in sacred texts. They create rites of passage for births, coming-of-age, marriages, and deaths that not only tie members of the community to one another but also to believers in past centuries, and thus the past itself. Secularism cannot produce any of these things and has therefore not forged the kind of tight communities that can comfort and console people during times of grief.

Freedman argues that there is a fundamental problem in secularism that will always block efforts to form the same kind of "thick" communities that religious belief provides. Community among persons is forged only when there is something more important than one's own interests to which all share a higher allegiance. And, Freedman says, "humanism suffers . . . from the valorization of the individual." When I am the final authority for determining right and wrong, and when nothing is more important than my right to live as I see fit, tight supportive community is eroded, perhaps even impossible.

Is Atheism a Blessing?

Just a few days after Samuel Freedman's article appeared, Susan Jacoby responded in the same pages with the op-ed piece "The Blessings of Atheism," which I wrote about in the previous chapter. She voiced her "exasperation at the endless talk about faith in God as the only consolation for those devastated by the unfathomable murders in Newtown, Conn . . . [that] nonbelief . . . has nothing to offer when people are suffering."[123] To counter that impression, Jacoby began by recounting how she became an atheist.

I trace my atheism to my first encounter, at age seven, with the scourge of polio. In 1952, a nine-year-old friend was stricken by the disease and clinging to life in an iron lung. After visiting him in the hospital, I asked my mother, "Why would God do that to a little boy?" She sighed in a way that telegraphed her lack of conviction and said: "I don't know. The priest would say God must have his reasons, but I don't know what they could be." Just two years later, in 1954, Jonas Salk's vaccine began the process of eradicating polio, and my mother took the opportunity to suggest that God may have guided his research. I remember replying, "Well, God should have guided the doctors a long time ago so that Al wouldn't be in an iron lung." (He was to die only eight years later, by which time I was a committed atheist.)

Jacoby went on to claim that "it is primarily in the face of suffering . . . that I am forcefully reminded of what atheism has to offer." As an atheist, she continued, she is free from the problem of evil that religious people must face. She did not need to ask, "as all people of faith must, why an all-powerful, all-good God allows such things to happen." This escape from the burden of the problem of evil "frees up" the atheist "to concentrate on the fate of this world." Instead of the doubt and confusion that she says must absorb believers in the face of tragedy, atheists can get to work to care for the victims of it and change things so that it doesn't happen again.

Finally, she says that it is possible when comforting others to show that "reason and emotion are not opposed but complementary." She quotes Robert Green Ingersoll, "the Great Agnostic" of the nineteenth century, who said at the graveside of his friend's child: "They who stand with breaking hearts around this little grave, need have no fear. The larger and nobler faith in all that is, and is to be, tells us that death, even at its worst, is only perfect rest. . . . The dead do not suffer."[124] Jacoby points to this as an example of secular consolation. Ingersoll was taking a very "rational" position—that there is no existence after death—and using it to comfort the grief stricken.

Jacoby is right that the secularist mind-set encourages activism against the forces that cause suffering. Religious systems that point to karma, or the illusory nature of this world, or to any afterlife at all can indeed lull people into a kind of passivity toward evil and injustice in the world. This is one point at which the secular approach may have it right as opposed to some other cultural and religious views of suffering.

But that may be the only point at which secularism has an advantage.

First, Jacoby exaggerates when she says that all people of faith *must* struggle over the problem of evil. We have seen in Charles Taylor's discussion of our age that the "problem of evil" was not widely felt by most people until populations began to inhabit the "immanent" frame—the secular mind-set, which valorizes individual reason and produces people "confident in their own powers of moral ordering." More robust beliefs in God, as we have seen, do not eliminate the problem of evil, but they keep it from becoming all-absorbing or debilitating.

Jacoby continues that atheists are freed to "advocate for social causes like justice for African-Americans, women's rights, prison reform and the elimination of cruelty to animals." In this she holds up Robert Green Ingersoll. But her comment seems to deliberately ignore two issues—one historical and one philosophical. The historical issue is that so many of the great social justice movements were religious in nature. Religion, then, can also free people for social justice.[125] It would be difficult historically to make the case that atheism has inspired more movements for social justice than religion has, so it is not clear how atheism provides a better resource for responding to suffering.

The philosophical issue is perhaps even greater. Jacoby assumes that although there is no God, definitions of justice and human flourishing—and of right and wrong—are nonetheless self-evident. But that is not the case. Within a religious framework, ethics and morality have some clear basis. They are grounded in the sources of authority that religion recognizes. But within a secular worldview, defining moral and just behavior becomes an enormous difficulty, and not only because there is disagreement about particular ethical standards. The deeper question for secular thinkers is what to base standards on so they are not purely arbitrary. At least since the eighteenth century, philosophers such as

David Hume have pointed out that science and empirical reason cannot be the basis of morality, since they can tell us how people live but not how they *ought* to live. Hume wrote that reason alone "is incompetent to answer any fundamental question about . . . morality, or the meaning of life."[126]

Harvard professor Michael Sandel in *Justice: What's the Right Thing to Do?* shows that there are at least three different, conflicting theories of justice vying for dominance in our society. Each theory depends on divergent beliefs about human nature and the meaning of human life, all of which rest on belief about the nature of things that can't be proven. Sandel provides an enormous number of examples—including abortion, immigration reform, and same-sex marriage—to show that there is no neutral "rational" basis for either side on these issues, that each side argues on the basis of different conceptions of freedom, different views of the proper relationship of the individual to community, and different definitions of a virtuous human life. Atheism, then, does not solve the big questions of what justice is and what our vision of the good society should be.[127]

Finally, Jacoby invokes Robert Green Ingersoll's claim in his funeral oration that "the dead do not suffer" to show that a strictly secular view of the world can be comforting. But Ingersoll was merely recycling Epicurus's notion that we need not fear death because we are nonexistent. As we have seen, this effort at comfort was, in Luc Ferry's words, "too brutal to be honest." It makes little sense to point to a state in which we are stripped of all love and everything that gives meaning in life—and tell people that they need not fear it. The secular consolation that "the dead do not suffer" seems thin in comparison to the Christian consolation of the resurrection. A secularist like Jacoby would respond, "but that belief isn't true," but Christians could say the same thing about secular beliefs. Putting aside the question of which set of beliefs is true, it is hard to maintain that the secular framework equips its followers as well for evil and suffering as religious faiths equip theirs.

If you are a parent facing the horror of your little child in a coffin, how do the two forms of comfort compare? The evidence—as anthropologists like Shweder show, and as the Newtown shootings show—is that when it comes to it, the vast majority of people will reach into nonsecular cultures and religions to survive their suffering.

One strongly atheistic woman commented on one of the many blog discussions about the president's Newtown speech. She admitted that the secular discourse simply doesn't work for most people. "In my adult life I believed in God for about thirty seconds," she wrote, "when they buried my son. There was an indescribably vivid sense of this departing spirit going . . . away. Then I came to my senses." She had the strongest intuition at that moment that this material world could not be all that existed. But even though she refused to follow that instinct, she recognized how powerful it is. "It's easy to see how people would be seduced," she added.[128]

This intuition—that we are not just a concatenation of matter and chemicals but also a soul—is, according to Shweder, one of the most widespread convictions of human beings in the world today and through the ages. Even this woman's deep, deliberate rejection of religious belief could not fend it off at the moment of grief. It is unrealistic, and maybe cruel, to insist that everyone must indeed reject it or be branded, in Richard Dawkins's term, "infantile."

Suffering and the Turn to the Spiritual

Both research and experience tell us that a majority of people reach for the spiritual to help them interpret and bear up under horrendous suffering. Victor Frankl, a Jewish psychiatrist who survived three years in the Nazi death camps, observed how some of his fellow prisoners were able to endure the horror and pass through it while others could not. The difference came down to what Frankl called meaning. The problem is that contemporary people think life is all about finding happiness. We decide what conditions will make us happy and then we work to bring those conditions about. To live for happiness means that you are trying to get something out of life. But when suffering comes along, it takes the conditions for happiness away, and so suffering destroys all your reason to keep living. But to "live for meaning" means not that you try to get something out of life but rather that life expects something from *us*. In other words, you have meaning only when there is something in life more important than your own personal freedom and happiness, something for which you are glad to sacrifice your happiness.[129]

Because this was the only way to survive the terror of the death camps, Frankl noted how often secular or nominally religious people turned to faith once they entered the horror of those places. Many prisoners developed a new "religious interest . . . the most sincere imaginable. The depth and vigor of religious belief often surprised the new arrivals." This included "improvised prayers and services in the corner of a hut, or in the darkness of the locked cattle truck."[130] Frankl argued that this increased faith was not only natural, but it was one of the only ways to go on in an environment that stripped you of all earthly sources of significance, security, and purpose.

After the Boston Marathon bombings, a staff writer for *The Atlantic,* Eleanor Barkhorn, noticed her social media feeds lit up with calls to "Pray for Boston." Barkhorn said, "It was jarring. . . . It was . . . strange to see so many non-religious friends talking about prayer. The majority of my Facebook friends who wrote about praying aren't especially observant. Maybe they go to church or synagogue on holidays, but not regularly—and they certainly don't post about prayer under normal circumstances. . . . What I saw on Twitter and Facebook . . . wasn't just faithful people reminding other faithful people to . . . pray. It was also the non-religious invoking prayer." Barkhorn went on to observe that the statement "There are no atheists in foxholes" is both patronizing and disproven. Plenty of people *become* atheists in foxholes. She also argued that the widespread compulsion to pray after a crisis is shortlived. But she gave a first-person account of how, as a young nonreligious resident in Manhattan after 9/11, she had felt "an involuntary urge to call on God's name" which eventually grew into a desire to read the Bible and finally into a full-blown Christian faith.[131]

A celebrated book by Andrew Solomon, *Far from the Tree,* examines the shock and response of parents who discover that the child born to them is not like them—but instead is deaf, a dwarf, has Down's syndrome, is autistic, or is chronically ill or disabled in some way. Solomon presents a series of well-written and sympathetic case studies of families who have faced each of these conditions and more. These children always represent a crisis to the family into which they come, and yet Solomon's bottom-line finding was: "This book's conundrum is that most of the families described here have ended up grateful for experiences they would have done anything to avoid."[132] This, of course, fits far better with the ancient cultures' understanding of "the sweet uses of adversity," of suffering as not the interruption of a life story but as a crucial part of a good life. One of the most interesting things to a reader is to see how often religion slips into so many of the descriptions of how families came to terms with their children. This is true despite the fact that Solomon himself is not religious and has no such agenda.

One set of parents, David and Sara, gave birth to an infant son who was blind and retarded. Their son Jamie grew up not able to sit up or roll over on his own and had to be permanently catheterized. Assured that Jamie's condition was anomalous, Bill and Sara had another child, a daughter who was healthy, and then another son, Sam, who turned out to be even more retarded and neurologically handicapped than Jamie. Incredibly to the detached reader, Sara told Solomon, "If we had known that the condition might be repeated, we would not have risked it. . . . Having said that, if I were told 'We can just wipe out that experience' [of having a second handicapped child] I wouldn't. . . . It absolutely blows my mind, the impact that a blind, retarded, nonverbal, nonambulatory person has had on people. He has a way of opening and touching people that we can't come near. That's part of our survival story—our marveling at how he has moved so many people."[133]

It is a remarkable story, but sprinkled through the account are many religious references, unsurprising in light of what we have seen in our study of cultures and history. The very day after they learned that their first child was blind and retarded, Sara said to David, "I don't know why I am saying this, but I feel very strongly that we need to have Jamie baptized." This impulse came as a surprise to them because neither had gone to church in years. And they still resisted much of religious doctrine, but, Sara explained, "I think I was acknowledging that Jamie had a soul." This was a crucial move for the parents to make. To love and care for their son, they had to know he was truly human. But if he consisted only of a body, that was a hard case to make. He lacked most of the capacities that we think of as making us human. Philosopher Martha Nussbaum lists the kinds of "capabilities" that in the secular view define someone who is human and therefore has rights. She includes: the use of imagination and thought, emotions, practical reason, affiliation ("having the social bases of self-respect"), play, and control over one's environment.[134] Of course Jamie had none of these. How could they avoid slowly sliding into thinking and treating him more like an animal or an object? They turned back to an older understanding of human nature, which consists of both body and soul, because all human beings, whether brilliant or retarded, are made in God's image. As Richard Shweder argues, the official secular narratives are inadequate for millions of sufferers in Western societies.

There are lots of other signs that the families in Solomon's book regularly resorted to "counter-discourses" to survive and even thrive in what would seem to be intolerable situations. The father of a son who is a dwarf is a devout Christian, and came to love his son by professing, "I believe there's a God. I believe God doesn't make junk."[135] Another parent of an autistic child points to her church as the biggest comfort she has. Jamie's sister, Liza, once took two weeks off work to read him *The Chronicles of Narnia,* a set of children's books by C. S. Lewis that is heavy with Christian symbolism. Even Solomon, not a religious person, said his own child was "richly and permanently human to me, possessed of a soul, and no alteration could change that."[136]

The Failure of the Secular

The secular view of life does not work for most people in the face of suffering. Why not? Let's begin to summarize our findings.

One reason is because human suffering comes in such an enormous variety of forms, stemming from a wide spectrum of different causes. The Western approach oversimplifies the complex causes of suffering, reducing it all to "victimization as the dominant account."[137] Of course this does account for suffering in many cases. Children who die by fire in an unsafe building are pure victims—victims of the builders who violated fire codes, and victims of an electrical mishap. But plenty of suffering—even much illness—is caused to some degree by the sufferers themselves. Too much of suffering simply doesn't fit into the straitjacket of Western analysis. Other cultures see suffering as caused by accident and mishap, sin and failure, destiny or God's will, and the struggle between good and evil. Some talk about the difference between "natural evil" (mishaps and destiny) and "moral evil" (sin and oppression). This spectrum of causes accounts well for the diversity of suffering's forms. The secular approach does not.

Another problem with our current Western culture's view is that, in the end, it is naïvely optimistic about human life. As Susan Jacoby and others suggest, the main response of the secular person to evil and suffering is not to find some meaning in it, nor to prepare to triumph over it in some future life, but to make the world better, to slowly but surely eliminate suffering right here. But the reason for all the emphasis on the here and now of this world is that secularism has no other happiness to offer. If you can't find it here, there really is no hope for you.

In his book *Straw Dogs: Thoughts on Humans and Other Animals*, philosopher John Gray looks at the epidemic of drug use and addiction in Western societies. "Drug use," he writes, "is a tacit admission of a forbidden truth [in Western culture.]" What is that truth? It is that "for most people happiness is beyond reach." Human life is unavoidably hard and unhappy for the vast majority of people and always will be. In the secular worldview, all happiness and meaning must be found in this lifetime and world. To live with any hope, then, secular people must believe that we can eliminate most sources of unhappiness for the majority of people. But that is impossible. The causes of suffering are infinitely complex and impossible to eliminate. In a startling admission, the nonreligious Gray argues this very point, that religious cultures were able by the nature of their beliefs to be far more realistic about how inveterate human misery is:

Religious cultures could admit that earthly life was hard, for they promised another in which all tears would be wiped away. Their humanist successors affirm something still more incredible—that in future, even the near future, everyone can be happy. Societies founded on a faith in progress cannot admit the normal unhappiness of human life.[138]

Author Ernest Becker, in *The Denial of Death,* likewise expresses his disgust with what he calls "scientific manipulators" who don't take the misery and horror of human life seriously enough. They give the impression that "we can change the world" with this or that technology, or that we can manage pain and suffering, we can "legislate the grotesque out of it, inaugurate a 'proper' human condition." This is why he feels that "in this sense, all science is 'bourgeois,' an affair of bureaucrats."

The Expansion of the Self

But perhaps suffering's main challenge to secular cultures is that it reveals the thinness of the World Story they give their adherents. As we have observed, every culture must give its people a story, an overarching narrative, about what human life is all about. Andrew Delbanco, in *The Real American Dream: A Meditation on Hope,* says that a cultural narrative must accomplish two things. First, it must give us hope. A narrative can give us hope only if it helps us "imagine some end to life that transcends our own tiny allotment of days and hours if we are to keep at bay the 'dim, back-of-the-mind suspicion that one may be adrift in an absurd world,'" and if it overcomes "the lurking suspicion that all our getting and spending amounts to nothing more than fidgeting while we wait for death."[139] Second, however, the narrative must enable a society to cohere instead of atomize into a million individual parts. It inspires us to put self-interest aside for the community, by delivering "the indispensible feeling that the world does not end at the borders of the self."[140]

Delbanco says that at the heart of every story is a big idea, "what life is all about," that enables the people of a society to identify themselves. He traces what he thinks have been the three big ideas of American culture—God, Nation, and Self. In the first years of U.S. society, the meaning of life was living for the glory of God.

Then, Delbanco argues, nineteenth-century Americans substituted the United States as a nation—its democratic values, expansion, and prosperity—for God and his kingdom. The hope for God's kingdom was transferred to a mission to make the world a better place through the values and power of America as redeemer-nation, "the greatest nation on earth." Here, Delbanco joins many other scholars who have made the same case. This move was most definitely a stage in the secularization of our society, a move deeper into the immanent frame. Nationalism and democracy were the new religion because Americans were invested in becoming self-made individuals. Alexis de Tocqueville said, even in the 1830s, that one of the "novel features" of America was its individualism. The American, he wrote, "exists only in himself and for himself alone."[141] So during this second stage of U.S. history, God was still believed in by the great majority, but he was becoming more remote, less involved in the workings of the world, less mysterious and majestic, leaving human beings capable of understanding and remaking the world.

But Delbanco believes that these older cultural "stories" have run their course. The Nation phase of American history still envisioned a higher good than individual freedom. As every culture always has, we were called to put our personal interests aside for something—the good of the country. But sometime in the later twentieth century, "something died," he wrote, namely "any conception of a common destiny worth tears, sacrifice, and maybe even death." Instant gratification was installed "as the hallmark of the good life." Both devotion to God and anything like American patriotism are laughed at among people of "advanced views" and so there is no "collective vision" left.[142] The contemporary person, for example, does not feel much guilt because "he no longer feels . . . there exists something in the world that transcends himself."[143]

> The history of hope I have tried to sketch in this book is one
> of diminution. At first, the self expanded toward (and was

sometimes overwhelmed by) the vastness of God. From the early republic to the Great Society, it remained implicated in a national ideal lesser than God but larger and more enduring than any individual citizen. Today, hope has narrowed to the vanishing point.[144]

What is being described is called expressive individualism by Robert Bellah in his landmark book *Habits of the Heart,* published just about the time that Delbanco saw the strong "turn toward the self" in our culture.[145] This is a very large subject, and writers on both the left and the right have warned about its consequences—from Tocqueville to sociologist Émile Durkheim, from Karl Marx to Edmund Burke, all of whom predicted a decaying social fabric and "the hell of loneliness."

But our interests in this book are narrower. Many express alarm over what "expanded self"—a self that says "I [have] to create my own happiness, to build my strength, to be the engine of my momentum"[146]—means for social cohesion. However, we are concerned about what it means for suffering. As Victor Frankl recognized in the death camps, people who are their own legislators of morality and meaning have nothing to die for, and therefore nothing to live for when life takes away their freedom. As Richard Shweder and Andrew Delbanco perceive, each in his own way, the "life story" that modern culture gives people does not have any ultimate goal more important than one's own comfort and power. As Frankl saw, when we have no meaning beyond personal happiness, suffering can lead very quickly to suicide.

A Different Story

We have been arguing that every culture gives its members a story about what life is all about, and the story of late modern culture—that life is about individual freedom and happiness—has no place for suffering. But the Christian story, as we will see, is utterly different. Suffering is actually at the heart of the Christian story. Suffering is the result of our turn away from God, and therefore it was the way through which God himself in

Jesus Christ came and rescued us for himself. And now it is how we suffer that comprises one of the main ways we become great and Christ-like, holy and happy, and a crucial way we show the world the love and glory of our Savior.

Pastor-theologian William Willimon tells this story from early in his ministry. A woman in his church had just given birth, and he went to the hospital to visit her. When he got there, the husband and wife were waiting for the doctor because they had received the ominous news that "there were problems with the birth." When the doctor arrived, he told the couple that the child had been born with Down syndrome, but he also had a minor and correctible respiratory condition. He said, "My recommendation is for you to consider just letting nature take its course, and then in a few days there shouldn't be a problem." The child would die "naturally" if they just left things as they were. The couple was confused and asked why they shouldn't fix the problem. The doctor looked at them and said that raising a Down syndrome child would create enormous amounts of stress in the marriage, and that studies showed that many parents of Down syndrome children separated or divorced. He then said, "Is it fair of you to bring this sort of suffering upon your other two children?"[147]

At the word *suffering*, the wife suddenly seemed to understand. She countered that her children had lived a safe and comfortable life with every advantage in the world. They had known, if anything, too little of suffering and the difficulty of life in the world. She spoke of "God's hand" and said, "I could certainly see why it would make sense for a child like this to be born into a family like ours. Our children will do just fine. When you think about it, it could be a great opportunity."

The doctor was dumbfounded and turned to the minister, urging him to "talk some reason into them." Willimon of course knew that the couple needed to be given good instruction as to what lay ahead so that they did not take up their parenting of this new child with naïveté. But, he wrote, the couple *was* using reasoning, though it was a reasoning foreign to the doctor. In the dominant cultural narrative—reflected in the reasoning of the doctor—"words like 'suffering' are unredeemably negative" because "it is important to avoid pain at all costs" since "our lives are [valued] by nothing more significant than our desires." The couple, however, was thinking about life through the logic of the Christian story, namely the Fall and the redemption of the world through Jesus Christ, and in that story, suffering can be redemptive, a way of serving others, and a way of glorifying God.[148]

The Call for Humility

In the Old Testament book of 2 Kings, we read the story of Naaman, a wealthy and powerful general of the Syrian army.[149] He was suffering terribly, dying slowly of leprosy. Hearing of a powerful God in Israel, he traveled there with both money and a threatening letter from his own ruler. He went to the king of Israel and demanded to be cured of his leprosy. Like so many of us today, Naaman thought money, influence, and expertise could address his suffering. So he went to the person in the culture who had the most of these things and expected a resolution. In response, the Israelite king tore his robes and replied: "Am I *God*? Can I kill and bring back to life?" (2 Kings 5:7). In other words, he said, "Don't look to me to do something only God can do!"

The whole Western world today needs to listen to this cry of the king of Israel. When we confront suffering, we think that what will solve it is a change in public policy, or the best expertise in psychology and therapy, or technological advances. But the world's darkness is too deep to be dispelled merely by such things. It is wrong, in our pride, to believe that we can control and defeat the darkness with our knowledge. Most of the time, we do not admit how dark the world is, but when events like 9/11 or the Newtown massacre happen, that fact presses down on us almost intolerably. And we should *not* be passive in the face of disasters and tragedies. If a change in public policy would prevent a particular form of the darkness from happening again, we should by all means do whatever it takes.

And yet it is crucial to realize at the same time that such measures will never be enough. Pain and evil in this world are pervasive and deep and have spiritual roots. They cannot be completely reduced to empirical causes that can be isolated and entirely eliminated. As Hamlet said,

"There are more things in heaven and earth than are dreamt of in your philosophy. . . ." Perhaps even more to the point is a line in J. R. R. Tolkien's novel *The Lord of the Rings*: "Always after a defeat and respite, [evil] takes another shape and grows again."[150] No matter what we do, human suffering and evil can't be eradicated. Even when you put all your force into stopping it—it just takes another form and grows in some new way. If we are going to face it, it takes more than earthly resources.

Naaman eventually turned not to wealth, technique, or expert power but to God himself. Instead of proudly trusting in his own or others' expertise, he was called to the soul work of humility. As a result, he not only got a cure for his body but a new relationship with God and a soul infused with grace and joy. Suffering led to his salvation. This does not even begin to answer the question "Why does God allow so much evil and suffering in the world to persist?" Nor does such an example justify suffering. And yet one of the main teachings of the Bible is that almost no one grows into greatness or finds God without suffering, without pain coming into our lives like smelling salts to wake us up to all sorts of facts about life and our own hearts to which we were blind.

For reasons past our finding out, even Christ did not bring salvation and grace to us apart from infinite suffering on the cross. As he loved us enough to face the suffering with patience and courage, so we must learn to trust in him enough to do the same. And as his weakness and suffering, thus faced, led to resurrection power, so can ours.

Life Story: Scars of Beauty and Depth

by Kendra

Silence. Stillness. "I'm sorry . . . but I can't seem to find a heartbeat," said the ultrasound technician. More silence. All of a sudden, everything in that dark room seemed darker and colder. Just moments before, my husband, John, and I were chatting with the technician. We had been waiting twenty long weeks to learn the gender of our child . . . hoping it would be the encouragement that we needed to carry us through the second half of this difficult season. But, in an instant, the room had grown cold and lifeless. As the technician stepped out to call the doctor, the darkness of the room echoed the darkness that began to invade our hearts. *It can't be true. . . . The doctor will come in, and he will find the heartbeat, and everything will be all right,* our hearts desperately willed. On a bleak February day and in one simple sentence, death had altered our hopes and dreams.

Not often is the news of a desired pregnancy met with a foreboding anxiety—joy, yes—but mixed with a fear of what is probably inevitable. For our family, the joyous news of a new life—a second baby on the way—brought with it the weight of holding both fear and hope all at once. This is our story of suffering and loss, mystery and peace, joy and sorrow.

Our first child, a baby girl, was born two years earlier. She came into the world beautiful and healthy, but my pregnancy with her was something quite opposite. A few weeks into the pregnancy, I was diagnosed with a rare condition of pregnancy called hyperemesis gravidarum (HG). Affecting about two percent of all pregnancies, HG is marked by rapid weight loss, malnutrition, and dehydration due to unrelenting nausea and vomiting. I lost twenty-five pounds in the first trimester, had repeated IVs to treat dehydration, intravenous medications, and depended on a powerful antinausea drug for the duration of the pregnancy. All the symptoms disappeared the day she was born and as my health continued to improve, we settled into the wonderful chaos of life with a newborn. In the end, it seemed a small price to pay for the abundant joy a longed-for child brings. Although the doctors told us it was very possible that I would experience HG again, our desire to have another child was stronger than our memory. Foolishly believing that experience had taught us something about managing the condition, we moved forward with trying to conceive.

Only one week after celebrating our good news—a positive pregnancy test—the condition returned. Unfortunately, this time, it promised to be an even more severe case. In fact, only .5 percent of all pregnancies are diagnosed with this severe a case of HG. My doctor immediately began an aggressive treatment plan, including hospitalization. A peripherally inserted central catheter (PICC) was inserted near my heart to administer the medications and nutrients my body needed to support the life growing inside me. I didn't eat for four months and I was weak and nauseated every waking moment, vomiting multiple times a day. A host of family and friends gave us round-the-clock care, took care of our daughter, prepared meals, sat with me, prayed for us. They were the hands and feet of Christ, and we have often wondered how we would have survived this time without our community. Their love literally nourished and sustained us.

Looking back, we see that the early weeks of this pregnancy were when our grieving really began. We knew that this would have to be our last pregnancy. Due to the "chemical incompatibility" that my body has with pregnancy, we could not intentionally put our family—or me—through the suffering again. We were just trying our very best to hold on and make it through each day, understanding it might be like this for the entire nine months.

We had made it to the halfway point of the pregnancy on that gray February day. Our hopes were lifted as we celebrated this significant milestone. However, instead of it being a celebration, we have come to view that day as the day our innocence was lost. *Babies are not supposed to die!* I often found myself thinking and, literally, screaming out. This tragic ending to months of physical suffering seemed too cruel. Yet we had to face an induced labor to deliver our second child, a son, whom we would never know in this life.

John Wilson was born peacefully the next morning. As we held his lifeless body, a torrent of emotion overcame us. The news of new life has a mysterious power that leads us into hope and we find ourselves dreaming of the future we will know with our child as they grow. We wept for the loss of this dream. As we commended him to God's keeping, I felt God's arms tenderly encircling us, joining us in our sorrow. Our dear friends and our church community planned a beautiful memorial service, and we began the process of letting go of the vision we had for our family.

The days following were profoundly dark and empty. I couldn't sleep—or even breathe, it seemed. I felt so very tender and limp. I'm a psychotherapist. . . . I know the stages of grief intellectually. But now here I was experiencing them firsthand. . . . Words to describe the feelings don't seem adequate. I believed that God could handle my emotions and I wasn't afraid to express them to him . . . often. There were moments of anger, but more often I felt anguish, despair, jealousy, bitterness, and profound sorrow. But somehow, in the midst of the range of emotions I felt daily, a strong and powerful peace found its way into my heart and brought comfort. I felt God's presence deeply, and slowly began the process of learning that, although He allows tragedies to befall us, he will not abandon us, nor deny us an intimate and life-giving relationship with Him. My relationship with him was growing in new ways and becoming more real. He was drawing me closer to him through each painful question and doubt. He was truly IN this dark place with us. The words of the psalmist, "The Lord is close to the brokenhearted and saves those who are crushed in spirit" (Ps 34:18 NIV), carried me through the days and months of healing. God was truly our refuge.

"Blessed are those who mourn" are not just words on a page anymore. We have experienced these words as the living and breathing Word of God. We have lived them and breathed them. Like most of you reading this, we feel sure we would NEVER have chosen to endure the fiery furnace of having a stillborn baby. However, we have been able to recognize the rich gifts we would never have received had we not been through this fire. God longs for us to experience a rich relationship with him and with one another. Each time I truly connect with another in their pain, I am thankful for the gift of my pain. It reminds me of our vulnerability and dependence. It is our nature to be strong and independent. Yet, there is no room for the ego in suffering. This stripping of my ego opens the doors to authentic relating to others. As I am drawn closer to others, I am experiencing God in the here and now.

In the days after losing our son, a friend told me that we would always "walk with a limp" from then on. Although our scars are not physical, the pain has left a mark on our hearts. But I like to think of these scars as unique marks of beauty and depth. Although our story does not end here—God brought four lives together in a miraculous and wondrous way to birth beauty from the ashes. We now enjoy the vibrancy of a life with two precious children, our nine-year-old daughter and a son, our miracle child, who is turning five this very week. We look forward to the day when we will be reunited with our first son in heaven, but until then, it is gratitude we feel for experiencing God in a very real and dynamic way, and we rejoice in the life he has given us.

FOUR

The Problem of Evil

"Since the order of the world is shaped by death, mightn't it be better for God if we refuse to believe in Him and struggle with all our might against death, without raising our eyes toward the heaven where He sits in silence?"

Tarrou nodded. "Yes. But your victories will never be lasting; that's all."

Rieux's face darkened. "Yes, I know that. But it's no reason for giving up the struggle."

"No reason, I agree. Only, I now can picture what this plague must mean for you."

"Yes. A never ending defeat."

—Albert Camus, *The Plague*[151]

The Problem of Evil in Context

The "problem of evil" is well known. If you believe in a God who is all-powerful and sovereign over the world and at the same time is also perfectly good and just, then the existence of evil and suffering poses a problem. The classic statement of it was given by David Hume, in his *Dialogues Concerning Natural Religion.* "Epicurus's old questions are yet unanswered. Is he willing to prevent evil but not able? Then he is impotent. Is he able but not willing? Then he is malevolent. Is he both able *and* willing? Whence then is evil?"[152] This has also been called the argument against God from evil, or just the argument from evil.

Many insist that this problem is the single strongest objection to the existence of God in general and the plausibility of Christianity in particular. Then why didn't I address this head-on in chapter one? My reason is because suffering is a lived reality that people and societies have wrestled with for centuries. Before suffering is a philosophical issue, it is a practical crisis—before it is about "why?" it is about "how?" How do I survive this? Therefore, we have looked at suffering historically and culturally, comparing and contrasting how various societies and people have actually engaged evil and sorrow. Our survey has shown that in order to do this, everyone has to have some working theory of what suffering is, what it means (and does not mean), and how we should respond to it. No one can function without some set of beliefs about it all.

If I had begun this volume with the traditional problem of evil against the existence of God, I would have inevitably given the impression that *only* belief in a traditional God is challenged by the existence of suffering. Most people who see the problems that suffering poses to classical theistic belief move toward a more secular way of thinking. But we have seen that secularism is also a set of beliefs, and it is probably the weakest of all worldviews at helping its adherents understand and endure the "terror of life." Christianity, though indeed having a problem with evil, does quite well when compared to alternatives. This becomes clear when we look at suffering from all perspectives—sociocultural, practical, and psychological. That is why I started the book in those areas before turning, in this chapter, to the philosophical. Nevertheless, suffering does indeed throw up problems for faith in God, and to those problems we must turn.

As we do so, we should also keep in mind what we learned from Charles Taylor's history of the development of secularity in Western culture. Awareness of the problem of God's relationship to evil is at least as old as the Greek philosopher Epicurus, who posed it three hundred years before Christ. But Taylor rightly points out that despite the discussions of philosophers, the argument from evil never had anything like popular appeal and broad attraction until some time after the Enlightenment. Things changed when Western thought came to see God as more remote, and to see the world as ultimately completely understandable through reason. These intellectual trends were reinforced by technological changes that eventually led to the development of the expanded, self-sufficient "buffered self." Human beings became far more confident in their own powers of reason and perception.

When people inside the immanent frame consider evil and God, the skeptical conclusion is already largely inherent in the premises. Modern discussions of the problem of suffering start with an abstract God—a God who, for the sake of argument, is all-powerful and all-good, but who is not glorious, majestic, infinitely wise, beginningless, and the creator and sustainer of all things. No wonder, then, that modern people are far more prone than their ancestors to conclude that, if *they* can see no good reason for a particular instance of suffering, God could not have any justifiable reasons for it either. If evil does not make sense to us, well, then evil simply does not make sense.

And so, while the philosophical issues and questions remain, the culture somewhat stacks the deck. Why keep this in mind as we hear the philosophical debate? It is always crucial to remember that our beliefs are formed not only through reason and argument but also through social conditioning.[153] Beliefs seem most plausible to us if they are held by people whom we admire and whose approval we desire. Our social and cultural locations make us much more open to some arguments and less open to others. The only way, therefore, to be as thoughtful, balanced, and unprejudiced as possible is to be highly aware of your cultural biases.

If a case comes before a judge involving a company in which the judge has an investment, she would recuse herself from the case because her objectivity could be suspect. We modern people are in the same situation. God is already questionable since our highest value is the freedom and autonomy of the individual self, and the existence of a being like God is the ultimate barrier to that. We are quick to complain about evil and suffering in the world because it aligns with our cultural biases. But we can't recuse ourselves from hearing this case as the judge can. We must consider the problem. I am only urging my readers, virtually all of whom will share at least some of our Western culture's biases, to be aware of their prejudices as we survey this subject.

The Argument(s) Against God from Evil

The problem of evil is widely felt among people today and does indeed pose a genuine challenge to belief in God. Any God who is all-powerful *and* all-good would be expected to stop horrendous evil and suffering, since he would not only want to prevent it, he would have the perfect ability to do so. Yet evil does indeed exist and persist. Therefore, this all-powerful and loving God either cannot exist or probably does not exist. The last sentence hints as a very important point. There are two forms that the argument against God from evil can take. They have been called the logical argument (which seeks to prove that there certainly is no such God) and the evidential argument (which reasons there *probably* is no such God.) We will look at the more ambitious "logical" argument first.

Up until the 1980s, the argument against God from evil was considered among academic philosophers to be conclusive, a proof that the traditional God of the Bible could not exist. It claimed that evil made Christianity not just less plausible but logically impossible. British philosopher John Mackie, in his oft reprinted article "Evil and Omnipotence," wrote: "It can be shown, not merely that religious beliefs lack rational support, but that they are positively irrational, that several parts of the essential theological doctrine are inconsistent with one another."[154]

But things began to change with the publication of Alvin Plantinga's book *God, Freedom, and Evil* in 1974, along with his more technical and rigorously argued book *The Nature of Necessity* the same year.[155] In these works, Plantinga argues that "the existence of evil is not logically incompatible (even in the broadly logical sense) with the existence of an all-powerful, all-knowing, and perfectly good God."[156] Plantinga and other philosophers who followed in his wake were so effective that twenty-five years later, it was widely conceded that the logical argument against God didn't work. The idea that evil disproves the existence of God, wrote philosopher William Alston, "is now acknowledged on (almost) all sides to be completely bankrupt."[157] Instead, skeptical thinkers began to formulate a new version, called the evidential argument against God. In this re-formulation, a much weaker claim was made, namely that suffering is not *proof* but *evidence* that makes the existence of God less probable, although not impossible.[158] As we will see later, the same arguments that brought down the stronger form of this case against God cast real doubts on the weaker form too.

All this shows that the confident assertion so common "on the street," that suffering and evil simply disproves the existence of God, has been almost entirely abandoned in professional and academic circles, "because the burden of proof of demonstrating that there is no possibility at all of the coexistence of God and . . . evil is just too heavy for the atheist to bear."[159] The argument against God from evil is no longer seen as being compelling.

How did this happen? We can begin to understand this recent history of philosophical debate by understanding a helpful distinction often made between a theodicy and a defense of God.

"Soul-Making" and Suffering

The distinction between a *theodicy* and a *defense* was made by Plantinga in *God, Freedom, and Evil*. The word *theodicy* was coined by the philosopher Gottfried Leibniz, meaning literally a justification of God's ways to human beings.[160] Anyone seeking to provide a theodicy has set a very high bar. A theodicy seeks to give an answer to the big "Why?" question. Its goal is to explain why a just God allows evil to come into existence and to continue. It attempts to reveal the reasons and purposes of God for suffering so listeners will be satisfied that his actions regarding evil and suffering are justified.

One of the first theodicies was that of "soul-making," formulated by the second-century theologian Irenaeus and promoted in contemporary form by author John Hick. This view says that the evils of life can be justified if we recognize that the world was primarily created to be a place where people find God and grow spiritually into all they were designed to be. This happens through "meeting and eventually mastering temptation . . . rightly making responsible choices in concrete situations," which results in "a positive and responsible character that comes from the investment of costly personal effort."[161] Hick argues that this kind of soul-making is an infinite good and cannot be achieved by simply being created in a state of innocence or virtue.

The soul-making theodicy helpfully forces us to examine our assumptions. Is the highest good that we become comfortable and trouble-free or that we become spiritually and morally great? If our lives do not go as we have planned, it is natural to question the wisdom of God, but our indignation is greatly magnified by an unexamined premise that God, if he exists, exists to make us happy, as we define happiness. Also, it is hard to imagine the development of virtues such as courage, humility, self-control, and faithfulness if every good deed was immediately rewarded and every bad deed immediately punished. No one would do things simply because they were right and loving to do. We merely would react instinctively to avoid pain and get pleasure. So the unfairness and difficulty of life in the world is a means by which we grow into something more than behaviorally conditioned animals.

However, the soul-making theodicy suffers from some glaring weaknesses. First, pain and evil do not appear in any way to be distributed according to soul-making need. Many people with bad souls get very little of the adversity they apparently need, and many with great souls get an amount that seems to go far beyond what is necessary for spiritual growth. Also, this theodicy does not speak to or account for the suffering of little children or infants who die in pain, or even for the suffering of animals.

God, Freedom, and Evil

The second and perhaps most prominent of these explanations is the free will theodicy. This has a long and ancient history going back to St. Augustine.[162] In its simplest form, it might be stated like this: God created us not to be robots or animals of instinct but free, rational agents with the ability to choose and therefore to love. But if God was to make us able to choose the good freely, then he had to make us capable of also choosing evil. So our free will can be abused and that is the reason for evil. But this greater good—for us, of having a rational soul, and for God, of having real loving sons and daughters rather than some kind of "pets"—is worth the evil that inevitably also comes. Jean-Paul Sartre puts this very well: "The man who wants to be loved does not desire the enslavement of the beloved. . . . If the beloved is transformed into an automaton, the lover finds himself alone."[163]

Along with this account of things usually goes an insistence that God has not actually created evil because it is not a distinct "thing" like other created objects. Augustine, who was later followed by Thomas Aquinas and others, taught that evil is, rather, the condition that results when some good thing that God made is twisted or corrupted from its original design or purpose. So there can be good without evil, but evil, being parasitic, cannot exist without the good on which it preys.[164] God, therefore, is not the author of evil but allowed it in order to achieve the greater good of human freedom and love.

Peter van Inwagen summarizes it like this: "The omniscient God knew that, however much evil might result from the elected separation from himself . . . the gift of free will would be, so to speak, worth it. For the existence of an eternity of love depends on this gift, and that eternity outweighs the horrors of the very long, but, in the most literal sense, temporary period of divine-human estrangement."[165]

The free will theodicy has become very popular, but it may be so partially because our culture inclines us to find it appealing. It sounds plausible to people in Western civilization, where we have been taught to think of freedom and choice as something almost sacred. But two problems immediately present themselves.

The first is that this seems to explain only a certain category of evil. It is customary to distinguish between *moral* evil, performed by human beings, and *natural* evil, which is caused by nonhuman causes such as disasters like hurricanes, floods, and earthquakes, as well as many forms of disease. The free will theodicy addresses moral evil—but how can it explain natural evil? Peter van Inwagen responds by offering an expanded version of the free will theodicy. In his St. Andrews University

Gifford lectures, he tells the Christian story of the Fall. In this story, humankind is blessed by God in a paradisiacal state but turns from God in disobedience and loses his protection and presence.[166] As van Inwagen explains, this means that "natural evil . . . is a consequence of an aboriginal abuse of free will."[167] So human free will can explain the violence of nature.

But a second problem looms—and it is, in my view, much more formidable. Is it really true that God could not create free agents capable of love without making them also capable of evil? The view that he could not has been called the libertarian understanding of free will. It says that God cannot lead us to do the right thing without violating our free will, and so evil is inevitable for free agents.

But the Bible presents God himself as sovereign and free (Ps 115:3), and not just capable of love but the very fountain and source of all love. Nevertheless, he himself cannot be evil. He cannot lie or break a promise (Num 23:19; Titus 1:2), he cannot be tempted by evil (James 1:13), he cannot deny or contradict his perfectly righteous and holy character (2 Tim 2:13; 1 Pet 1:16). If God has a free will yet is not capable of doing wrong—why could not other beings also be likewise constituted? Also biblical authors teach us that eventually God will give us a suffering-free, evil-free world filled with redeemed human beings. Suffering and death will be banished forever. That means we will be in God's world but not be capable of choosing evil. Yet we will obviously still be capable of love.

Finally, many Christian theologians point out the biblical teaching on the nature of freedom differs sharply from modern views. The Bible characterizes all sin as slavery, never as freedom. Only when we are completely redeemed from all sin will we experience complete freedom (cf. Rom 8:21). We are free only to the extent that we do what God built us to do—to serve him. Therefore, the more capable you are to commit evil, the *less* free you are. Not until we attain heaven and lose the capability of evil are we truly and completely free. How, then, could the ability to sin be a form of freedom?[168]

There is another strand of biblical teaching that undermines the free will theodicy. The theodicy assumes that if God gives us the gift of free will, then he cannot control the outcomes of its usage. But the Bible shows in many places that God can sovereignly direct our choices in history without violating our freedom and responsibility for our actions. For example, Jesus' crucifixion was clearly foreordained and destined to happen, and yet all the people who, by God's plan, brought it about were still making their choices freely and thus were responsible for what they did (cf. Acts 2:23). This indicates that it is possible to be free and nevertheless to have our course directed by God—at the same time, compatibly. There are scores of other examples of this. So God can give free will and still direct the outcomes of our choices to fit into his plan for history.[169]

There is a final question about the premises underlying the free will theodicy. It assumes that despite the horrendous evils of history, merely having freedom of choice is worth it. But is it? What if you saw a child walking into the path of an oncoming car? Would you say: "I can't violate her freedom of choice! She will have to take the consequences."? Of course not. You would not consider her freedom of choice more important than saving her life. You would violate her freedom of will as fast as you could possibly do it. You would snatch her out of the path of the car and teach her how to keep that from happening again. Why couldn't God have done that with us? Assume that the Fall of humankind happened the way the Bible says. Why couldn't God have shown Adam and Eve a lurid, detailed full-length movie of all that would happen to them and to their descendants if they ate of the tree? Surely he could have scared them and convinced them to avoid eating the forbidden fruit.

In short, could the gift and maintenance of free will be the only or main reason God allows evil? The purpose of a theodicy is to reveal sufficiently God's reasons for allowing evil and suffering so that we think it justified. Does the free will theodicy do this—does it really answer most of the questions? I don't believe it does, nor do sizable numbers of other people.[170] If God has good reasons for allowing the pain and misery we see, the reasons must extend beyond the mere provision of freedom of choice.

The Problem with All Theodicies

There are other theodicies that have been presented throughout history. One has been called the natural law theodicy, put forward by C. S. Lewis in his book *The Problem of Pain* and by Oxford philosopher Richard Swinburne.[171] It argues that a world created by God must have a natural order to it—it could not be random, operating differently every moment. If we break natural laws, they must rebound on us. For example, imagine a physical world without a law of gravity. But if we have gravity, then if you jump off a cliff, you will be hurt or killed—whether you are a good person or a bad one. Without natural laws, life is impossible, but suffering is then inevitable. The natural evils that hurt so much are the by-products of something that brings us even greater good.

But most suffering does *not* happen in an orderly way, proportionate to bad choices. If people only got hurt when they did something stupid like jumping off a cliff, it would be painful, yet it would feel fair. But natural evil does not come to us like that. People do not die only by falling off cliffs but also because the cliff comes down in an avalanche and buries innocent people walking by. Suffering is so often random and horrific, and it comes upon people who seem to have done nothing to warrant it.

This does not exhaust the list of theodicies. Some are ingenious but perhaps too complicated, such as the plenitude theory that God could have created innumerable universes, and the distribution of evil could be different in each one but equitable across them all.[172] Others are too simple, like the punishment theodicy, which looks at the beginning of Genesis and concludes that all suffering can be justified because humankind rebelled against God, and the suffering of the world is just our deserved punishment for sin.

But as the book of Job so vividly shows us, that does not explain why, if suffering is punishment for sin, it does not fall on people in proportion to the goodness or evil of their character. Why does God allow the distribution of the "punishment" to be so random and unfair? And this view has one of the same problems of the free will theodicy. Why could

God not have convinced our human forebears to follow him without violating their free will, avoiding the punishment? And since in the Bible we understand that God will someday end evil and suffering, why does a loving and all-powerful God allow it to continue?

Taken all together, the various theodicies can account for a great deal of human suffering—each theodicy provides some plausible explanations for some of the evil in the world—but they always fall short, in the end, of explaining all suffering. It is very hard to insist that any of them show convincingly how God would be fully justified in permitting all the evil we see in the world. Peter van Inwagen writes that no major Christian church, denomination, or tradition has ever endorsed a particular theodicy.[173] Alvin Plantinga himself wrote: "I must say that most attempts to explain *why* God permits evil—*theodicies*, as we may call them—strike me as tepid, shallow and ultimately frivolous."[174] And we can add to these warnings the book of Job itself. Surely one of the messages, as we will see, is that it is both futile and inappropriate to assume that any human mind could comprehend all the reasons God might have for any instance of pain and sorrow, let alone for all evil. It may be that the Bible itself warns us not to try to construct these theories.

In the past few decades, therefore, most Christian thinkers and philosophers have turned away from the very project of seeking full theodicies. Instead, they have increasingly (and to my mind, rightly) recommended that believers not try to formulate theodicies but rather simply mount a *defense*. A defense shies away from trying to tell a full story that reveals God's purposes in decreeing or allowing evil. A defense simply seeks to prove that the argument against God from evil fails, that the skeptics have failed to make their case. A defense shows that the existence of evil does *not* mean God can't or is unlikely to exist. In making a theodicy, the burden of proof is upon the believer in God. He or she must provide an account so convincing that the listener says to the believer, "Now I see why all the suffering is worth it." But in a defense, the burden of proof is upon the skeptic. Why?

On the surface, these two statements—"There's a good, omnipotent God." and "There is evil in the world."—are not a direct contradiction. It is up to the skeptic to make a compelling case that they actually contradict each other. He or she must provide an argument so convincing that the listener says to the skeptic: "Now I see why, if evil exists, God cannot or at least is not likely to exist." But that is not at all an easy case to make.

The Logical Argument and the "Noseeums" Objection

Peter van Inwagen suggested that a person using evil as an argument against the existence of God might say something like this:

> *Skeptic*: "If there were an omnipotent, morally perfect being who knew about the evils we know about—well, they wouldn't have arisen in the first place, for he'd have prevented their occurrence. Or if, for some reason, he didn't do that, he'd certainly remove them the instant they began to exist. But we observe evils, and very long-lasting ones. So we must conclude that God does not exist."[175]

In short, the argument is:

1. A truly good God would not want evil to exist; an all-powerful God would not allow evil to exist.
2. Evil exists.
3. Therefore, a God who is both good and powerful cannot exist.

But the believer in God could respond by pointing out that the argument against God from evil has a hidden premise, namely that God does not have any good reasons to allow evil to exist. He might say:

> *Believer*: "It may be that someone has a very strong desire for something and is able to obtain this thing, but does not act on this desire—because he has reasons for not doing so that seem to him to outweigh the desirability of the thing . . . [so] God might have reasons for allowing evil to exist that, in his

mind, outweigh the desirability of the non-existence of evil."[176]

If God has good reasons for allowing suffering and evil, then there is no contradiction between his existence and that of evil. So in order for his case not to fail, the skeptic would have to reply that *God could not possibly have any such reasons.* But it is very hard to prove that.

To show the skeptic that his premise is untrue, the believer could point out that we ourselves often allow suffering in someone's life in order to bring about some greater good. Doctors often inflict painful procedures and treatments on people, all for the purpose of the greater good of better health and longer life. Parents who punish bad behavior with the loss of toys or privileges are causing pain (especially from the child's perspective), but the alternative is that the child will grow into an adult with no self-control and would therefore experience far greater suffering. And most people will grant some truth to the saying attributed to Nietzsche: "Whatever doesn't kill me makes me stronger." Many can point to adversity in their lives that, however excruciating, taught them lessons that helped them avoid greater suffering later.[177] So the principle of allowing pain for the good reason of bringing about a greater happiness is valid and one we understand and use ourselves. That means there is no automatic inconsistency between God and the existence of evil and suffering.

The skeptic's response could be that the inconsistency is not between God and suffering in general but rather between God and the kinds and magnitude of evil and suffering we see in the world. Helpless people often experience horrendous violence and pain that have no obvious purpose toward instruction and character growth. Yes, says the skeptic, there can be good reasons for allowing some kinds of suffering but not the magnitude and types of suffering that exist in the world today. God could not have any warrant for allowing that.

But we can discern another implicit assumption *inside* the first hidden premise. The assumption is—"if *I* can't see any reasons God might have for permitting that evil . . . then probably he doesn't have any."[178] But that premise is obviously false. Remember that the argument against

God from evil starts with the idea of an omnipotent God. It says, "If God is infinitely powerful as you say—why doesn't he stop evil?" But a God who is infinitely more powerful than us would also be infinitely more knowledgeable than us. So the rejoinder to the skeptic is "If God is infinitely knowledgeable—*why* couldn't he have morally sufficient reasons for allowing evil *that you can't think of*?" To insist that we know as much about life and history as all-powerful God is a logical fallacy, howsoever much the immanent frame of our culture would incline us to feel that way.

Philosopher Stephen John Wykstra came up with the illustration of the "noseeums" to reveal this fallacy in the argument from evil.[179] Wykstra was responding to the writings of William Rowe, who argued that because we could not see any "outweighing good" that might justify God's allowing suffering, therefore there "*are* no such goods." Wykstra responds by pointing to a particular species of insect. "In the Midwest we have 'noseeums'—tiny flies which, while having a painful bite, are so small you 'no see 'um.'"[180] Just because you cannot see noseeums does not mean they are not there. Alvin Plantinga carries on the illustration:

> I look inside my pup-tent: I don't see a St. Bernard. It is then probable that there is no St. Bernard in my tent. That is because if there were one, it is highly likely I would have seen it. It's not easy for a St. Bernard to avoid detection in a small tent. Again I look inside my tent and I don't see any noseeums. . . . This time it is not particularly probable that there are no noseeums in my tent. . . . The reason is that even if there were noseeums there I wouldn't see 'em; they're too small to see. And now the question is whether God's reasons, if any, for permitting such evils . . . are more like St. Bernards or more like noseeums. . . . Given that God *does* have a reason for permitting these evils, why think we would be the first to know? . . . Given that he is omniscient and given our very substantial epistemic limitations, it isn't at all surprising that his reasons . . . escape us.[181]

Here we see the Achilles heel of the "logical" argument against God—the case that evil means God *cannot* exist. We also can understand why it has fallen on such hard times. If you have a God infinite and powerful enough for you to be angry at for allowing evil, then you must at the same time have a God infinite enough to have sufficient reasons for allowing that evil.

And we also now can see why Charles Taylor is right, that the "problem of evil" was not widely perceived to be an objection to God until modern times. Human beings operating within the immanent frame have far more confidence in their reasoning powers and their ability to unlock the mysteries of the universe than did ancient people. The belief—that because we cannot think of something, God cannot think of it either—is more than a fallacy. It is a mark of great pride and faith in one's own mind.

The Evidential Argument and the Butterfly Effect

But what about the less ambitious form of the argument—what has been called the evidential argument against God that says, more modestly, that evil and suffering simply make God's existence improbable? A skeptic might say, "Of course we can't prove that there couldn't be a God, or that there couldn't be any sufficient reason for allowing evil. But have you watched a little child die by degrees—eaten out from the inside by cancer? While evil may not technically disprove the existence of a good and powerful God, it still makes his existence highly unlikely."[182]

The problem with this argument is that it isn't fundamentally any different from the logical argument. It rests on the same premises and has the same Achilles heel. If we are unable to prove that God has no morally sufficient reasons for evil, we are certainly unable to assess the level of probability that he has such reasons. To insist that we have a sufficient vantage point from which to evaluate percentages or likelihood is to again forget our knowledge limitations. If there is an infinite God and we are finite, there would be no way for us to lay odds on such things.

Imagine a ball on the crest of a hill that could roll off the hill into any one of several valleys, setting off avalanches and changing landscapes and lives. The route of the ball, however, depends on innumerable tiny differences in initial position and thrust, irregularities in the terrain, and even weather conditions like the wind or atmospheric pressure. Can we know exactly where the ball will go when it is released, and what percentage probability there is for entering each valley? No. The variables are too many to calculate. In the field of chaos theory, scientists have learned that large, macroscopic systems—such as weather—can be sensitive to the tiniest changes. The classic example is the claim that a butterfly's fluttering in China would be magnified through a ripple effect so as to determine the path of a hurricane in the South Pacific. Yet no one would be able to calculate and predict the actual effects of the butterfly's flight.

Now, what if every event in time, even the most insignificant, had similar massive and infinitely complex ripple effects? Ray Bradbury depicted this famously in his science fiction short story "A Sound of Thunder." In the story, the time-travel guide Travis is telling the time traveler Eckels that when he visits the past, he must be absolutely sure not to step off the metal path provided for him. Otherwise he might do something like step on a mouse. That would mean all future descendants of that mouse—maybe millions—would disappear. That would mean that all sorts of other animals that fed on those mice would starve and not have descendants. That would mean that some human beings who would have gotten those animals to eat do not—and would lead them to move or to starve. And for one man or woman to die meant whole families, eventually whole nations, wouldn't exist.

> The stomp of your foot, on one mouse . . . the effects of which could shake our earth and destinies down through Time, to their very foundations. . . . Perhaps Rome never rises on its seven hills. Perhaps Europe is forever a dark forest. . . . Step on a mouse and you leave your print, like a Grand Canyon, across Eternity. . . . So be careful. Stay on the Path. Never step off![183]

Now, if even the effects of a butterfly's flight or the roll of a ball down a hill are too complex to calculate, how much less could any human being look at the tragic, seemingly "senseless" death of a young person and have any idea of what the effects in history will be? If an all-powerful and all-wise God were directing all of history with its infinite number of interactive events toward good ends, it would be folly to think we could look at any particular occurrence and understand a millionth of what it will bring about. The history-butterfly effect means that "only an omniscient mind could grasp the complexities of directing a world of free creatures toward . . . previsioned [good] goals. . . . Certainly many evils seem pointless and unnecessary to us—but we are simply not in a position to judge."[184]

The Visceral Argument from Evil

The philosophical arguments and counterarguments we have surveyed are usually written about and discussed with a detached, dispassionate tone. But most people who, in the face of actual evil, object to God's existence do so not for philosophical reasons but for visceral ones. Peter van Inwagen distinguishes these two modes as the "global" and the "local" problem of evil. In his lecture on the local problem, he recounts the true story of a woman who was assaulted by a man who not only raped her but then chopped off her arms at the elbows, leaving her to die. Somehow she crawled to the side of a road, where she was rescued. She survived but must now live her life without arms and with the memory of the horror of that night.[185]

Our response to such an incident comes initially from deep within. It evokes a feeling in the stomach before it produces a set of propositions in the head. We might say, "You can keep all your long chains of syllogistic reasoning. I know the arguments. I know the existence of this kind of cruelty does not technically disprove the existence of a personal God. But *it makes no sense* that things like this are justified in any way. This is just *wrong—wrong*. I don't *want* to believe in a God who would let this happen—whether he exists or not." That is the visceral argument against

God from evil. It is not fair to call it mere emotion, a passing feeling. Evil can make God implausible, unreal to the heart. What can be said in response?

The visceral argument is not a strictly logical operation, and yet it has a moral logic to it. Years ago, I sat with a young family whose husband and father had just been killed, electrocuted while doing some simple maintenance in the crawl space under his house. His dead body was still nearby and the ambulance was on its way. Only the oldest of his three children, a son age nine, was able to articulate what everyone was feeling. "It's not right! A boy needs his dad. It's *not* right." Like Dylan Thomas, while we may know in our mind that death and suffering are the way of things, we "rage, rage" against them.

Probably the classic example of the visceral argument in our times comes in Elie Wiesel's *Night*.[186] He vividly describes how the very first night in the Nazi death camp devastated him. That first night, he wrote, "turned my life into one long night, seven times cursed and seven times sealed." He looked at the furnaces turning human beings, including little children, into "wreaths of smoke." The fires of those furnaces utterly destroyed his faith in God.

> Never shall I forget those flames which consumed my faith forever. . . . Never shall I forget those moments which murdered my God and my soul and turned my dreams to dust.[187]

How can you "argue" with this? It is only with great respect for Wiesel's experience and brilliance as a writer that we must nevertheless point out that there were others who saw the same sights and came out with their faith in God intact, even strengthened.[188] As we have seen, Victor Frankl described how death camp inmates responded in very different ways to the terror. Many lost all hope, but others found it, including religious hope. J. Christiaan Beker, a former professor at Princeton Theological Seminary, lived in a forced labor camp in Berlin as a Nazi slave, eventually hiding from the Germans in an attic for months, in constant fear of betrayal or discovery. He saw many of the sights of horrendous evil and suffered, as a result, from a manic-depressive condition all of his life. Nevertheless, it was during his enslavement that he determined to become a Christian theologian, and eventually to write *Suffering and Hope: The Biblical Vision and the Human Predicament.*[189] The message of the book is that the Christian hope of the resurrection and the renewal of the world enables us to view "the present power of death in terms of its empty future and therefore in the knowledge of its sure defeat."[190]

The Boomerang Effect

So not everyone who experiences radical evil automatically loses faith in God. And this must mean that even the visceral reaction to suffering has within it some arguments, some assumptions, that may not be conscious at first. We do not simply *respond* to nauseating, gut-wrenching evil. Deep down we are telling ourselves something about it, we are interpreting it in a particular way. As Blaise Pascal wrote, "At first a thing pleases or shocks me without my knowing the reason, and yet it shocks me for that reason which I only discover afterwards. . . . The heart has its reasons, which reason does not know."[191]

There is a moral assumption in the minds and hearts of those who find suffering weakening their faith rather than strengthening it. The assumption is that God, if he exists, has failed to do the right thing, that he has violated a moral standard. Evil is only evil if it contravenes a moral norm. When we say, "I can't believe in a God who would allow this," we are saying that God is somehow complicit with evil.

But this creates a conundrum for the skeptic who disbelieves in God. It is inarguable that human beings have moral *feelings*. A moral feeling means I feel some behavior is right and some behavior wrong and even repulsive. Now, if there is no God, where do such strong moral instincts and feelings come from? Today many would say our moral sense comes from evolution. Our feelings about right and wrong are thought to be genetically hardwired into us because they helped our ancestors survive. While that explanation may account for moral feelings, it can't account for moral *obligation*. What right have you to tell people they are obligated to stop certain behaviors if *their* feelings tell them those things are right, but you feel they are wrong? Why should your moral feelings take precedence over theirs? Where do you get a standard by which your moral feelings and sense are judged as true and others as false? On what basis do you say to someone, "What you have done is evil," if their feelings differ from yours?

We can call this a conundrum because the very basis for disbelief in God—a certainty about evil and the moral obligation not to commit it—dissolves if there truly is no God. The ground on which you make your objection vanishes under your feet. So not only does the argument against God from evil not succeed, but it actually has a "boomerang effect" on the users. Because it shows you that you are assuming something that can't exist unless God does. And so, in a sense, you are relying on God to make an argument against God. The most famous victim of this boomerang experience was C. S. Lewis.

For years, Lewis rejected the existence of God because he believed the logical argument from evil against God worked. But eventually, he came to realize that evil and suffering were a bigger problem for him as an atheist than as a believer in God. He concluded that the awareness of moral evil in the world was actually an argument *for* the existence of God, not against it. Lewis describes his awakening to this point in *Mere Christianity*,[192] but he gives a longer exposition in his essay *De Futilitate*. Lewis explains that "there is, to be sure, one glaringly obvious ground for denying that any moral purpose at all is operative in the universe: namely, the actual course of events in all its wasteful cruelty and apparent indifference, or hostility, to life."[193] So the existence of cruelty and evil in the world was the reason Lewis could not believe there was a good God, a "moral purpose" operating behind the universe.

But then he began to realize that evil in the world was "precisely the ground which we cannot use" to object to God. Why? "Unless we judge this waste and cruelty to be real evils we cannot . . . condemn the universe for exhibiting them. . . . Unless we take our own standard to be something more than ours, to be in fact an objective principle to which we are responding, we cannot regard that standard as valid."[194] Here was the conundrum for Lewis as an atheist. His objection to the existence of God was that he could perceive no moral standard behind the world—the world was just randomly evil and cruel. But then, if there was no God, my definition of evil was just based on a private feeling of mine. So Lewis wrote: "In a word, unless we allow ultimate reality to be moral, we cannot morally condemn it."[195] And he concluded with a vivid idea:

> The defiance of the good atheist hurled at an apparently ruthless and idiotic cosmos is really an unconscious homage to something in or behind that cosmos which he recognizes as infinitely valuable and authoritative: for if mercy and justice were really only private whims of his own with no objective and impersonal roots, and if he realized this, he could not go on being indignant. The fact that he arraigns heaven itself for disregarding them means that at some level of his mind he knows they are enthroned in a higher heaven still.[196]

So this leaves us with a question. What if evil and suffering in the world actually make the existence of God *more* likely? What if our awareness of absolute evil is a clue that we know unavoidably at some level within ourselves that God actually does exist? Alvin Plantinga writes that a secular way of looking at the world "has no place for genuine moral obligation of any sort . . . and thus no way to say there is such a thing as genuine and appalling wickedness. Accordingly, if you think there really is such a thing as horrifying wickedness (. . . and not just an illusion of some sort), then you have a powerful . . . argument [for the reality of God]."[197]

A. N. Wilson, writer and critic, abandoned the Christianity of his youth but more recently wrote an article, "Why I Believe Again." Crucial to his return was his work on a book on the Wagner family and Nazi Germany. It showed him "what sort of mad world is created by those who think that ethics are a purely human construct."[198] A recent faith-journey memoir titled *Faith and Other Flat Tires* shows us that this boomerang effect is not something that only academics like Lewis, Plantinga, or Wilson can feel. Andrea Palpant Dilley was raised by

Quaker medical missionaries in Kenya, where she was exposed to far more death and darkness than most children in Western countries ever see. By the time she was a teenager, she began to question God's goodness, and by the time she was in her twenties, she had rejected Christianity altogether. What drove her away was her anger at God over suffering and injustice.

But one night she was in a philosophical discussion with a young man about the existence of God. He was arguing that morality was relative—different to every culture and person. In conclusion, he said, "I think morals are totally subjective: therefore God is unnecessary." Dilley heard herself responding: "But, if morals are totally subjective, then you can't say Hitler was wrong. You can't say there's anything unjust about letting babies starve. And you can't condemn evil. How tenable is that? . . . You have to consent to an objective moral standard, up here." She waved her hand in the air, drawing a horizontal line. "And the possibility of a divine moral mind comes into play." She realized that she was taking the first steps back into belief.[199]

Later, Dilley concluded:

> When people ask me what drove me out the doors of the church and then what brought me back, my answer to both questions is the same. I left the church in part because I was mad at God about human suffering and injustice. And I came back to church because of that same struggle. I realized that I couldn't even talk about justice without standing inside of a theistic framework. In a naturalistic worldview, a parentless orphan in the slums of Nairobi can only be explained in terms of survival of the fittest. We're all just animals slumming it in a godless world, fighting for space and resources. The idea of justice doesn't really mean anything. To talk about justice, you have to talk about objective morality, and to talk about objective morality, you have to talk about God.[200]

In summary, the problem of senseless suffering does not go away if you abandon belief in God. If there is no God, why have a sense of outrage and horror when unjust suffering occurs to any group of people? Violence, suffering, and death are completely natural phenomena. On what basis do you say cruelty is wrong? Two famous thinkers gave very different answers to those questions. Dr. Martin Luther King Jr., in his "Letter from Birmingham Jail," said that if there were no higher divine law—that defined what justice is—there would be no way to tell if any particular human practice or experience was unjust or not. But when Friedrich Nietzsche heard that a natural disaster had destroyed Java in 1883, he wrote a friend: "Two hundred thousand wiped out at a stroke—how magnificent!" Nietzsche was relentless in his logic. Because there is (he said) no God, all value judgments are arbitrary. All definitions of justice are just the results of your culture or temperament.

As different as their views were, King and Nietzsche agreed on one point. If there is no God or higher divine law, then violence is perfectly natural. So abandoning belief in God doesn't help with the problem of suffering at all and, as we will see, it removes many resources for facing it.

Life Story: Hope in Christ

by Mary

Both my parents were destroyed by alcoholism. I was three when they divorced.

My mother loved me and tried her best, but drinking became her refuge, binges and craziness the norm. I was repeatedly locked out of my house for such things as losing a piano competition or dumping vodka down the drain and had to break the basement window to get back inside.

I was seventeen when Jesus found me. A friend invited me to church and I clung to the minister's reassuring words of God's unfailing love. I was hopeful my life would change.

I married a man six years my senior. At first, our relationship comforted me, but he became violent. I was hit repeatedly, once with a dog chain; strangled; kicked in the stomach; and pushed off a dock and down the steps. Unbelievably, I convinced myself I still loved him.

At twenty-three, I found my father again. I thought he would protect and defend me, so I left my husband. Instead, my father sexually abused me. I plummeted into utter despair and attempted suicide. Failing, I screamed at God for allowing me to live. Where was He?

I sought counseling with an extremely intelligent, kind young deacon. After a year, we fell in love, but he was already married. We struggled and pleaded with God for help, but ultimately gave in to sin. He divorced and we were married. We did not deserve the blessing of the three beautiful children God gave us. For the first time, I had a family.

My children were under six when I began experiencing severe headaches, hearing loss, and partial facial paralysis. A specialist discovered a massive brain tumor. Parts of the tumor still remain inoperable and are now causing new complications. I remember feeling strangely calm. Though our lives were turned upside down, my family was still intact.

My children grew and though they were brought up in the church, they were also becoming strongly influenced by the world. All were arrested at some point. The youngest was diagnosed with a schizophrenic disorder. The oldest was incarcerated for two years. We were devastated.

Shortly after, my husband suffered two strokes, leaving his personality drastically altered. I discovered our finances were in ruin. We eventually lost our house. I was so crushed, I could barely speak to a therapist.

Life has not changed. But God is changing me.

What I discovered about heartaches and problems, especially the ones that are way beyond what we can handle, is that maybe those are the problems He does permit precisely because we cannot handle them or the pain and anxiety they cause. But He can. I think He wants us to realize that trusting Him to handle these situations is actually a gift. His gift of peace to us in the midst of the craziness. Problems don't disappear and life continues, but He replaces the sting of those heartaches with hope, which has been an amazing realization.

I have come to believe that life will not always be as it is now. I find even more comfort in being able to stop focusing on all the heartache, and focus on the One who will someday take heartache away completely and forever.

I spent my entire life looking for, and never finding, a recipe to go from despair to hope. It did not come from anything I did or didn't do. Hope comes not in the solution to the problem but in focusing on Christ, who facilitates the change.

PART TWO

Facing the Furnace

FIVE

The Challenge to Faith

The other gods were strong, but Thou was weak.
They rode, but Thou didst stumble to a throne.
But to our wounds only God's wounds can speak,
And not a god has wounds but Thou alone.

—Edward Shillito, from "Jesus of the Scars"

Answers for the Heart

We said that the visceral argument against God happens at the heart level. Pascal's insightful phrase "reasons of the heart" refers neither to mere irrational feelings nor simply to logical propositions. They are best described as intuitions—explanations that not only give some light to the mind but are also existentially comforting or satisfying. A "reason for the heart," unlike an abstract proposition, affects and changes attitudes and actions. I propose that there are three powerful themes of Christian teaching that can serve us in this way when it comes to the pain and suffering of life. Each one not only helps enrich our understanding of suffering but directly affects our attitudes, giving us a new frame of heart capable of facing adversity.

The first set of Christian teachings that frame the heart in this way are the doctrines of creation and fall. Genesis 1 and 2 show us humankind put by God into a world without death or suffering. The evil we see today was not part of God's original design. It was not God's intent for human life. That means that ultimately, even a peaceful death at the age of ninety years old is *not* the way things were meant to be. Those of us who sense the "wrongness" of death—in any form—are correct. The "rage at the dying of the light" is our intuition that we were not meant for mortality, for the loss of love, or for the triumph of darkness. In order to help people face death and grief we often tell people that death is a perfectly natural part of life. But that asks them to repress a very right and profound human intuition—that we were not meant to simply go to dust, and that love was meant to last.

Genesis 3 confirms this intuition in great detail, showing us the origin of the world's darkness and how it unfolded out of our refusal to let God be our lord and king. When we turned from God and lost that relationship, all other relationships fell apart. Because we rejected his authority everything about the world—our hearts, emotions, bodies, our relationships to other people, and our relationship to nature itself—stopped working as it should.

The Fall of humankind means that the original design of the world is broken. In the Garden, men and women were called to work—to care for and cultivate the earth. When Adam and Eve sinned, part of the curse was that now "thorns and thistles" would grow out of the ground as well as flowers and food. This means that the good pattern of the life God created here is not completely eradicated, but it now falls far short of its original intent. It should be that hard work would always lead to prosperity, but now sometimes you can work hard and injustice or disaster wipes it away. The doctrine of the Fall, then, gives us a remarkably nuanced understanding of suffering.

On the one hand, this teaching rejects the idea that people who suffer more are always worse people than those who suffer less. That was the self-righteous premise of Job's friends who sat around him and said, "The reason this is happening to you and not to us is because we are living right and you are not." At the end of the book, God expresses his fury at Job's "miserable comforters." The world is too fallen and deeply broken to divide into a neat pattern of good people having good lives and bad people having bad lives. The brokenness of the world is inherited by the entire human race. As Jesus says, the sun shines and the rain falls on both the just and the unjust (Matt 5:45).

The individual sufferer is not necessarily receiving a due payment for specific wrongdoings.

But on the other hand, while we must never say that every particular instance of suffering is caused by a particular sin, it is fair to say that suffering and death in general is a natural consequence and just judgment of God on our sin. Therefore we cannot protest that the human race, considering our record, deserves a better life than the one we have now.

All of this comprises a "reason of the heart" for sufferers because, when accepted, it brings the relief of humility. Often the unstated assumption of many people is that it is God's job to create a world in which things benefit us. We saw how the Deism of the eighteenth century explicitly promoted this idea though it was at loggerheads with the book of Genesis and the rest of the Bible. Nevertheless, this idea has captured the hearts of most people, as sociologist Christian Smith points out. From his research he concluded that most young American adults are "practical Deists"—though few of them have ever heard the term. Smith means that they see God as a being whose job it is to meet their needs. The implicit but strong cultural assumption of young adults is that God owes all but the most villainous people a comfortable life. This premise, however, inevitably leads to bitter disillusionment. Life is nasty, hard, brutish, and always feels too short. The presumption of spiritual entitlement dooms its bearers to a life of confusion when things in life inevitably go wrong.

When we stand back to consider the premise—that God owes us a good life—it is clearly unwarranted. If there really is an infinitely glorious God, why should the universe revolve around us rather than around him? If we look at the biblical God's standards for our behavior—the Golden Rule, the Ten Commandments, and the Sermon on the Mount—and then consider humanity's record against those norms, it may occur to us that the real riddle of evil is not what we thought. Perhaps the real puzzle is this: Why, in light of our behavior as a human race, does God allow so much *happiness*? The teaching of creation and fall removes the self-pity that afflicts people with the deistic view of life. It strengthens the soul, preparing it to be unsurprised when life is hard.

The Renewal of the World

The second Christian doctrine that speaks so well to our hearts is that of the final judgment and the renewal of the world. Many people complain that they cannot believe in a God who judges and punishes people. But if there is no Judgment Day, what about all the enormous amount of injustice that has been and is being perpetrated? If there is no Judgment Day, then there are only two things to do—lose all hope or turn to vengeance. Either it means that the tyranny and oppression that have been so dominant over the ages will never be redressed, and in the end it will make no difference whether you live a life of justice and kindness or a life of cruelty and selfishness, or it means that, since there is no Judgment Day, we will need to take up our weapons and go and hunt down the evildoers now. We will have to take justice into our own hands. We will have to be the judges, if there is no Judge.

And so the biblical doctrine of Judgment Day, far from being a gloomy idea, enables us to live with both hope and grace. If we accept it, we get hope and incentive to work for justice. For no matter how little success we may have now, we know that justice *will* be established—fully and perfectly. All wrongs—what we have called moral evil—will be redressed. But it also enables us to be gracious, to forgive, and to refrain from vengefulness and violence. Why? If we are not sure that there will be a final judgment, then when we are wronged, we will feel an almost irresistible compulsion to take up the sword and smite the wrongdoers. But if we know that no one will get away with anything, and that all wrongs will be ultimately redressed, then we can live in peace. The doctrine of Judgment Day warns us that we have neither the knowledge to know exactly what people deserve, nor the right to mete out punishment when we are sinners ourselves (Rom 2:1–16, 12:17–21). So belief in Judgment Day keeps us from being too passive or too violently aggressive in our pursuit of truth and justice.

But it is what lies on the far side of Judgment Day that is of the deepest consolation to sufferers. Peter van Inwagen writes:

At some point, for all eternity, there will be no more unmerited suffering: this present darkness, "the age of evil," will eventually be remembered as a brief flicker at the beginning of human history. Every evil done by the wicked to the innocent will have been avenged, and every tear will have been wiped away.[201]

As we have said, there is no fully satisfying theodicy that completely shows why God is justified in allowing evil. Nevertheless, the Christian doctrine of the resurrection and the renewal of the world—when all the biblical promises and implications are weighed and grasped—comes the closest to any real explanation we have. The resurrection of the body means that we do not merely receive a consolation for the life we have lost but a restoration of it. We not only get the bodies and lives we had but the bodies and lives we wished for but had never before received. We get a glorious, perfect, unimaginably rich life in a renewed material world.

Often we can see how bad things "work together for good" (Rom 8:28). The problem is that we can only glimpse this sometimes, in a limited number of cases. But why could it not be that God allowed evil because it will bring us all to a far greater glory and joy than we would have had otherwise? Isn't it possible that the eventual glory and joy we will know will be infinitely greater than it would have been had there been no evil? What if that future world will somehow be greater for having once been broken and lost? If such is the case, that would truly mean the utter defeat of evil. Evil would not just be an obstacle to our beauty and bliss, but it will have only made it better. Evil would have accomplished the very opposite of what it intended.

How might that come about? At the simplest level, we know that only if there is danger can there be courage. And apart from sin and evil, we would never have seen the courage of God, or the astonishing extent of his love, or the glory of a deity who lays aside his glory and goes to the cross. For us here in this life, the thought of God's glory is rather remote and abstract. But we must realize that the most rapturous delights you have ever had—in the beauty of a landscape, or in the pleasure of food, or in the fulfillment of a loving embrace—are like dewdrops compared to the bottomless ocean of joy that it will be to see God face-to-face (1 John 3:1–3). That is what we are in for, nothing less. And according to the Bible, that glorious beauty, and our enjoyment of it, has been immeasurably enhanced by Christ's redemption of us from evil and death. We are told that the angels long to endlessly gaze into the gospel, into the wonder of what Jesus did in his incarnation and atonement (1 Pet 1:12).

Paul speaks mysteriously that we who know Christ and the power of his resurrection also know "the fellowship of sharing in his sufferings"[202] (Phil 3:10–11). Alvin Plantinga points to the teachings of older Reformed theologians, such as Jonathan Edwards and Abraham Kuyper, who believed that because of our fall and redemption, we will achieve a level of intimacy with God that cannot be received any other way. And therefore the angels are envious of it.[203] What if, in the future, we came to see that just as Jesus could not have displayed such glory and love any other way except through his suffering, we would not have been able to experience such transcendent glory, joy, and love any other way except by going through a world of suffering?

And why could it not be that our future glory will actually so "swallow" the evil of the past that in some unimaginable way even the memory of the evil won't darken our hearts but only make us happier? C. S. Lewis's fantasy story of heaven and hell—*The Great Divorce*—depicts hell and all the people within it as having become microscopically small. He writes that, when on earth, people say "no future bliss can make up" for a particular instance of suffering, "not knowing that Heaven, once attained, will work backwards and turn even that agony into a glory."[204] This is an effort to convey the same idea that J. R. R. Tolkien does when he envisions a time in which "everything sad is going to come untrue."[205]

The Wounds of God

The final doctrines that serve as resources for our hearts are the doctrines of the incarnation and the atonement.

Peter Berger is a sociologist, not a theologian, but he knows that every culture must provide a way to make sense of suffering for its members. Berger sees in the Bible two basic ways it does that. In the Old Testament book of Job, we have the most difficult and severe truth about suffering—namely, that in the end we cannot question God. Job calls on God to explain why such sorrows and griefs have come upon him. But in response, "the questioner is radically challenged to his right to pose the question in the first place."[206] God confronts Job with his own finitude, his inability to understand God's counsels and purposes even if they were revealed, and his status as a sinner in no position to demand a comfortable life. Berger admits that this view of things has a strong logic to it, but that all by itself such a vision would be "hard to sustain for most people . . . only possible for certain religious 'virtuosi.' "[207] Fortunately for us, that is not the Bible's last word on suffering.

Berger says that the "unbearable tension of this problem brought about . . . by the Old Testament" is met with "the essential Christian solution of the problem." And that solution is that "the incarnate God is a God who suffers. Without this suffering, without the agony of the cross, the incarnation would not provide that solution of the problem of [suffering] to which, we would contend, it owes its immense potency." Berger then quotes Albert Camus, who wrote: "Only the sacrifice of an innocent god could justify the endless and universal torture of innocence. Only the most abject suffering by God could assuage man's agony."[208]

Berger sees the brilliance of the solution. He writes:

> Through Christ the terrible otherness of the Yahweh of the thunderstorms [in Job] is mellowed. At the same time, because the contemplation of Christ's suffering deepens the conviction of man's unworthiness, the old [repentant] surrender is allowed to repeat itself in a more refined . . . manner. . . . [For] Christ's suffering does not justify God, but man.[209]

The book of Job rightly points to human unworthiness and finitude, and calls for complete surrender to the sovereignty of God. But taken by itself the call might seem more than a sufferer could bear. Then the New Testament comes filled with an unimaginable comfort for those who are trusting in God's sovereignty. The sovereign God himself has come down into this world and has experienced its darkness. He has personally drunk the cup of its suffering down to the dregs. And he did it not to justify himself but to justify *us,* that is, to bear the suffering, death, and curse for sin that we have earned. He takes the punishment upon himself so that someday he can return and end all evil without having to condemn and punish us.

The New Testament teaches that Jesus was God come in the flesh— "in him all the fullness of the Godhead dwelled bodily" (Col 2:9). He was God yet he suffered. He experienced weakness, a life filled "with fervent cries and tears" (Heb 5:7). He knew firsthand rejection and betrayal, poverty and abuse, disappointment and despair, bereavement, torture, and death. And so he is "able to empathize with our weaknesses" for he "has been tempted in every way, just as we are—yet without sin" (Heb 4:15). On the cross, he went beyond even the worst human suffering and experienced cosmic rejection and a pain that exceeds ours as infinitely as his knowledge and power exceeds ours. There is no greater inner agony than the loss of a love relationship. We cannot imagine, however, what it would be like to lose not just a human relationship that has lasted for some years but the infinite love of the Father that Jesus had from all eternity. The separation would have been infinitely unbearable. And so Jesus experienced Godforsakenness itself on the cross when he cried out, "My God, my God! Why have you forsaken me?"

Here we see the ultimate strength—a God who is strong enough to voluntarily become weak and plunge himself into vulnerability and darkness out of love for us. And here we see the greatest possible glory—the willingness to lay aside all his glory out of love for us.

There is no other religion that even conceives of such a thing. Christian minister John Dickson once spoke on the theme of *the wounds of God* on a university campus in Sydney, Australia. During the question time, a Muslim man rose to explain "how preposterous was the claim that the Creator of the universe should be subjected to the forces of his own creation—that he would have to eat, sleep, and go to the toilet, let alone die on a cross." Dickson said his remarks were intelligent, cogent, and civil. The man went on to argue that it was illogical that God, the "cause of all causes" could have pain inflicted on him by any lesser beings. The minister felt he had no knockdown argument, no witty comeback. So finally he simply thanked the man for making the uniqueness of the Christian claim so clear. "What the Muslim denounces as blasphemy the Christian holds precious: God has wounds."[210]

So Peter Berger is right. The answer of the book of Job—that "God knows what he's doing, so be quiet and trust him"—is right but insufficient. It is inadequate because alone it is cold and because the New Testament gives us more with which to face the terrors of life. We turned from God, but God did not abandon us. Only Christianity, of all the world's major religions, teaches that God came to earth in Jesus Christ and became subject to suffering and death himself.

See what this means? Yes, we do not know the reason God allows evil and suffering to continue, or why it is so random, but now at least we know what the reason is not. It cannot be that he does not love us. It cannot be that he does not care. He is so committed to our ultimate happiness that he was willing to plunge into the greatest depths of suffering himself. He understands us, he has been there, and he assures us that he has a plan to eventually wipe away every tear. Someone might say, "But that's only half an answer to the question 'Why?' " Yes, but it is the half we need.

If God actually provided an explanation of all the reasons why he allows things to happen as they do, it would be too much for our finite brains. Think of little children and their relationship to their parents. Three-year-olds cannot understand most of why their parents allow and disallow what they do. But though they aren't capable of comprehending their parents' reasons, they are capable of knowing their parents' love and therefore are capable of trusting them and living securely. That is what they really need. Now, the difference between God and human beings is infinitely greater than the difference between a thirty-year-old parent and a three-year-old child. So we should not expect to be able to grasp all God's purposes, but through the cross and gospel of Jesus Christ, we can know his love. And that is what we need most.

In Ann Voskamp's book *One Thousand Gifts*, she shares her journey to understand the senseless death of her sister, crushed by a truck at the age of two. In the end, she concludes that the primary issue is whether we trust God's character. Is he really loving? Is he really just? Her conclusion:

> [God] gave us Jesus. . . . If God didn't withhold from us His very own Son, will God *withhold* anything we need? If trust must be earned, hasn't God unequivocally earned our trust with the bark on the raw wounds, the thorns pressed into the brow, your name on the cracked lips? How will he not also graciously give us all things He deems best and right? He's already given us the incomprehensible.[211]

The Light in the Darkness

This is a dark world. There are many ways we keep that darkness at bay, but we cannot do it forever. Eventually the lights of our lives—love, health, home, work—will begin go out. And when that happens, we will need something more than what our own understanding, competence, and power can give us.

In Isaiah 9:2 and Matthew 4:16, we are told that in the birth of Jesus, "the people walking in darkness have seen a great light; on those living in the land of the shadow of death a light has dawned." But, you may say, if Jesus is the light of the world, why when he came into the world did he not *do* something about the suffering and darkness? Children still die premature and horrible deaths. The poor are still downtrodden. Young fathers still die in accidents, leaving widows and orphans to fend for themselves. There are still wars and rumors of wars. Why didn't he stop it all?

But what if when Jesus came to earth he had not died young but had come to put down injustice and end evil? What would the result have been for us? Remember Tolkien's dictum: "Always after a defeat and a respite . . . [evil] takes another shape and grows again."[212] He's right. Consider the scientific and technological advances that have brought untold benefits in health care and communication. The communication revolution has even been credited with bringing down the Iron Curtain and ending the Cold War. Yet many well-informed people now are afraid that terrorists will use that technology to bring down whole sectors of the electronic grid and wipe out trillions in wealth and bring on a world-wide depression. Nuclear energy is also a great source of power when harnessed properly, yet we know the likelihood of nuclear proliferation and nuclear terrorism. When a new development pushes back evil in one form, evil always finds a way to use that development to bring itself home to us in new shapes and forms.

Why? It is because the evil and darkness of this world comes to a great degree from *within* us. Martin Luther taught that human nature is *in curvatus in se,* curved in on itself. We are so instinctively and profoundly self-centered that we don't believe we are. And this curved-in-ness is a source of a vast amount of the suffering and evil we experience, from the violence and genocides in the headlines down to the reason your marriage is so painful. Philosopher John Gray is an atheist, but on this point he agrees with the book of Genesis.

> In comparison with the Genesis myth, the modern myth in which humanity is marching to a better future is mere superstition. As the Genesis story teaches, knowledge cannot save us from ourselves. If we know more than before, it means only that we have greater scope to enact our fantasies. . . . The message of Genesis is that in the most vital areas of human life there can be no progress, only an unending struggle with our own nature.[213]

Now do you see what would have happened at Jesus' first coming to earth if he'd come with a sword in his hand and a power to destroy all sources of suffering and evil? It would have meant there would be no human beings left. If you don't think that is fair, I would argue that you don't know your own capabilities, your own heart.

But Jesus did not come to earth the first time to bring justice but rather to bear it. He came not with a sword in his hands but with nails through his hands. Christian teaching for centuries has been this: Jesus died on the cross in our place, taking the punishment our sins deserve, so that someday he can return to earth to end evil without destroying us all.

Jesus did not come back the first time with a political program to cast off the Roman oppression—as good as that may have been. He did not want to do merely the thing we human beings can (and must do)—oppose and prevent the latest form of evil. No, he had a more radical program. He was born into the world and died on the cross and rose from the dead to begin that program. His death and resurrection created a people in the world who now have a unique and powerful ability to diminish the evil in their own hearts as well as a mandate to oppose and endure without flagging the evil they find in their communities and society. And it was all because the Son of God entered into human suffering to turn evil on its head and eventually end evil, sin, suffering, and death itself for good.

The Bible says that Jesus is *the* light of the world. If you know you are in his love, and that nothing can snatch you out of his hand, and that he is taking you to God's house and God's future—then he can be a light for you in dark places when all other lights go out. His love for you now—and this infallible hope for the future—are indeed a light in the darkness, by which we can find our way.

Life Story: Forgiveness

by Georgianna

My daughters and I love fiction—especially stories that have happy endings. Our life with their father and my husband, Ted, had been so happy and blissful. So much so, that if God said to me, "I am going to allow a painful crisis in your family, and *all of you will suffer*," I would calmly reply, "Okay, Father, let Your will be done." We could handle anything together.

On May 13, 2011, our youngest daughter, Jane, had an accident. She tipped backward in her seat and fell, hitting her head on the hardwood floor. I assessed her immediately, as a trained infant and pediatric nurse practitioner. She showed no signs of injury. My sister, also a nurse practitioner, agreed that she appeared healthy.

We took Jane to her scheduled pediatrician's visit on May 16, 2011. I told the doctor what had happened, and he thought it would be prudent to obtain a skull X-ray. We took Jane to the children's hospital, where the X-ray revealed a skull fracture. A CT scan confirmed that there were no other complications. I obviously felt terrible, and had many questions, but we were comforted and assured by the medical staff. We praised God all the way home for protecting Jane from more severe injuries.

A week later, I was home alone with Anne, Paige, and Jane. Suddenly, there were police detectives and Child Protective Services (CPS) workers at our house. They had come to investigate a report of "severe child abuse." Their questions were shocking, accusatory, and confusing. Even more appalling, my daughters witnessed it all.

The report of "severe child abuse" came from a new doctor at the hospital who only viewed the X-ray, and made the report to CPS based on nothing more. Because Jane was under twelve months old, the report was automatically classified as a criminal case.

All three of our daughters were removed from our custody.

There was no evidence of abuse, past or present, in any of our children. There were no risk factors for abuse in our family. There were no previous injuries in any of our children. Every medical professional who actually examined Jane and spoke with our family ruled out the possibility of abuse.

In spite of the truth, our family was torn apart, and was not reunited until nine months later. Ted and I were not allowed to live in the same house as our girls, so we were forced to move out, and were allowed only supervised visitation.

I will never forget the first night away from our daughters. I was *raging*, crying out to God, screaming in agony. Then something powerful happened. A calmness and warmth spread through me. I was suddenly aware that God was right there, holding me, raging with me at the injustice, weeping with us, His children. In that moment, I had never felt more protected in all my life.

I certainly did not remain one hundred percent trusting or peaceful over the following nine months. Every second felt like evil persecution. Our children were suffering. I was being falsely accused of "severely abusing" Jane. I was also being personally and professionally attacked on many levels. I had spent over a decade working as a nurse with high-risk families. I was specifically trained to prevent child abuse and neglect.

In addition to the emotional assault on our family, we also experienced the enormous financial burden of legal defense, case-related consultations, associated medical bills, and counseling, and I wasn't allowed to return to work since I worked with children.

So what happened to that deep, peaceful awareness of my Father's presence and protection? It was still in me, grounding me, giving me strength to get through another day. Despite each day's disappointments, frustrations, and sorrows, I slept soundly each night. Each morning, I thanked God for recharging me.

During the day, I frequently wrestled with God. I often brooded when He didn't "make things right." I was so weary of waiting for the truth to prevail. There were countless court meetings, petitions, hearings, CPS visits, police procedures, legal proceedings, rumors, expert opinions, off-the-record tips, and massive amounts of paperwork. Most of the time, I accepted the courage God was giving me to handle these daily challenges. Other times, I crumbled under the pressure. Over time, I learned that God didn't mind how strong or weak I was on any given day. He was the same. This was the true miracle—that my family lived and survived in the fiery furnace with God's provision, not that God ultimately rescued us from it.

We often found ourselves speaking words of hope and encouragement to others. I never, however, concealed my true feelings about what was happening or how I was struggling. God made me vulnerable enough to touch people's hearts, but resilient enough to testify about His provision. Many said, "If that happened to me, I would fall apart; I wouldn't survive; My anger would make me do something regrettable. But you are so strong, so faithful, so patient!" Every time someone said this, I felt a spark of joy, because I loved being God's instrument. I did feel all of those awful and hopeless emotions, but God was strong for me. I did fall apart, often, but God always put me back together. I did relish the thought of revenge at times, but God replaced my bitterness with mercy. God was the patient One, not me!

We finally made it to Juvenile Court trial. Although it was technically a criminal investigation as well, the police had performed many investigative procedures, and since they never uncovered any evidence against us, we were never charged criminally. The judge was respected as a fair and objective judge by all. The CPS attorney had the opposite reputation. While on the stand, I often felt hurt, angry, annoyed, defeated, tricked, betrayed, and helpless, but the whole time I could feel God with me, fighting for me. After the third day of trial, once Ted and I were alone, I cried, "Thank you, God, for the privilege of this suffering, for being with us in it, and for shining through us during this suffering. . . ."

On the fourth day, the judge made a declaration that astonished everyone. He dismissed the entire case as unfounded—without even hearing our defense. I whispered "thank You," over and over. Our attorney said to us, "This isn't my victory, or your victory. This is God's victory. Thank Him, not me."

When the battle was over, there were battle wounds that needed tending. Initially, we were so relieved and overjoyed by freedom that we did not anticipate the emotional task ahead. Despite the reunification of our family, our daughters continued to suffer the effects of our crisis.

Ted and I also faced some symptoms of post-traumatic stress, but even so, the predominant mood in our home was relief. We felt peace and joy with fresh intensity. I felt a renewed sense of awe and gratitude for the gift of my children. It was amazing how the lingering hurt coexisted with the delight, how our grieving was simultaneous with our healing.

February 2013 marked only the one-year anniversary of our trial. The most powerful facilitation to our recovery has been forgiveness. I think injustice is very difficult to forgive. Personally, it would have been impossible to forgive without God's intervention.

After our exoneration, my family attempted repeatedly to contact the children's hospital that ignited the whole ordeal. The chief of staff finally agreed to a meeting with the physician who reported us. Our intention was to have a collegial discussion about the events, in an effort to prevent similar harm to other families.

I recounted every appalling detail of our family's experience to the chief of staff and the head of Child Abuse Pediatrics (the one who reported us). As I spoke, I felt confident and calm, never angry or bitter.

When I finished, the chief of staff apologized, saying, "Mistakes were made, and I am very sorry for what your family had to go through." Then the physician who made the misdiagnosis of child abuse echoed the same apology.

When we were leaving the office, I *hugged the doctor who had reported us.* Trust me, I did not feel like showing love to that person, but God did. That was the most powerful healing and reconciliation I have ever experienced. God changed me in that moment, more than He had changed me through the entire tribulation. He miraculously changed my perspective—I suddenly saw myself in this flawed woman facing me. How many mistakes have I made in my life? How many people have I hurt, intentionally or unintentionally? How many times have I allowed pride to prevent me from doing the right thing? How, after all, was I different from my accuser?

I believe our story does have a happy ending, but the truth is, our story is never-ending. And I praise God that He is still writing chapters of my life. My family and I are humbly grateful for the suffering our Father endured with us. Without it, we would be comfortably living our "old normal," instead of courageously living our "new normal."

SIX

The Sovereignty of God

Everything difficult indicates something more than our theory of life yet embraces.

—George MacDonald[214]

We have looked at suffering and evil from cultural, historical, and philosophical perspectives. Along the way, we have contrasted various views with Christianity and as a result we have already laid the groundwork for a biblical theology of suffering. Now we will take what we have already learned and lay out an outline of what the Bible as a whole tells us about pain and suffering.

Compared to the other worldviews we have considered, the Bible's picture of suffering is, I would argue, the most nuanced and multidimensional. When weighing the biblical material, we see two foundational balances.

Suffering is both just and unjust.

God is both a sovereign and a suffering God.

These two sets of paired truths, held together without jettisoning one in favor of another, leads to a remarkably rich and many-sided understanding of the causes and forms of suffering. It also affords sufferers a great range of resources and approaches for facing it, without a one-size-fits-all prescription.

In this chapter and the next, we will look at these two pairs of complementary truths about suffering, and will then revisit God's final answer to evil in the cross and new creation.

Suffering as Justice and Judgment

The first chapters of the Bible, Genesis 1–3, say that suffering in the world is the result of sin, particularly the original sin of humankind turning away from God. After Adam and Eve disobey their Creator, God describes what the fallen world will look like. It is virtually a catalogue of all forms of suffering—including spiritual alienation, inner psychological pain, social and interpersonal conflict and cruelty, natural disasters, disease, and death (Gen 3:17ff). All this natural and moral evil is understood as stemming from the foundational rupture of our relationship with God. And suffering begins when Adam and Eve are expelled from the Garden of Eden (Gen 3:23–24). Their exile is the original infliction of suffering as judgment.

Paul looks back to this when he writes:

> I consider that our present sufferings are not worth comparing with the glory that will be revealed in us. . . . For the creation was subjected to frustration, not by its own choice, but by the will of the one who subjected it, in hope that the creation itself will be liberated from its bondage to decay and brought into the freedom and glory of the children of God (Rom 8:18, 20–21).

The word *frustration* can also be translated as "futility." To be futile is to fall short of your purpose, to stretch and exert but see it all come to nothing. The world is now in a cursed condition that falls short of its design. Human beings were not created to experience death, pain, grief, disappointment, ruptured relationships, disease, and natural disasters.[215] The world we were made to live in was not supposed to be like that. A frustrated world is a broken world, in which things do not function as they should, and that is why there is evil and suffering.

But Paul adds that this judgment does not represent God's abandonment of us. Rather, his judgment of the world was purposeful. Even as he judged the world with suffering, he had in view a plan for the redemption of all things. God judged the world "in hope" of a final redemption from evil that would be glorious. This little verse has an enormous depth behind it. It suggests that once human beings turned from God, there were only two alternatives, either immediate destruction or a path that led to redemption through great loss, grief, and pain, not only for human beings but for God himself. There is even a hint here that the future glory will be somehow even greater for all the suffering. Nevertheless, for the present, we live in the shadows.

The Bible is emphatic, then, that the existence of suffering in the world is really a form of justice. But suffering-as-judgment does not end with original sin and the initial expulsion from the Garden. God often gives out rewards and punishment in history to peoples and individuals on the basis of their deeds, or simply to allow people to reap the natural consequences of what they have sown. The book of Proverbs is filled with examples of what has been called retributive justice.[216] Stinginess often leads to want because the miser has no friends (Prov 11:24-26); a lazy and undisciplined person can suffer hunger (Prov 19:15); a person who chooses the wrong friends often comes to grief (Prov 13:20). Much of the wisdom literature is very clear that suffering comes in all these instances because certain behavior goes against the grain of the universe, violating God's moral order as much as trying to fly off a cliff violates the law of gravity.

Suffering as Injustice and Mystery

However, while the Bible tells us that suffering in the world is the result of human sin in general, it is just as emphatic that individual instances of suffering may not be the result of a particular sin. As one scholar summarizes it, "The fact of suffering was held to be the result of sin, especially original sin, but this did not mean that each instance of suffering could be causally linked to a specific sin and its divine punishment."[217]

The most prominent example of this is the case of Job. Job's suffering is greater than his friends'. This leads his friends to conclude smugly that

Job's moral life must be inferior to theirs. As the book shows so vividly, this was a proud, cruel, and mistaken belief, and one that God himself condemns with great forcefulness at the end of the book. Job's friends forgot one half of the crucial dual principle. While the human race as a whole indeed deserves the broken world it inhabits, nevertheless evil is not distributed in a proportionate, fair way. Bad people do not have worse lives than good people. And, of course, the best people often have terrible lives. Job is one example, and Jesus—the ultimate "Job," the only truly, fully innocent sufferer—is another.

The book of Ecclesiastes also points to cases of unfair, unmerited, and seemingly inexplicable suffering. The writer sees that "the wise have eyes in their heads, while the fool walks in darkness," but then he comes to realize "that the same fate overtakes them both" (Eccles 2:14). The hard worker and the wise man often lose everything while the wicked prosper. He says, "In the place of judgment—wickedness was there, in the place of justice—wickedness was there" (Eccles 3:16). At the beginning of his fourth chapter, the author says he took another look at "all the oppression that was taking place under the sun" and

> I saw the tears of the oppressed—
> and they have no comforter;
> power was on the side of their oppressors—
> and they have no comforter.
> And I declared that the dead,
> who had already died,
> are happier than the living,
> who are still alive.
> But better than both
> is the one who has never been born,
> who has not seen the evil
> that is done under the sun. (Eccles 4:1–3)

And so, he writes: "I hated life, because the work that is done under the sun was grievous to me. All of it is meaningless, a chasing after the wind" (Eccles 2:17). The Hebrew term for "meaningless" or "vanity" used here is akin to the "futility" visited on the world in the wake of human sin.

Proverbs, Ecclesiastes, and Job sit literally alongside one another in the "wisdom literature" section of the Bible, and it is important to recognize their differing yet complementary perspectives on suffering. While Proverbs tends to emphasize the justice of suffering and how much suffering is directly related to wrongdoing, Job and Ecclesiastes vividly show how much of it is *not*.

The biblical story of creation was unique among ancient accounts of the world's origin. Other accounts describe the world as coming into existence through a battle or struggle between divine beings or other supernatural forces. In these views, there are multiple power centers in constant conflict and tension. That meant that the world was basically a chaotic place, a place where anything could happen, depending on which power gained the upper hand. This view has resurfaced today in the writings of scientific materialists who see the universe as the production of violent, unguided forces. In this kind of world, the most important trait is strength and power.

But Old Testament scholar Gerhard von Rad points out the uniqueness of the Hebrew Scriptures.[218] There we read that creation was the result of one all-powerful God without a rival, who made the world not in the way a warrior wins a battle but more as an artist crafts something of wonder and beauty. As an artist, he creates for the sheer joy of it (Prov 8:27–31). And therefore the world has a pattern to it, a *fabric*. A fabric is a complex underlying designed order or structure.

Biblical wisdom, according to von Rad, is to "become competent with regard to the realities of life."[219] Since the world was made by a good and righteous God, the fabric of the world has a moral order to it. That order is not based on power but on righteousness. Power and self-interest may appear successful in the short run, but they do not ultimately "work" in a world created by a good and just God. Therefore cruel, selfish power is not only sinful, but stupid. It brings about loneliness, emptiness, and destruction. Faithfulness, integrity, unselfish service, and love are not only right but wise, because they fit the fabric of reality.

Except. While Proverbs points to the fact that, in general, hard work leads to prosperity, and laziness leads to want—it doesn't always work that way. Job and Ecclesiastes supplement Proverbs' understanding of the world. Our world has been created by God and therefore has a foundational moral order to it. And yet something is wrong with that order now. It is partly, though not fully, broken. Biblical scholar Graeme Goldsworthy tells us that, while Proverbs shows us the reality of God's order, Job points to its "hiddenness" and Ecclesiastes to its "confusion."[220] At the end of the book of Job, God appears and insists that the moral order of the universe is still intact, but it is in large part hidden from human eyes. So while there is still a certain amount of "poetic justice" in which evildoers fall into the very traps they set for others, much suffering is disproportionate and unfairly distributed. The good can and do die young.

The New Testament testifies to the same view of things. In John 9, Jesus heals a blind man and takes pains to show his disciples that he was not in that condition because of his sin or that of his parents, but in order to fulfill God's inscrutable purposes. Thus, suffering people should not automatically be blamed for their condition.

This biblical idea not only contrasts with the teachings of karma, it goes against common sense. Psychologist Mel Lerner has demonstrated that most people have a deep desire to believe "people get what they deserve and deserve what they get." They tend to assign blame to victims of tragedy especially if it is not possible to punish a perpetrator.[221] This comes from a normal human impulse to make sense of things, but it also likely stems from the deep human need to believe we are in control of our own lives. People want to believe "that couldn't happen to me—because I'm wiser, I'm better, I know what I'm doing." The Bible's assessment is less flattering to non-sufferers and kinder to those who are hurting. Much suffering is mysterious and unjust.

Suffering as the Enemy of God

Evil is an intrusion into God's good creation. And often evil and suffering occur without regard to an individual's relative moral decency or deserts. But even though, as we will see, the Bible is insistent that suffering is not outside of God's control, it is crucial to understand evil as an enemy of God. David Bentley Hart, in an essay written after the 2004 tsunamis that killed so many, writes

> . . . of a child dying an agonizing death from diphtheria, of a young mother ravaged by cancer, of tens of thousands of Asians swallowed in an instant by the sea, of millions murdered in death camps and gulags and forced famines. . . . Our faith is in a God who has come to rescue His creation from the absurdity of sin and the emptiness of death, and so we are permitted to hate these things with a perfect hatred. . . . As for comfort, when we seek it, I can imagine none greater than the happy knowledge that when I see the death of a child, I do not see the face of God, but the face of His enemy. It is . . . a faith that . . . has set us free from optimism, and taught us hope instead.[222]

Something of this truth can be seen when Jesus comes to visit the family of his recently deceased friend Lazarus, in John 11. When he approaches the tomb, most translations say he was "once more deeply moved" or "he groaned in himself" (v. 38). But these translations are too weak. The Greek word used by the gospel writer John means "to bellow with anger." It is a startling term. Theologian B. B. Warfield writes: "What John tells us, in point of fact, is that Jesus approached the grave of Lazarus in a state, not of uncontrollable grief, but of irrepressible anger."[223] Why did the sight of Lazarus's tomb and his family's grief enrage Jesus? In some ways, his anger and tears seem inappropriate. He knows full well that he is about to turn all the grieving and mourning into shouts of wonder and joy—he is about to raise Lazarus from the dead (vv. 42–44). So why is he quite literally furious? And what is he furious at? Warfield, relying on John Calvin's commentary on the same passage, gives a remarkable answer.

> The spectacle of the distress of Mary and her companions enraged Jesus because it brought poignantly home to his consciousness the evil of death, its unnaturalness, its "violent tyranny" as Calvin (in verse 38) phrases it. In Mary's grief, he "contemplates"—still to adopt Calvin's words (in verse 33)— "the general misery of the whole human race" and burns with rage against the oppressor of men. Inextinguishable fury seizes upon him; his whole being is discomposed and perturbed. . . .
>
> It is death that is the object of his wrath, and behind death him who has the power of death, and whom he has come into the world to destroy. Tears of sympathy may fill his eyes, but this is incidental. His soul is held by rage: and he advances to the tomb, in Calvin's words again, "as a champion who prepares for conflict.". . . What John does for us in this particular statement is to uncover to us the heart of Jesus, as he wins for us our salvation. Not in cold unconcern, but in flaming wrath against the foe, Jesus smites in our behalf. He has not only saved us from the evils which oppress us; he has felt for and with us in our oppression, and under the impulse of these feelings has wrought out our redemption.[224]

So Jesus is furious at evil, death, and suffering and, even though he is God, he is not mad at himself. This means that evil is the enemy of God's good creation, and of God himself. And Jesus' entire mission was to take evil on and end it. But, as we have seen, evil is so deeply rooted in the human heart that if Christ had come in power to destroy it everywhere he found it, he would have had to destroy us too. Instead of coming as a general at the head of an army, he went in weakness to the cross in order to pay for our sins, so that someday he will return to wipe out evil without having to judge us as well. He will be able to receive us to himself because he bore our judgment himself on Calvary.

In passages like John 9 and 11 Jesus teaches that, though God has imposed suffering and evil as just punishment on us and will put things right on Judgment Day, suffering in the meantime is often unjust and always something that God himself hates. As Ronald Rittgers summarizes: "Christ upholds the . . . justice model [that suffering is due to sin]. When he rebukes people for speculating about the eighteen who were killed when the Tower of Siloam fell on them (Luke 13:4–5) or when he chastises the disciples for trying to connect a man's blindness with a specific sin (John 9:1–12) he does not deny the model . . . rather he opposes a simplistic and self-aggrandizing application of it."[225]

Suffering, Justice, and Wisdom

Already we can see how this first set of paired biblical teachings—that suffering is both just and unjust—leads us toward wisdom about how to face suffering. As von Rad observed, wisdom is an awareness of complex reality. Part of reality is that suffering is something that God has justly imposed on the world. We owe God everything, since he created us and sustains our life every moment. It is only reasonable and right that we love him more than anything else and serve him rather than our own interests and impulses. But we do not—we live for ourselves and we sin. Therefore we do not deserve a good world, a world made for our benefit.

But another controlling reality is that the creation order—the fabric of this world—is frayed or broken through. Suffering and pain are distributed disproportionately so that often the innocent suffer more and the wicked suffer less. In light of this second reality, we must be very slow to assume that suffering has come upon us or others because of not living right. We must not look at parents with children gone off the rails, or racial groups with a lot of poverty and crime, or gay people who are dying of AIDs and assume that, if we are not suffering in the same way as they, we are morally superior to them in God's eyes. And when suffering comes upon us inexplicably, as it did to Job, it means that we can indeed cry out in our confusion. We have a warrant for being in deep distress, and there is truth in our feeling that we are suffering unjustly.

If we ignore either of these truths, we will be out of touch with the universe as it really is. If we forget the first truth—that, in general, suffering is just—we will fall into proud, resentful self-pity that bitterly rejects the goodness or even the existence of God. If we forget the second truth—that, in particular, suffering is often unjust—we may be trapped in inordinate guilt and the belief that God must have abandoned us. These teachings eliminate what could be called both the "I hate thee" response—debilitating anger toward God—and the "I hate me" response—devastating guilt and a sense of personal failure. Counselors know what an enormous number of people fall into one or the other—or both—of these abysses. This balance—that God is just and will bring final justice, but life in the meantime is often deeply unfair—keeps us from many deadly errors. If we end up in one abyss or the other, it will be due to being unwise, "incompetent with regard to the realities of life."

The Sovereignty of God

The second pair of balancing truths we must begin to consider is the twin teachings that God is a sovereign and yet suffering God. These are the biblical teachings that correspond to the philosophers' depiction of an "all-powerful" and "all-good" God. The Bible goes beyond such abstractions, presenting God as not merely omnipotent but sovereign over every event in history, and it also shows us God as not merely "good and loving" but as entering our world and becoming subject to greater evil, suffering, and pain than any of us have ever experienced. Rittgers writes that unless we know both of these truths, suffering cannot have any meaningfulness nor any ultimate solution:

> The God of the Bible . . . both suffers with humanity—
> supremely on the cross—and yet is in some sense also sover-

eign over suffering. *Both* beliefs were (and are) essential to the traditional Christian assertion that suffering ultimately has some meaning and that the triune God is able to provide deliverance from it.[226]

What do we mean, first, when we say that God is sovereign over history and therefore over suffering? The doctrine of the sovereignty of God in the Bible has sometimes been called compatibilism.[227] The Bible teaches that God is completely in control of what happens in history and yet he exercises that control in such a way that human beings are responsible for their freely chosen actions and the results of those actions. Human freedom and God's direction of historical events are therefore completely compatible. To put it most practically and vividly—if a man robs a bank, that moral evil is fully his responsibility, though it also is part of God's plan.

It is crude but effective to think of this in percentages. We think that either God has planned something or that a human being has freely chose to do it—but both cannot be true at once. Perhaps we grant that the event is due 50 percent to God's activity and 50 percent to human agency. Or maybe it is 80-20, or 20-80. But the Bible depicts history as 100 percent under God's purposeful direction, and yet filled with human beings who are 100 percent responsible for their behavior—at once.

This way of thinking is counterintuitive to both ancient and modern ways of thinking. The Greek notion of "fate" or the Islamic notion of "kismet" are quite different from the Christian doctrine of God's sovereignty. The Greek myth of Oedipus tells of the main character who, the oracle predicts, is fated to kill his father and marry his mother. Though Oedipus and all around him do all they can to avoid this fate, all of their schemes to avoid this destiny only end up hastening it. The destined end is reached despite everyone's choices. The Christian concept of God's sovereignty is quite different. God's plan works *through* our choices, not around or despite them. Our choices have consequences, and we are never forced by God to do anything—we always do what we most want to do. God works out his will perfectly through our willing actions.

The Bible everywhere presupposes this "compatibilism" between God's plan and our actions, and at many places explicitly teaches it.[228]

In Isaiah 10, God calls Assyria "the rod of my anger" (v. 5). He says he is using Assyria to punish Israel for its sins, and yet he nonetheless holds Assyria responsible for what it is doing. "I send him [Assyria] against a godless nation [Israel]," says God, "but this is not what he intends, this is not what he has in mind, his purpose is to destroy" (v. 6–7). While God uses Assyria as his rod according to his wise and just plan, that nation's inner motivation is not a passion for justice but merely a cruel and proud desire to dominate others. And so God will judge the instrument of his judgment. Assyria's actions are part of God's plan, and yet the Assyrians are held accountable for their free choices. It is a remarkable balance. On the one hand, evil is taken seriously as a reality. And yet there is an assurance that in the end, it can never triumph.

God is called the one "who works out everything in conformity with the purpose of his will" (Eph 1:11). "*Everything*" that happens fits in accord with, in harmony with, God's plan. This means that God's plan includes "little things." Proverbs 16:33 says, "The lot is cast into the lap, but the disposal thereof is from the Lord." Even the flip of the coin is part of his plan. Ultimately, there are no accidents. His plan also includes bad things. Psalm 60:3 reads, "You have made your people see hard things; you have given us wine to drink that made us stagger."

Suffering then is not outside God's plan but a part of it. In Acts 4:27–28, the Christian disciples pray to God, "In this city, there were gathered together against your holy servant Jesus . . . Herod and Pontius Pilate, along with the Gentiles and the peoples of Israel, to do whatever your hand and your plan had predestined to take place." Jesus' suffering and death was a great act of injustice, but it was also part of the set plan of God.

God's Plans and Our Plans

According to the Bible, God plans our plans. Proverbs 16:9 says, "The heart of man plans his way, but the Lord establishes his steps." The author assumes that while we make our plans, they only fit into the larger plans of God.

There are many texts that weave free will and divine sovereignty together in ways that startle us. In Genesis 50:20, Joseph explains how his brothers' evil action of selling him into slavery was used by God to do great good. "You intended me harm, but God intended it for good to accomplish what is now being done, the saving of many lives." Notice Joseph assuming that what they did was evil—they "intended" harm, it was deliberate. Yet he says God's plan overruled and used Joseph's troubles and sorrows for his own good purposes. The New Testament version of Joseph's saying is Romans 8:28—"All things work together for good to them who love God."

In Acts 2:23, Peter again tells us Jesus was crucified "according to the definite plan" of God, and yet the hands that put him to death were guilty of injustice and "lawlessness." In other words, the death of Jesus was destined to happen by God's will—it was not possible that it would not happen. Yet no one who betrayed and put Jesus to death was forced to do it. They all freely chose what they did and were fully liable and responsible for their decisions. Jesus himself puts these truths together in one sentence: "The Son of Man will go [to his death] as it has been decreed, but woe to that man who betrays him" (Luke 22:22).

One of the most fascinating examples of this biblical perspective is found in the account of Moses' confrontation with Pharaoh in Exodus 7–14. Moses continually calls Pharaoh to release the Israelites from bondage and declares that this is the will of God. Over several chapters the text tells us Pharaoh "hardened" his heart and he stubbornly refused to let the people go. This obstinate refusal led to untold misery and death for the Egyptians. But the text is fascinating, because it tells us that God hardened Pharaoh's heart (Ex 7:3; 9:12; 10:1; 11:10; 14:4, 8) almost the same number of times it tells us Pharaoh hardened his own heart (Ex 8:15, 32; 9:34; 10:3; 13:15). So which is it? Did God do it or did Pharaoh do it? The biblical answer to both is yes.

Look at the sins in the life of the patriarch Jacob, whose life is recounted in the book of Genesis. Jacob deceived his father and robbed his brother; as a result, he had to flee his homeland and experienced great suffering and injustice in a foreign land. Yet there he met the love of his life and had the children through which Jesus was descended. It is clear that his sin did not put him into a "plan B" for his life. It was all part of God's perfect plan for him and even for the salvation of the world. Was he therefore not responsible for his sin? No, he was. Did he not suffer consequences for his foolish behavior? Yes, he did. But God was infallibly in control, even as Jacob was completely responsible.

In the end, the Christian concept of God's sovereignty is a marvelous, practical principle. No one can claim to know exactly *how* both of these truths fit together.[229] And yet even in our own ordinary experience, we know something of how to direct people along a path without violating their free will. Good leaders do this in part—why would the infinite God not be able to do it perfectly? The sovereignty of God is mysterious but not contradictory. It means that we have great incentive to use our wisdom and our will to the best effect, knowing God holds us to it and knowing we will suffer consequences from foolishness and wickedness. On the other hand, there is an absolute promise that we cannot ultimately mess up our lives. Even our failures and troubles will be used for God's glory and our benefit. I don't know a more comforting assurance than that. "God performs all things for me!" cries the psalmist (Ps 57:2).

This teaching has both high-level and practical implications for how we approach suffering. At one level, this means that, as Don Carson writes: "It must be the case that God stands behind good and evil in somewhat different ways; that is, he stands behind good and evil *asymmetrically*."[230] While moral evil cannot be done outside the bounds of God's purposes, "the evil is not morally chargeable to him" since the perpetrators are responsible.[231] Yet since all good impulses in the human heart come ultimately from God (James 1:17)[232]—when good things happen, they *are* directly attributable to him.

At the most practical level, we have the crucial assurance that even wickedness and tragedy, which we know was not part of God's original design, is nonetheless being woven into a wise plan. So the promise of Romans 8, "that all things work together for good," is an incomparable comfort to believers.

Life Story: Dependence on God

by Russ and Sue

RUSS: The first decade of our marriage was marked by cycles of privilege and crisis. The perpetual jostling of high-flying careers and sudden unemployment and trying to jump-start new careers made it very difficult to feel any sense of security. It was, however, preparation for the unrelenting challenges that lay ahead.

In 2000, our world was in upheaval from the unexpected news of cancer.

SUE: The night before I was to hear the results of my biopsy, I was in anguish and despair. Suddenly an undeniable presence entered the room. An overpowering sense of calm overwhelmed me and I heard, "It will be all right, I am with you." That chilling moment was a gift that not only lulled me to sleep that night but gave me the strength to hear that I was diagnosed with Hodgkin's lymphoma. It would sustain me throughout my ordeals.

No sooner had we celebrated the end of chemotherapy when the cancer returned with a vengeance. This necessitated a stem cell transplant and high-dose chemotherapy with a 50-50 chance of survival, followed by radiation. It was clearly evident how little control we had.

RUSS: We spent three weeks together through the stem cell procedure as Sue's immunity was reduced to zero. We faced the issue of mortality, had deep talks and quiet contemplation. I felt such closeness to God and my wife, as if in a peaceful, parallel universe. The most difficult thing was how to handle the "what if"

God were to allow her to die. I needed to truly be able to say "Your will, not mine." She went on to recover and God spared me the torment.

SUE: The treatment eliminated the cancer but a year later caused pulmonary fibrosis, an incurable, progressive scarring of the lungs. Over time, the only option for survival was a double lung transplant.

I prayed desperately to be spared the procedure, but the disease outpaced a cure. The support we received through the church, friends, neighbors, and family was a testimony to God's faithful hand. After three failed attempts, the replacement lungs were a match. As doctors operated, I could see angels entering their bodies. I awoke two days later euphoric. My first thought was "Lord, you did it!" I was blessed with more time. My thoughts were then with my donor who in death became my lifesaver.

RUSS: The first night at home, we felt a mutual sense of awe, tremendous joy, and deep reverence toward God. A glimpse of heaven was revealed when for a brief night we felt love and intimacy with Him deepen to a completely different level. It was an unforgettable experience of shared relief and contentment, utter bliss so intense that neither of us wanted it to end. It was quite literally a mountaintop experience that encourages us to this day.

Our joy in the days that followed was immense, but in the fourth month, signs of rejection and chronic lung disease ensued, along with talk of re-transplantation.

These volatile and unresolved medical issues are a source of deep frustration and sadness and place difficult burdens on our family. Yet somehow, God eases the pain, exhaustion, and anger when we cannot bear any more, and encourages us forward. His face appears in the gracious actions of others, and our gratitude runs alongside our sorrow. We know that God is holding us up, working on our behalf. We feel it, see it, and are uplifted by it.

We've come to accept that we will not have the life of stability and comfort we had hoped. We've come to realize that we should not have been striving for stability and comfort but for *total* dependence on God, from whom we draw strength. This requires a daily effort to give up all to Him. Our real comfort is the promise that "in heaven our joy will be made greater as a result of the depth of our distress." We may be crippled still, but empowered by our renewed faith. God has helped us to persevere and that gives us the hope and strength to carry on.

SEVEN

The Suffering of God

It seems to me quite disastrous that the idea should have got about that Christianity is an other-worldly, unreal, idealistic kind of religion that suggests that if we are good we shall be happy. . . . On the contrary, it is fiercely and even harshly realistic, insisting that . . . there are certain eternal achievements that make even happiness look like trash.

—Dorothy L. Sayers, *Creed or Chaos?*

God is sovereign over suffering and yet, in teaching unique to the Christian faith among the major religions, God also made himself vulnerable and subject to suffering. The other side of the sovereignty of God is the suffering of God himself. As Ronald Rittgers said, holding both of these together—as paradoxical as they seem at first—is crucial to grasping the unique Christian understanding of suffering. In earlier chapters, we have already learned that "the *main reason* that Christians insist that God can be trusted in the midst of suffering is that . . . God himself has firsthand experience of suffering."[233]

We can't overemphasize the importance of this. Rittgers and Peter Berger both identify this truth as the counterweight and the complement to the teaching that God is sovereign and uses suffering as part of his often inscrutable purposes. Yes, he is Lord of history, but he is also the vulnerable one who entered that history and became subject to its darkest forces. Yes, God often seems to be absent, but Jesus himself experienced the searing pain of that absence when he cried, "My God, my God, why have you forsaken me?" Yes, God is king, but is a king who came to earth and went not to a throne but to a cross. Yes, God is glorious, but there is no greater glory than this—that he laid his glory and power aside and became weak and mortal.

> Though he was in the form of God, he did not count equality with God something to be grasped, but emptied himself, by taking the form of a servant, being born in the likeness of men. And being found in human form, he humbled himself by becoming obedient to the point of death, even death on a cross (Phil 2:6–8 ESV).

How did the sovereign God become the suffering God? The suffering of God is indicated already in the Hebrew Scriptures, long before the coming of Jesus into the world.

The Old Testament shows us a God who so deliberately sets his heart upon us that our condition affects him. In the book of Jeremiah, God speaks of Israel as "Ephraim" and says, "Is not Ephraim, my dear son, the child in whom I delight? Though I often speak against him, I still remember him. Therefore my heart yearns for him; I have great compassion for him" (Jer 31:20). In a famous outburst in Hosea 11, God cries, "How can I give you up, Ephraim? How can I hand you over, Israel? . . . My heart is changed within me; all my compassion is aroused. I will not carry out my fierce anger, nor will I turn and devastate Ephraim again" (Hosea 11:8–9). Another striking example of this same theme is Genesis 6:5–6: "The Lord saw how great man's wickedness on the earth had become. . . . The Lord was grieved that he had made man on the earth, and his heart was filled with pain" (NIV-1984). Old Testament scholar Derek Kidner says that these are "the boldest terms, counterpoised elsewhere [in the Bible] if need be, but not weakened."[234]

Kidner means that these passages of the Bible must be put alongside those that talk of God's omnipotence, sovereignty, holiness, absolute self-sufficiency, infinity, and eternal nature. As biblical theologian Alec Motyer puts it: "The living God [is] a self-maintaining, self-sufficient reality that does not need to draw vitality from outside."[235] Put another way, God depends on no one and nothing, but everything depends on him. God does not need our love and worship. He needs nothing to complete himself, as we do. We must not look at these passages that talk of God's emotions and grief without seeing what the rest of the Bible says; otherwise we might come up with a God as "halting . . . ever-changing, in process of growth" or needing our love.[236]

But we must not go to the other extreme either. Theologians some-times have spoken of the "impassibility of God;" namely that God could not be capable of emotions, of either joy and pleasure or pain and grief.[237] But this goes beyond the language and teaching of the Scrip-ture. We must not play down the poignancy of what is said in passages like Hosea 11 and Genesis 6. "The word *grieved*," Kidner writes about Genesis 6:6, "is akin to the 'sorrow' and 'pain' [inflicted on human be-ings for their sin] in Genesis 3:16, 17: *already God suffers on man's ac-count*."[238]

We all know how heart involvement leads to suffering. The more you love someone, the more that person's grief and pain becomes yours. And so even in the first chapters of Genesis, we see God is suffering because of our suffering, because of the misery of the world. Here we have no abstract deity, no "divine principle," no "rational structure behind the universe." This is not merely the "spark of divine life in every living thing." This is a transcendent but personal God who loves us so much that his heart is filled with pain over us. That would be remarkable enough. But then there is Jesus himself.

The Suffering of God the Son

The gospels show us Jesus experiencing the ordinary pressures, difficul-ties, and pains of normal human life. He experienced weariness and thirst (John 4:6), distress, grief, and being "troubled in heart" (Mark 3:5; John 11:35; 12:27). His suffering was such that throughout his life he offered up prayers "with loud cries and tears" (Heb 5:7; cf. Luke 22:44). He knew what it was like to be completely misunderstood by his best friends and rejected by his family and hometown (John 7:3–5; Matt

13:57; Mark 3:21). He was also tempted and assaulted by the devil (Matt 4:2ff). And amazingly, we are told that Jesus "learned" from what he suffered (Heb 5:8). Don Carson concludes, "The God on whom we rely knows what suffering is all about, not merely in the way that God knows everything, but by *experience*."[239]

But at the end of his life we come to the *Passion*, literally the sufferings of Jesus. He was abandoned, denied, and betrayed by all the people he had poured his life into, and on the cross he was forsaken even by his father (Matt 27:46). This final experience, ultimately unfathomable to us, means infinite, cosmic agony beyond the knowledge of any of us on earth. For the ultimate suffering is the loss of love, and this was the loss of an eternal, perfect love. There is nothing more difficult than the disruption and loss of family relationships, but here we see that "God knows what it is like to suffer, not just because he sees it in far greater clarity than we, but because he has personally suffered in the most severe way possible . . . the agony of loss by death, the separation from a beloved . . . [and] the disruption of his own family (the Trinity) by the immensity of his own wrath against sin."[240] That is, in order to satisfy justice, in order to punish sin so that in love he could forgive and receive us, God had to bear the penalty for sin within himself. God the Son took the punishment we deserved, including being cut off from the Father. And so God took into his own self, his own heart, an infinite agony— out of love for us.

The early-nineteenth-century Scottish preacher Robert Murray M'Cheyne stretches to give us a sense of what he called "the infinity of Christ's sufferings" on the cross. As he reflects on Jesus' cry that God had forsaken him, M'Cheyne writes:

> He was without any comforts of God—no feeling that God loved him—no feeling that God pitied him—no feeling that God supported him. God was his sun before—now that sun became all darkness. . . . He was without God—he was as if he had no God. All that God had been to him before was taken from him now. He was Godless—deprived of his God. He had the feeling of the condemned, when the Judge says,

"Depart from me, ye cursed . . . who shall be punished with everlasting destruction from the presence of the Lord and from the glory of his power." He felt that God said the same to him. I feel like a little child casting a stone into some deep ravine in the mountain side, and listening to hear its fall—but listening all in vain. . . .

Ah! This is the hell that Christ suffered. The ocean of Christ's sufferings is unfathomable. . . . He was forsaken in the [place] of sinners. If you close with him, as your surety, you will never be forsaken. . . . "My God, my God, why hast thou forsaken me?" [The answer?] For *me*—for *me*. The ocean of Christ's sufferings is unfathomable.[241]

And yet we are not finished with what the Bible tells us about God's suffering. In Acts 9 we have the account of the conversion of St. Paul. As a zealous Pharisee, Saul (later Paul) had been persecuting Christians. When Jesus appears to him on the road to Damascus, he asks him, "Saul, why do you persecute *me*?" (Acts 9:4). Here we see that Jesus so identifies with his people that he shares in their suffering. When they are hurt or in grief, so is he.

Sometimes the New Testament puts it the other way around and speaks about Christians sharing in Christ's sufferings. Peter encourages his readers that when they go through the fiery trials—the furnace—Jesus is not merely spiritually present with them, "you share in Christ's sufferings" (1 Pet 4:13; cf. Col 1:24). Peter is saying that we and he suffer together. Now, it is quite clear in the Bible that Jesus' sufferings achieved our redemption completely, and we can contribute nothing to his saving work. That is why, when Jesus died, he said that his work was "finished"—the debt was fully paid (John 19:30). As we saw Luther argue so forcefully—our suffering does not earn or merit any salvation. Nevertheless, we can have the remarkable comfort of knowing that because we are connected by Christ through the Spirit, because we are in union with him, part of his Body, that we have "fellowship" with Jesus in his sufferings (Phil 3:10).

Perhaps the best way to understand this is to put it in the following way. Dan McCartney writes: "Christ learned humanhood from his suffering (Heb 5:8). [And therefore] we learn Christhood from our suffering."[242] Just as Jesus assumed human likeness through suffering (Heb 2:18; 4:14–15), so we can grow into Christ's likeness through it, if we face it in faith and patience. "So we do not lose heart. Though our outer self is wasting away, our inner self is being renewed day by day. For this light momentary affliction is preparing us for an eternal weight of glory beyond all comparison" (2 Cor 4:16–17).

When believers in Jesus suffer, he is quite literally with us in our furnace of trouble, in some way actually feeling the flames too.

The Suffering Sovereign

These two truths must be held together as they are in the Bible—both true, not contradicting but rather complementing the other. As Don Carson and Dan McCartney point out, one error is to fall into the belief that God is not capable of emotions or suffering. This gives us a God more like a Platonic ideal than the God of the Bible. It also may undermine the historic Christian belief that Jesus was fully God while emptied of his glory and living a human life. God learned suffering by experience. On the other hand, there are an increasing number of theologians who are so glad to emphasize the suffering of God that they lose the idea of divine sovereignty, depicting God as one who is not all-powerful and not able to stop suffering in the world.[243] Ronald Rittgers writes: "The idea that God has a causal relationship to adversity and misfortune is rejected by many contemporary theologians. The notion of God as co-sufferer is welcomed, but the idea of God as agent of suffering is shunned."[244]

But, Rittgers adds, "the God who has no causal relationship to suffering is no God at all, certainly not the God of the Bible . . . who is both suffering and sovereign. Both beliefs were (and are) essential to the traditional Christian assertion that suffering ultimately has some meaning."[245] That is absolutely right. If God is out of control of history, then suffering is not part of any plan; it is random and senseless. This would be the secular view of things that Richard Shweder sketches. On the other hand, if God has not suffered, then how can we trust him?

In other words, it is because God is all-powerful and sovereign that his suffering is so astonishing. If God were somehow limited or out of control, his suffering would not be so radically *voluntary*—and therefore not so fully motivated by love. That is why the sight of God's agony on the cross is so profoundly moving and consoling. Albert Camus writes: "In that Christ has suffered, and had suffered voluntarily, suffering was no longer unjust. . . . If everything, without exception, in heaven and earth is doomed to pain and suffering, then a strange form of happiness is possible.[246] Elsewhere Camus observes: "[Christ] the god-man suffers too, with patience. Evil and death can no longer be entirely imputed to him since he suffers and dies. . . . The divinity ostensibly abandoned its traditional privilege, and lived through to the end, despair included, the agony of death."[247]

Peter Berger says that Camus, an "insightful critic" of Christianity, nevertheless understands the "immense religious potency" of this answer to the problem of suffering.[248] If God is no exception—if even he has suffered—then we cannot say he doesn't understand, or that his sovereignty over suffering is being exercised in a cruel and unfeeling way, or that he is a cold king who lets things happens without caring about what we are going through. As Camus argues, the cross makes it impossible to say such facile things. Since even he has not kept himself immune from our pain, we can trust him.

That leads to many rich and powerful practical implications. Because suffering is both just and unjust, we can cry out and pour out our grief, yet without the toxic additive of bitterness. Because God is both sovereign and suffering, we know our suffering always has meaning even though we cannot see it. We can trust him without understanding it all. When one of my sons was around eight years old, he began to exert his will and resist his parents' directions. One time I told him to do something and he said, "Dad, I'll obey you and do this—but only if first you explain to me why I should do it." I responded something like this: "If you obey me only because it makes sense to you, then that's not obedience, it's just agreement. The problem is that you are too young to understand most of the reasons why I want you do to this. Do it because you are eight and I'm thirty-eight—because you are a child and I'm an adult and your father."

We can easily see why children need to trust their parents even when they do not understand them. How much more, then, should we trust God even though we do not understand him. It is not just that the differential in wisdom between him and us is infinitely greater than the difference between a child and a parent. It is not just that he is sovereign and all-powerful. We should also trust him because he earned our trust on the cross. So we can trust him even when he hasn't shown us yet the reason why. He is good for it.

The Final Defeat of Evil

The book of Revelation is a dizzying text, and touches on many subjects. But I have always profited from meditating on how it addresses suffering and evil.

In chapter 6, the author John has a vision of "the souls of those who had been slain because of the word of God and the testimony they had maintained" (Rev 6:9). These are people who had been unjustly put to death for their faith. They cry out for justice, asking God, "How long, Sovereign Lord, holy and true, until you judge the inhabitants of the earth . . . ?" (Rev 6:10). This is an agonized cry that has echoed down the years throughout the books of the Bible. "How long, Lord, will you look on? Rescue me from their ravages" (Ps 35:17). "Where is the God of justice?" (Mal 2:17). "Why do you tolerate the treacherous? Why are you silent while the wicked swallow up the righteous?" (Hab 1:13).

But theologian Louis Berkhof writes: "The Bible teaches us to look forward to a final judgment as the decisive answer of God to all such questions, as the solution of all such problems, and as the removal of all the apparent discrepancies of the present." Berkhof then lists passages such as Matthew 25:31–46, John 5:27–29, Romans 2:5–11, and Revelation 20:11–15, which speak of the "great white throne" and all people who ever lived, "great and small," standing before the throne with the "books opened" and every person judged with justice. "These passages," says Berkhof, "do not refer to a process, but to a very definite event at the end of time."[249]

However, the Bible does not merely tell us that evil is punished, as important as that is. In our world, sometimes evildoers are caught and brought to justice, but while we can *punish* evil, we cannot *undo* evil. Imprisoning or executing murderers, for example, cannot bring back the dead they killed or repair the lives they have ruined. But the book of Revelation promises much more than a Judgment Day. Berkhof tells us that Judgment Day is "accompanied by . . . the coming of Jesus Christ, the resurrection of the dead, and the renewal of heaven and earth."[250]

In Revelation 5, John has a vision of God sitting on a throne with a sealed scroll in his hand. Many scholars have agreed that this scroll is "the meaning and purpose of history, the great plan of God for all time." It is sealed with seven seals, and John begins to weep because it appears to him that no one has the ability to open the scroll, that is, "to interpret and carry out the plan of God."[251] But then he hears others tell him not to weep, for "a Lamb, looking as if it had been slain" (Rev 5:6), stands forth and opens the scroll seal after seal. And why is he able to share the throne and open the scroll? It is because of his redemptive suffering. The song goes:

> *You are worthy to take the scroll*
> *and to open its seals,*
> *because you were slain,*
> *and with your blood you purchased for God*
> *persons from every tribe and language and people and nation. You*
> *   have made them to be a kingdom and priests to serve our God,*
> *and they will reign on the earth* (Rev 5:9–10).

Over the next few chapters, the seals are opened and great judgments are carried out, exercises in immense power. Inexorably, we move toward Judgment Day and the renewal of all things. And now we see what at first looks simply like an irony. The New Testament shows us that virtually every kind of evil was thrown at Jesus at the end of his life. He was abandoned, betrayed, and denied by friends. He was handed over by a fickle mob. He was given a sham trial and was tortured and killed, a victim of injustice. On display was the whole range of sin and malevolence—cowardice, lies, vested interests, nationalism and racism, corrupt religious and political institutions, and behind it all the power of Satan himself (John 13:27). Christopher Wright sums it up: "The cross was the worst that human [and non-human] evil and rebellion against God could do."[252]

But look how it backfired. Who is opening the seals on the scroll and carrying out judgments against the forces of darkness? A wounded lamb! That is hardly a figure we would associate with strength and power, and that is the whole point. The Bible says that at the very moment Jesus was dying on the cross, he was "disarming the powers . . . triumphing over them by the cross" (Col 2:15). Through his death, he absorbed the curse for human disobedience (Gal 3:10–14) and so defeated sin and death and the evil forces behind them. For those who are "in Christ Jesus . . . there is no condemnation" (Rom 8:1)—death has no more ultimate claim on us. And so it is a wounded lamb who now is able not simply to judge wrongdoing but actually to undo the damage that evil has wreaked on the creation.

This is not just an irony—this is the ultimate strategy for the defeat of evil. Without the suffering of Jesus, evil wins. It results in the destruction of the entire human race. It is only Jesus' suffering that makes it possible to end suffering—to judge and renew the world—without having to destroy us. Theologian Henri Blocher says that here we come to "the threshold of the secret and hidden wisdom," the deepest look we have into the mystery of how the cross of Jesus answers the problem of evil.[253]

Blocher, in his book *Evil and the Cross,* argues that if evil were purely "local"—"an imperfection in every finite being"—Christ could have simply come to teach people a different way. If evil were, on the other hand, only some entity—some external force in the universe—then "it would have been sufficient to deploy a superior force against it."[254] But evil is neither simply the result of flawed individuals nor merely of a single powerful being like the devil. It stems from both as well as from the effects of a corrupted created order. And ultimately we can't see all the roots and sources of evil—it is a mystery.

But we can see this—at the cross, evil is "turned back on itself." Or, as John Calvin expressed it, on the cross, destruction was destroyed, "torment tormented, damnation damned . . . death dead, mortality made immortal."[255] Blocher writes:

> At the cross evil is conquered as evil. . . . Evil is conquered as evil because God turns it back upon itself. He makes the supreme crime, the murder of the only righteous person, the very operation that abolishes sin. The manoeuvre is utterly unprecedented. No more complete victory could be imagined. . . . God entraps the deceiver in his own wiles. Evil, like a judoist, [tries to] take advantage of the power of the good, which it perverts; the Lord, like a supreme champion, replies by using the very grip of the opponent.[256]

This is certainly the ultimate defeat of evil, for this strategy used evil's own weight and force against it as, Blocher says, in judo. He goes on: "This . . . sin of sins, the murder of the Son . . . provides the opportunity for love to be carried to its very peak, for there is no greater love than to give one's life for one's friends (John 15:13)." Evil is defeated because God uses it to bring about its very opposite—courage, faithfulness, selfless sacrifice, forgiveness. But there's more. The cross doesn't simply provide an inspiring example of love. "The requirement of [justice] . . . that evil be punished by death . . . permits our Brother and Head to intervene in love and take over the debt in place of the guilty party. . . . At the cross, evil is conquered by the ultimate degree of love in the fulfillment of justice."[257] Blocher concludes by rightly claiming that this Christian answer to evil is both more optimistic *and* more pessimistic than the alternatives—at once:

We have no other position than at the foot of the cross. After we have been there we are given the answer of the wisdom of God, which incenses the advocates of optimistic theodicies or of tragic philosophies. God's answer is evil turned back upon itself, conquered by the ultimate degree of love in the fulfillment of justice. This answer consoles us and summons us. It allows us to wait for the coming of the crucified conqueror. He will wipe away the tears from every face, soon.[258]

So, while Christianity never claims to be able to offer a full *explanation* of all God's reasons behind every instance of evil and suffering—it does have a final *answer* to it. That answer will be given at the end of history and all who hear it and see its fulfillment will find it completely satisfying, infinitely sufficient. Dostoevsky expressed this as well as anyone ever has when he wrote:

I believe like a child that suffering will be healed and made up for, that all the humiliating absurdity of human contradictions will vanish like a pitiful mirage, like the despicable fabrication of the impotent and infinitely small Euclidean mind of man, that in the world's finale, at the moment of eternal harmony, something so precious will come to pass that it will suffice for all hearts, for the comforting of all resentments, for the atonement of all the crimes of humanity, of all the blood that they've shed; that it will make it not only possible to forgive but to justify all that has happened.[259]

No More Tears

Henri Blocher is right to look to both the past and the future here. The cross secured the defeat of evil in the past, on Calvary, but now it also guarantees a final experience of that defeat in the future, in the renewal of all things, when every tear will be wiped away. In the vision of St. John, even before the opening of the seals, it is said:

Never again will they hunger;
never again will they thirst.
The sun will not beat down on them,
nor any scorching heat.
For the Lamb at the center of the throne
will be their shepherd;
he will lead them to springs of living water.
And God will wipe away every tear from their eyes (Rev 7:16–17).

The climax of the book of Revelation depicts the "new heaven and new earth" (Rev 21:1). There will "no longer be any curse" (Rev 22:3)—the curse that fell on creation at the Fall is lifted. And as a result, "he will wipe every tear from their eyes. There will be no more death or mourning or crying or pain, for the old order of things has passed away" (Rev 21:4). This is poetic language of course, but the message is clear. There will be no more evil, suffering, sin, or pain. The suffering of Jesus has ended suffering.

As we observed before, the Bible teaches that the future is not an immaterial "paradise" but a new heaven and a new earth. Matthew 19:28 and Acts 3:21 speak of the "regeneration" or "restoration of all things." Peter says that we look for the day in which we will have a new heaven and new earth (2 Pet 3:13), and Paul teaches that the creation will gloriously be liberated from its bondage to decay and death (Rom 8:19–22).

It is this new world that John saw in his vision in Revelation 21 and 22. Here ultimately, Christianity holds out a hope unlike any other. The secular view sees no future good of any kind, and other religions believe in an eternity or heaven that is a consolation for the losses and pain of this life and all the joys that might have been. But as we have said, Christianity offers not merely a consolation but a restoration—not just of the life we had but of the life we always wanted but never achieved. And because the joy will be even greater for all that evil, this means the final defeat of all those forces that would have destroyed the purpose of God in creation, namely, to live with his people in glory and delight forever.

Life Story: The Ring

by Andi

I dropped to my knees when I got to the side of my bed. It was time to end the day, but I couldn't yet. The ring had to come off. It was time.

That afternoon, a judge had declared my divorce final. Though the demise of our marriage had appeared inevitable for a while, I hadn't stopped wearing my wedding ring, a symbol of my confidence that no matter how hopeless things looked, God could turn them around in an instant. But now here I was, thirty years later, kneeling alone by the side of my bed. I sobbed, but it wasn't the sorrow. I dissolved as these images were eclipsed by an overwhelming awareness of God's faithfulness to me through it all. Never had I felt abandoned by him. Confused by his allowing life to be excruciatingly hard for so long when I knew he could restore? Yes. On the verge of complete mental, emotional, and physical collapse at times? Yes. Like I had lost my bearings spiritually? Yes.

In fact, one night it all came to a head and I experienced a true spiritual crisis. Where was this God I had been counting on? Was he real? If he was, did he care? I was in no shape to compose an articulate prayer. There was a lot of sobbing and groaning. When I could form words, I cried out, "I could never watch someone I love suffer like this and not stop it! You say you love me, but I can't square that with what I see happening. This feels cruel. I've got to know you are who you say you are or I cannot go on." I didn't need to know his reasons . . . I needed Him.

The next morning, wise words from a trusted friend came to me: "Andi, you need to force-feed yourself the Scriptures. Through them the Holy Spirit can speak to places in your heart where human words just can't reach."

I needed to be touched that deeply, so the next morning I opened my Bible. My eyes fell on these words in Psalms: "You, O

God, are strong, and you, O Lord, are loving." They came like smelling salts to my fainting heart, silencing torturous fear and doubt. My heart was infused with a deep assurance that He loved me and was very near. I was immediately steadied. It didn't matter anymore that I couldn't square this with what I saw unfolding in my life.

Kneeling by my bed that night, my heart broke, unable to contain my gratitude for God's persistent love through a mess that should have driven him away. . . . Instead he came closer than ever.

As I slipped the ring off, a prayer poured from my heart. "Now I want to give you the devotion I thought I would be giving to an earthly husband. You alone are worthy of my whole heart's trust, and it's yours for the rest of my life."

How could a vow of such loving trust pour from a heart that had just lost so much . . . and be made to the One who had been my only hope? The only explanation is that while so much was dying, something was coming to life.

I had been changed by the experience of this unstoppable love constantly moving toward me when I was coming to him with nothing to offer but weakness, confusion, and need. I cannot adequately explain what happened. I just know that, in the end, this prayer was the only possible response.

As I got up off my knees and climbed into bed, I thought, *I should get myself a new ring to remind me of this vow I've made to the Lord tonight.*

The next morning, I met with a group of women with whom I had been meeting weekly for prayer. We never talked a lot about what we were going to pray for, we just prayed.

During the time of silence with which we always began, I noticed one of them coming over and kneeling in front of my chair. She took a ring off her finger, held it out to me, and said, "I feel like the Lord wants you to have this ring. He wants you to know that you are his beloved, and he is betrothing himself to you for the rest of your life. He will be your protector and provider. He will never leave you or forsake you. He will be with you forever."

The ring she handed me was much more beautiful and valuable than any ring I would have gotten myself. I had mentioned nothing about getting a new ring.

I can't tell you how many times, in the years since, a glance at that ring calmed my fear, filled my loneliness, and comforted me in grief.

I wanted a ring to remind me of my commitment to the Lord. Instead, I ended up with one that will forever remind me of his commitment to me.

EIGHT

The Reason for Suffering

Lord, with what care hast thou begirt us round! . . .
Pulpits and Sundays, sorrow-dogging sin,
Afflictions sorted, anguish of all sizes,
Fine nets and stratagems to catch us in.

George Herbert, "Sin"

Peter Berger says that all people and cultures long to "bestow meaning on the experience of suffering and evil." I have been arguing that no culture or worldview has ever done this with the thoroughness of Christianity. According to Christian theology, suffering is not meaningless—neither in general nor in particular instances. For God has purposed to defeat evil so exhaustively on the cross that all the ravages of evil will someday be undone and we, despite participating in it so deeply, will be saved. God is accomplishing this not in spite of suffering, agony, and loss but *through* it—it is through the suffering of God that the suffering of humankind will eventually be overcome and undone. While it is impossible not to wonder whether God could have done all this some other way—without allowing all the misery and grief—the cross assures us that, whatever the unfathomable counsels and purposes behind the course of history, they are motivated by love for us and absolute commitment to our joy and glory.

So suffering is at the very heart of the Christian faith. It is not only the way Christ became like and redeemed us, but it is one of the main ways we become like him and experience his redemption. And that means that our suffering, despite its painfulness, is also filled with purpose and usefulness.

On Not Wasting Your Suffering

We live in a time in which this ancient idea of suffering's "usefulness" is resisted. Psychologist Jonathan Haidt explains that people who face imminent death but survive often develop post-traumatic stress disorder that may permanently debilitate them. The condition can leave them "anxious and over reactive," liable to "panic or crumble more easily when faced with later adversity." Research on stress shows that it is generally bad for people's health. Stressors include death of a spouse (or, for a non-adult, a parent or sibling), separation and divorce, personal injury or illness, job loss, and financial reversals. Studies show that these can lead to depression, anxiety disorders, and physical illness, particularly heart disease.[260]

Nevertheless, Haidt maintains that there is empirical support for the ancient view that "people need adversity, setbacks, and perhaps even trauma to reach the highest levels of strength, fulfillment, and personal development."[261] He relates a true story of a friend of his whom he names "Greg." Greg was a young assistant college professor whose wife left him for another man, taking their two young children with them. Greg faced years of legal expense and fights over the custody of the children. Eventually he won custody but then found himself a single parent with a full-time, poor-paying job. He had almost no hope of finishing the book on which his academic career depended, and he worried about the mental health of his children.[262]

But several months later, Haidt visited Greg and discovered that many people had rallied around him. He learned how his church helped him with meals and child care and strong emotional and spiritual support. His parents had sold their home in the west and moved nearby to help him raise the children. And then, after relating all of this, Haidt wrote that Greg "said something so powerful I choked up." He observed how in the middle of many operas there was a crucial aria, a "sad and moving solo" in which the main character turned sorrow into something beautiful. And Greg said:

> This is my moment to sing the aria. I don't want to, I don't want to have this chance, but it's here now, and what am I going to do about it? Am I going to rise to the occasion?[263]

The psychologist listened and knew that "to have framed things in such a way showed that [Greg] was already rising." Haidt recounts what he calls the "post-traumatic growth" of his friend after that. "With the help of family, friends, and deep religious faith . . . [he] rebuilt his life, finished his book, and two years later found a better job. . . . He now experiences more joy from each day with his children than he did before the crisis." Greg said that the experience had "radically changed his perspective about what mattered in life." Career was now not nearly as important to him as it had been, and this freed him to be a much better father. He now found himself "reacting to others with much greater sympathy, love, and forgiveness. He just couldn't get mad at people for little things anymore."[264]

Haidt points out that the three benefits of suffering seen in Greg's life often appear in others' lives as well. First, people who endure and get through suffering become more resilient. Once they have learned to cope, they know they can do it again and live life with less anxiety. Romans 5:3–4 sums it up: "Suffering produces endurance, and endurance produces character, and character produces hope." Second, it strengthens relationships, usually bonding the sufferer permanently into a set of deeper friendships or family ties that serve to nurture and strengthen for years.

But the third benefit is perhaps the most significant—suffering "changes priorities and philosophies."[265] Psychologist Robert Emmons has sorted people's life goals into four basic categories—personal achievement and happiness, relationships and intimacy, religion and spirituality, and "generativity" (contributing something lasting to society). People who invest much or most of their energy into the goals of personal achievement and happiness are the most vulnerable to the adverse circumstances of life.[266] Efforts to seek God, deeper relationships, and the good of society sometimes can be directly enhanced by suffering, but our freedom and comfort never are. And so trouble and trials tend to force us out of certain life agendas and into others.

Haidt puts this in another way. Everyone operates out of a life story that integrates the events of life into a "coherent and vitalizing" narrative. People who have never suffered are likely to have naïve stories about life's meaning. He gives the example of a woman who thought of herself as a brilliant but unfulfilled artist who had been forced by her parents into a mundane job. Her life story led to unrealistic views of her own abilities and to a great deal of self-pity and resentment toward life in general. It also contributed to her failure to find any qualified spouse candidate, who (she felt) had to be extremely creative and perfectly compatible with her. Haidt concluded that adversity offered her a prospect. "She is a mess of mismatched motives and stories, and it may be that only through adversity will she be able to make the radical changes she would need to achieve coherence."[267] He went on to write: "Trauma . . . shatters belief systems and robs people of their sense of meaning. In doing so, it forces people to put the pieces back together, and often they do so by [turning to] God or some other higher principle as a unifying principle."[268]

Haidt makes a crucial disclaimer when he says, "I don't want to celebrate suffering, prescribe it for everyone, or minimize the moral imperative to reduce it where we can. I don't want to ignore the pain that ripples out from each diagnosis of cancer."[269] He is indeed right, and as we have seen, the Bible agrees with his view. God is grieved at our grief. The Bible is filled with cries of lament and shouts of "Why?" that God does not denounce. And yet—God is so committed to defeating evil that he is ready to help us use it for good even in our individual lives right now. Haidt, James Davies, and other psychologists are arguing that there is a common sense as well as empirical basis for the idea that suffering produces endurance, character, and hope.

The Bible of course assumes this and tells us much more about the various meanings and benefits of suffering, and the various purposes it can accomplish in our lives. What are those purposes?

To Glorify God

According to all branches of Christian theology, the ultimate purpose of life is to glorify God. That means that the first—but perhaps hardest to grasp—purpose for our suffering is the glory of God. The words *suffering* and *glory* are linked in a surprising number of biblical passages.

Paul says repeatedly that our sufferings prepare for us an eternal glory (Rom 8:17–18; 2 Cor 4:17). Peter adds that our sufferings enhance our eventual joy at our future glory (1 Pet 4:13). Then, in Ephesians 3:13, Paul tells his readers that his imprisonment and sufferings are for *their* glory. Finally, in 1 Peter 1:6–7, the apostle explains why his readers are "suffering grief in all kinds of trials." "These have come," he writes, "so that the proven genuineness of your faith—of greater worth than gold, which perishes even though refined by fire—may result in praise, glory and honor when Jesus Christ is revealed." Our sufferings, if handled properly, bring the Lord glory.

Many of the most popular churches today teach that God will make you happy, healthy, and prosperous, that he is there for your personal benefit. If we tacitly accept that view of things, we may find it offensive to hear someone say that tragedies and evil can honor and glorify God. And indeed, to simply say such a thing to someone who is watching their mother or child die from cancer would be confusing and cruel.

C. S. Lewis, in his book *Reflections of the Psalms,* confesses that for many years after becoming a Christian he was confused and embarrassed by God's calls to us to glorify and praise him, to tell him about his greatness and rejoice in his excellencies. Lewis pointed out that, among humans, such a desire for praise was seen as completely despicable. "We all despise the man who demands continued assurance of his own virtue, intelligence, or delightfulness."[270]

However, Lewis began to think about how praise and glorying worked in other ways. He noticed that when we say that a work of art is admirable, we don't mean that it "deserves" praise in the way that a good student deserves a high mark. Rather, we mean the artwork demands admiration because it is the only "adequate or appropriate response to it" and that if we do not give it that praise, "we shall be stupid, insensible, and great *losers,* we shall have missed something." And of course, he concluded then that "God would be, by his very nature, the 'supremely beautiful and all-satisfying Object.' "[271]

From there, Lewis reasons that God commands us to glorify him because it is only by doing this that we will ever find the rest, satisfaction, and joy in him that we were made for. He directs us to do this not only because it is simply right but also because we need it. The psalmist tells us that it is "fitting . . . to praise him" (Ps 33:1; 147:1). It *fits* to glorify God—it not only fits reality, because God is infinitely and supremely praiseworthy, but it fits *us* as nothing else does. All the beauty we have looked for in art or faces or places—and all the love we have looked for in the arms of other people—is only fully present in God himself. And so in every action by which we treat him as glorious as he is, whether through prayer, singing, trusting, obeying, or hoping, we are at once giving God his due and fulfilling our own design.

The God of Glory

So much of Christian faith and practice hinges on the concept of the glory of God. But what is that?

The theology books struggle when they try to define it. I believe it is because the glory of God is actually the combined magnitude of all God's attributes and qualities put together. The glory of God means what can be called *his infinite beyondness.* He is not a "tame" God, a God at hand. He is not someone you can always figure out, or expect to figure out. This is a God beyond our comprehension, and it is one of the aspects of the biblical God that modern people dislike the most. We are always saying, "I can't believe in a God who would do this" or "I can't believe in a God who would judge people." One of the things that may mean is that we don't want a glorious God, one beyond our comprehension.

The glory of God also means his *supreme importance.* The Hebrew word for "glory" is *kabod,* which means "weight"—literally God's weightiness. Fortunately, we have an English word that has the same lexical range and that functions in the same way—it is the word *matter*. Matter means "as opposed to the immaterial, something solid, something substantial," but it can also mean "importance." And therefore, when the Bible says that God is glorious, it means he should matter, and does matter, more than anything else or anyone else. And if anything matters to you more than God, you are not acknowledging his glory. You are giving glory to something else.

When J. R. R. Tolkien's *Lord of the Rings* trilogy was published in the 1950s, a woman named Rhona Beare wrote Tolkien and asked him about the chapter in which the Ring of Power is destroyed in the fires of Mount Doom. When the ring is melted, the Dark Lord's entire power collapses and melts away with it. She found it inexplicable that this unassailable, overwhelming power would be wiped out by the erasure of such a little object. Tolkien replied that at the heart of the plot was the Dark Lord's effort to magnify and maximize his power by placing so much of it in the ring. He wrote: "The Ring of Sauron is only one of the various mythical treatments of the placing of one's life, or power, in some external object, which is thus exposed to capture or destruction with disastrous results to oneself."[272]

Tolkien means something like this: It is one thing to love somebody and get a lot of joy out of the relationship. But if that person breaks up with you and you want to kill yourself, it means you have given that person too much glory, too much weight in your life. You may have said in your heart, "If that person loves me, then I know I am somebody." But if that person then takes the relationship away, you collapse and melt down because you have ascribed more glory and honor to him or her than to God. If anything matters more to you than God you are placing yourself and your heart into something external. Only if you make God matter the most—which means only if you glorify him and give him the glory—will you have a safe life.

There is one more thing to say about God's glory—it is his *absolute splendor and beauty*. The word for "glory" in the Old Testament means importance, the word for "glory" in the New Testament (the Greek word *doxa*) means "praise and wonder; luminosity, brilliance, or beauty."

Jonathan Edwards once said: "God is glorified not only by His glory's being seen, but by its being rejoiced in."[273] It is not enough to say, "I guess he is God, so I have got to knuckle under." You have to see his beauty. Glorifying God does not mean obeying him only because you have to. It means to obey him because you *want* to—because you are attracted to him, because you delight in him. This is what C. S. Lewis grasped and explained so well in his chapter on praising. We need beauty. We go to lengths to put ourselves in front of beautiful places, or surround ourselves with beautiful music, or hang out with beautiful people. But these will leave us empty if we don't learn to see all of these things as mere tributaries and God himself as the fountain, the headwaters of it all.

So to see God as glorious is not only to admit his incomprehensibility and beyondness, and make him the thing that matters the most, but it is also to work your heart so it finds him the most pleasurable and beautiful thing you know.

No Graven Image

How, then, can we glorify God in our suffering—and how can suffering help us glorify God?

In 1966, Elisabeth Elliot, who had been a missionary to the Aucas (Waorani) of the South American Amazon rain forest, wrote a novel entitled *No Graven Image*.[274] It is the story of a young unmarried woman named Margaret Sparhawk who had dedicated her life to translating the Bible for remote tribes whose languages had not yet been written down. She took up Bible translation work among the Quechua people of the mountains of Ecuador. Key to her work was the discovery of a man, Pedro, who knew the unwritten dialect that Margaret needed to learn in order to translate the Bible into that particular language. He began to teach her the language, and her painstaking work of systematically recording and documenting it moved forward.

One day, Margaret is feeling grateful as she travels to see Pedro. She remembers the Bible verse "Wait for the Lord; be strong, and let your heart take courage." And she prays to God, "I've been waiting, Lord. Waiting and waiting. . . . You know I waited a long time to be a missionary to mountain Indians. . . . You seemed to say translation and medical work. So you gave me Pedro. . . . Just being here today is an answer to prayer."[275] She thinks of all it has taken to bring her to where she is that day—the support of friends, financial help from many people in the United States, years of training, years of building relationships, and of course the provision of the one man who knew both Spanish and the dialect she needed. God now seemed to be bringing things together. Margaret imagines the possibility of bringing the Bible to a million people in remote regions of the mountains.

Finally, she arrives at Pedro's home and discovers that he has an infected, painful wound in his leg. As part of her duties Margaret provided ordinary medical care and therefore she had with her a syringe and some penicillin. Pedro asks her for an injection and she decides to give it. But within seconds, Pedro begins to experience anaphylaxis, a severe, whole-body allergic reaction to the penicillin. The entire family gathers around in tears as he lies convulsing.

"Can't you see he's dying?" his wife, Rosa, cries to her. "You killed him."

Margaret is astonished at what is happening and prays, "Lord God, Father of us all, if You've never heard me pray before, hear me now. . . . Save him, Lord, save him."[276] But Pedro worsens and begins to retch, bent over in tormented spasms. Rosa puts both of her hands on the top of her head and begins the death wail of women in her community. But Margaret continues to pray in her mind, "O Lord, what will become of Rosa? . . . What will become of *Your work*? You started all this, Lord. It wasn't I. You led me here. You answered prayers and gave me Pedro—he is the only one. . . . O Lord, remember that. There is no one else."[277]

But Pedro dies, and indeed it means her work is over. All the years of labor are wiped away. "As for the translation of the Bible, of course, I cannot go ahead without an informant. God knew about that when Pedro died. I do not write prayer letters [to my supporters] anymore, for I have nothing to say about my work. It seemed, on the night of Pedro's death, as though *Finis* were written below all I had done."[278]

The book ends with a profoundly confused young missionary. There is no last-minute reversal, and no "silver lining." She stands at Pedro's grave and thinks, "And God? What of Him? 'I am with thee,' He had said. With me in *this*? He had allowed Pedro to die, or—and I could not then nor can I today deny the possibility—He had perhaps caused me to destroy him. And does He now, I asked myself there at the graveside, ask me to worship Him?"[279]

The answer was yes—as my wife, Kathy, and I learned a few years later when we listened to Elisabeth Elliot's lectures in the theological seminary where we were graduate students. She pointed to the last page, where, she said, was the key line.

> "God, if He was merely my accomplice, had betrayed me. If, on the other hand, He was God, He had freed me."[280]

She went on to explain to us that the graven image, the idol of the title, was a God who always acted the way we thought he should. Or more to the point—he was a God who supported our plans, how *we* thought the world and history should go. That is a God of our own creation, a counterfeit god. Such a god is really just a projection of our own wisdom, of our own self. In that way of operating, God is our "accomplice," someone to whom we relate as long as he is doing what we want. If he does something else, we want to "fire" him, or "unfriend him," as we would any personal assistant or acquaintance who was insubordinate or incompetent.

But at the very end, Margaret realizes that the demise of her plans had shattered her false god, and now she was free for the first time to worship the True One. When serving the god-of-my-plans, she had been extraordinarily anxious. She had never been sure that God was going to come through for her and "get it right." She was always trying to figure out how to bring God to do what she had planned. But she had not really been treating him *as* God—as the all-wise, all-good, all-powerful one. Now she had been liberated to put her hope not in her agendas and plans but in God himself. If she could make *this* change, it would bring a rest and security she had never had. In short, suffering had pointed her to a glorious God, and it had taught her to treat him as such. And when she did so, it freed her from the desperate, doomed, exhausting effort to seek to control all the circumstances of her life and of those she loved.

Elliot's novel was extraordinarily bold, and it offended traditional religious as well as secular sensibilities. In spite of the fact that we expect young children to trust adults that they cannot understand, most modern people are horrified to be asked to trust a God they cannot understand. But the novel was just as outrageous to many in the evangelical Christian world. Many readers wrote Elliot and protested vehemently that God would *never* allow such a thing to happen to a woman who had so prayerfully dedicated her life to his cause. A leading evangelical pastor told her with much satisfaction that he had personally kept the book off the Christian "book of the year" list.

However, Elisabeth told us, her own actual life experience had run almost exactly parallel to this novel—and actually had been even worse. In *These Strange Ashes,* an account of her first years as a Bible-translating missionary in South America, she tells of a man named Macario, who was "God's answer to prayer . . . the key to the whole of the language work; he was (God knew) the only man on earth who spoke both Spanish and Colorado with equal ease." But he was senselessly murdered, shot to death. Their translation work "now came to a sudden full stop."[281]

Later a flood and then a theft robbed the translators of their card files—in which they had invested years of work.[282] And after all this, Elisabeth married Jim Elliot, one of five young missionaries who were trying to reach out to the then isolated and hostile Waorani people of the Amazonian rain forest. One evening they sang a hymn, "We rest on thee, our Shield and our Defender," and the next day they traveled into the forest, met a party of Waoranis, and were all speared to death, leaving behind many widows and orphans.[283] All the Christians who were indignantly telling the author that God would never allow such things to happen to faithful believers simply didn't know what they were talking about.

In her 1996 epilogue to *Through Gates of Splendor,* the account of the missionaries' deaths, she challenged both the secular and traditional religious views of God and suffering as simplistic and naïve. She warned against trying to "find a silver lining" that would justify what happened. She wrote:

> We know that time and again in the history of the Christian church, the blood of martyrs has been its seed. We are tempted to assume a simple equation here. Five men died. This will mean x-number of Waorani Christians. Perhaps so. Perhaps not. . . . God is God. I dethrone Him in my heart if I demand that He act in ways that satisfy my idea of justice. It is the same spirit that taunted, "If Thou be the Son of God, come down from the Cross." There is unbelief, there is even rebellion, in the attitude that says, "God has no right to do this to five men unless . . ."[284]

The theme that runs through all of Elliot's work is that to trust God when we do not understand him is to treat him as God and not as another human being. It is to treat him as glorious—infinitely beyond us in his goodness and wisdom. But, as Jesus says, the hour at which God's glory was most brilliantly revealed was on the cross (John 12:23, 32). There we see that God is so infinitely, uncompromisingly just that Jesus had to die for sin, but also that God is so absolutely loving that Jesus was willing and glad to die. This is consummate wisdom—that God's love and justice, seemingly at odds, could both be fulfilled at once. And so to trust God's wisdom in our suffering, even when we don't understand it, is to remember the glory and meaning of the cross. Elliot reasons like this: "Those hands that keep a million worlds from spinning into oblivion were nailed motionless to a cross—for us. . . . Can you trust him?"[285]

So one of the purposes of suffering is to glorify God by simply treating him as the infinite, sovereign, all-wise, and yet incarnate and suffering God that he is. This glorifies God to God—the most fitting thing that can be done. And if we do what fits God and our souls, we will find, as Elisabeth Elliot argues, a rest not based on circumstances.

Glorifying God to Others

Trusting God in suffering also glorifies him to others. When believers handle suffering rightly, they are not merely glorifying God to God. They are showing the world something of the greatness of God—and perhaps nothing else can reveal him to people in quite the same way. "It is commendable if someone bears up under the pain of unjust suffering out of a conscious commitment to God," writes Peter (1 Pet 2:19). Patient endurance of suffering, when onlookers know that the sufferers are Christians, can reveal the power of God. Paul puts it even more vividly: "We always carry around in our body the death of Jesus [suffering], so that the life of Jesus may also be revealed in our body" (2 Cor 4:10).

In the early church, the first martyr was Stephen, who was stoned to death for his public preaching of the gospel. The account of his death is told in Acts 6:8–8:1. When he was on trial for his life, we are told he was not fearful but radiant—"his face was like the face of an angel" (Acts 6:15). And as he was dying under the hail of stones, he prayed aloud, "Lord Jesus, do not hold this sin against them" (Acts 7:60). The young scholar Saul of Tarsus was present and saw the entire scene (Acts 7:58, 8:1). Later Saul is on his way to imprison Christians and destroy the church in Damascus when he meets the risen Christ. Jesus says, "Saul, Saul, why do you persecute me? It is hard for you to kick against the goads" (Acts 26:14). Goads were sharp sticks used to move animals in a right direction, and Jesus is indicating that although Saul was angrily opposed to Christianity, there was something deep inside that was pushing him unwillingly toward acknowledging its truth. Many believe that one of those "goads" was the seemingly inexplicable joy, peace, and lack of bitterness that Stephen showed as he was dying. How could Stephen have been that calm? How could he have been that sure that he was right with God? That able to forgive people even as they were killing him? It didn't make sense. The way Stephen bore up under suffering was more than just "commendable"—it stuck in Saul's soul.

This was perhaps the first example of what later Christian writers such as Ambrose, Cyprian, Ignatius, and Polycarp said over and over. Christians died so well, leaving onlookers wondering where they got their power. "Christians used suffering to argue for the superiority of their creed . . . [because] they suffered better than pagans."[286] Paul never forgot the principle after his conversion. That is why later he could write to believers not to be discouraged by his imprisonment (Eph 3:13) because his suffering was a way to show people his Savior's character. He said to the Philippians, "I want you to know, brothers, that what has happened to me has really served to advance the gospel. As a result, it has become clear throughout the whole palace guard and to everyone else that I am in chains for Christ" (Phil 1:12–13).

In October of 2006, a gunman took hostages in a one-room schoolhouse of an Amish community in Lancaster County, Pennsylvania. After shooting ten victims, five of whom died, ages seven to thirteen, he killed himself. Within hours after the suicide-murders, members of the Amish community visited the killer's parents and expressed sympathy for their loss and support for the hard days ahead. When the gunman was buried a few days later, his young widow and her three children were amazed to discover that half those attending the funeral were Amish, who showed nothing but support and concern for the murderer's family. An entire Christian community faced their suffering with the same peace that Stephen did in Acts 7. The forgiveness and love shown by the Amish community toward the shooter and his family was the talk of the entire country. The way they handled their suffering had been a powerful testimony to the truth of their faith and to the grace and glory of their God.

It is worth noting that the testimony of the Amish to Christ was so powerful that many observers felt the need to mute it. A made-for-TV film about the incident created a fictional character, Ida Graber, an Amish mother of one of the murdered children. In the movie, she is so filled with doubts and anger at God, and so unable to forgive the gunman, that she almost leaves her faith. Those who were actually involved with the Amish after the shootings countered that, despite the deep grief and pain, there was simply no one in the community who had their faith shaken or who could not forgive.[287] The film showed—without aiming to—that the secular filmmakers who lived within the "immanent frame" couldn't really comprehend an attitude toward God that enabled people to accept mysterious providence and dispense forgiveness without bitterness toward either God or the shooter.

Four years after the incident, a group of sociologists published a book about it.[288] One of their main conclusions was that our secular culture is not likely to produce people who can handle suffering the way the Amish did. Many pundits and commentators across the country tried to claim the Amish's startling love as "the best in 'us,'" ignoring the profoundly and distinctively Christian roots of what they did. The *Amish Grace* scholars called that out as naïve. They argued that the Amish ability to forgive was based on two things. First, it was grounded in deep reflection and meditation on Christ forgiving his tormentors and killers.[289] At the heart of their faith was a man dying for his enemies, and if you are a member of a community that speaks and sings about it—rehearses and celebrates it—constantly, then the practice of forgiving even the murderers of one's children will not seem impossible.

But second, the authors pointed out that at its heart, forgiveness is a form of "self-renunciation"—it means giving up your right to pay back. As sociologists, they knew that the Christian view is that the meaning of life is to give up one's individual interests for the sake of God and others, it is to give up one's freedom in order to live according to God's will and to the benefit of one's neighbor. But this is directly opposed to how Americans are taught to live.

We live in an individualistic, consumeristic society, a society in which we are taught not self-renunciation but self-assertion—that your freedom, interests, and needs must always come first.[290] A culture promoting self-assertion, however, will usually produce revenge as a response to suffering, while a counterculture like the Amish, promoting self-renunciation, will much more likely produce forgiveness as a response. "Most of us have [therefore] been formed by a culture that nourishes revenge and mocks grace," the authors conclude, and they are right.[291]

And that is why peace and love in the face of evil and suffering—whether shown by the Amish in Lancaster, or Stephen in Jerusalem, or Jesus himself on the cross—is one of the greatest testimonies possible to the world of the reality of God, to his glory and his grace.

Glorifying God When No One Sees

The martyrdom of Jim Elliot had a visible impact on a generation of young Christian leaders. But what about suffering that virtually no one sees? Can that glorify God? Yes.

Joni Eareckson Tada is a woman who has been in a wheelchair most of her life. When she was seventeen, she had a diving accident and suffered an injury that left her a quadriplegic, paralyzed from the shoulders down. During the first two years after the injury, Joni experienced depression, bitterness, thoughts of suicide, and doubts about her Christian faith. When she was in a rehabilitation hospital in the Baltimore area, she shared a room with three or four other young women who also had some kind of debilitating condition. One of the people in her room was a girl named Denise Walters.[292]

Denise had been a happy, popular seventeen-year-old high school senior in Baltimore, Maryland. One day when she was bounding up the steps at the high school, she stumbled because her knees felt rather weak. By the end of the day, she could hardly walk. She went home and went to bed. When she woke up to go to dinner, she found she was paralyzed from the waist down. Not long afterward, she was paralyzed from the neck down, and then went blind. Just like that. It was a rare form of rapid-progression multiple sclerosis.

She lay motionless in her bed at Greenoaks Rehabilitation Hospital, unable to move or see, or barely able to talk. It was difficult to have any kind of conversation with her. Her roommates could have brief, fragmentary talks with her, but that was it. It wasn't long before she had no visitors but her mother. But Denise and her mother were Christians, and every night her mom came in and read the Bible to her and prayed with her dying daughter. Denise knew she was dying, but death was not coming quickly enough to be considered merciful in any way. She lay there in a lonely hospital bed for eight long years.

Then she died.

Joni shares how troubling Denise's life was to her. As her book explains, she first had to come to grips with her own loss and suffering. She recounts all the questions that pressed down on her every day. "Why did this happen to me? I am a Christian committed to Jesus: Why am I in a wheelchair for the rest of my life? How can God bring any good out of this? Why should I trust a God who allowed this to happen to me?" Nevertheless, slowly but surely, she began to make progress. She had begun to discover some of the reasons why suffering can be meaningful. Many of them had to do with a deeper understanding of God's glory. She came to see that suffering is a way to testify to others about the glory of God. If others see you being patient under the suffering, it can show them that God is real.

But when Denise died, Joni struggled because here, it seemed, was a person who had loved Christ, and who never complained, but whose suffering seemed to be completely pointless. Nobody saw her. "Nobody ever told her 'I want the kind of life you have. How do I get it?' Her suffering seemed to be for nothing."[293]

When Joni heard that Denise had finally died, she shared her struggle with some of her friends. One of them opened a Bible and turned first to Luke 15:10, which talks about the angels rejoicing in heaven over a repentant sinner. Then she turned to Ephesians 3:10, where it says that the angels are looking at what happens inside the church. If they had thought of it, they also could have gone to the book of Job. There the suffering of Job is watched by a great council of angels and by the devil as well. And suddenly Joni got it.

The secular worldview says there is only *this* world. The here-and-now material universe is the only reality. The natural is real, there is no supernatural. The immanent is real, there is no transcendent—no angels and demons, no spirits and souls, no God or devil. If you live within the secular "immanent frame," as Charles Taylor says, you would be completely cut off from the hope that then came to Joni. " 'I get it!' I lit up. . . . So her life wasn't a waste, I reasoned. . . . Someone *was* watching her in that lonely hospital room—a great many someones."[294]

To understand Joni's insight, do this thought experiment. What if I told you that tomorrow, for one day, there would be a special camera that was going to put everything you said, everything you did, and everything you *thought*, on television? It would beam it around the world and probably a billion people would see it. Would that make any difference in how you lived tomorrow? I think it would. It would bestow enormous meaning and significance on even the most fleeting thoughts and minor actions. It would be somewhat frightening, of course, because you would need to be on your best behavior. But it would also be thrilling. You might say, "There are a couple of things I have always wanted to tell the world. Now I really can." It would make an enormous difference. It would make the day incredibly meaningful.

But if Christianity is true—this is already happening. Don't you see that you are already on camera? There is an unimaginable but real spiritual world out there. You are already on the air. Everything you do is done in front of billions of beings. And God sees it, too. As Joni wrote about her friend Denise, "Angels and demons stood amazed as they watched her uncomplaining and patient spirit rising as a sweet smelling savor to God."[295]

No suffering is for nothing.

Suffering and Glory

Paul said to his Ephesian readers, discouraged because of his imprisonment, "My suffering is for your glory." Why? Because that is how it works. Suffering and glory are closely linked. Suffering glorifies God to the universe and eventually even achieves a glory for us. And do you know why suffering and glory are so tied to each other? It is because of Jesus. Philippians 2 tells us Jesus laid aside his glory. Why? Charles Wesley's famous Christmas carol tells you.

> *Mild he lays his glory by; born that men no more may die;*
> *Born to raise the sons of earth. Born to give them second birth.*

Jesus lost all his glory so that we could be clothed in it. He was shut out so we could get access. He was bound, nailed, so that we could be free. He was cast out so we could approach.

And Jesus took away the only kind of suffering that can really destroy you: that is being cast away from God. He took that so that now all suffering that comes into your life will only make you great. A lump of coal under pressure becomes a diamond. And the suffering of a person in Christ only turns you into somebody gorgeous.

Jesus Christ suffered, not so that we would never suffer but so that when we suffer we would be like him. His suffering led to glory. And you can see it in Paul. Paul is happy to be in prison because "my sufferings are for your glory," he says. He is like Jesus now. Because that is how Jesus did it. And if you know that that glory is coming, you can handle suffering, too.

Life Story: The Canvas of Suffering

by Gigi

Growing up in the inner city of Oakland, California, in a predominantly black community, I identified as brown, even though I was Brazilian and Amish. With time, I became very passionate about how the gospel engages social issues such as poverty, race, and socioeconomic issues, and I devoted my life to serving in low-income areas for these very purposes. All the while viewing such issues through the lens of a person of color.

Then, in 2009, I moved to South Africa. Overnight, I became white.

I was well aware that South Africa continues to be one of the most racially polarized countries in the world. In 2010, I married an amazing black South African man, becoming one of very few interracial couples in this country. We instantly became a threat to the very fabric of a society built on racial hierarchy and separation, even post-Apartheid. Wherever we went, we felt the piercing stares of the masses.

Just before we met, my husband had planted a church in the largest township in South Africa: Soweto. Townships in South Africa, by definition, are exclusively black communities begun during the oppressive system of Apartheid. Today, they are vibrant communities full of life, culture, and beautiful people, as well as poverty, crime, and much suffering.

In short, overnight I became a "white" woman living in the largest all-black residential area in a country still hemorrhaging from its long legacy of racial distrust, hatred, and anger. I never could have expected what awaited me in this beautiful country among these beautiful and broken people. I longed to be an agent of healing among such devastation, and I continually prayed that God would make me more like Him to serve here. Little did I know how He intended to answer that prayer. It seems that some fruit comes only from suffering.

One month before our wedding, my husband's closest friend and his most trusted leader in the church was exposed in having multiple moral failures with vulnerable young women in our church. As it turned out, he'd been living a double life for quite some time and hid it from all of us. Having been an elder, he was removed from leadership to go through a restoration process. Though he appeared repentant with his words, it soon became apparent that he was out for vengeance.

On our wedding night, while we slept, there was a fire in our room, which quickly filled with smoke. I woke up feeling like I was choking. We were taken to the hospital and told by the doctors that we never should have survived. They said we both should have died that night.

As a result of the smoke inhalation, chest X-rays showed, I had gotten pneumonia very badly. I was barely conscious for those two weeks of our honeymoon and I don't even remember most of it. We came home after two weeks to a divided church and vicious rumors circulating. The elder who had been living a double life had made appointments with each of our leaders alleging that we had grossly mistreated him after his sin was exposed. He told many of our trusted leaders and members that I, in particular, had refused to forgive him and wouldn't even speak to him. Given the great mistrust of white people in this community—and seeing as how I was now considered white—people readily accepted his story as truth. Within six months, we lost seventy-five percent of our church as a result of these lies. We lost most of our closest friends in this web of deceit, and many of them walked out of our lives with unashamed hatred toward us.

My health continued to decline. I found out that I had contracted a medically incurable tropical disease, which caused severe exhaustion and weakness most of the time.

By 2011, our thriving, vibrant ever-growing church had dwindled down to thirty people, many of whom still questioned if we could be trusted. As a result of the rumors, some people lost confidence in us, and our salary was cut almost in half. We struggled to pay rent, buy food and gas, and live day to day.

I felt utterly lost and alone, hated and alienated among the very people I left everything to love and serve. I also felt abandoned by God.

By October of 2011, I was so sick that I struggled to live day to day. Living in a poor community in South Africa also meant that pollution was really bad where we lived. My doctor told us that if I continued to live in Soweto, I would likely die within two years.

This shook us to the core. After much prayer, however, we felt the Lord was saying otherwise; that we were to stay and I would be restored.

As we neared the end of 2011, a momentum was finally building in the church again. We had been gutted by the countless trials and were still trying to recover, but the process of rebuilding had begun. We thought the worst was over . . . only to find it was yet to come.

During these two years full of rejection and hatred and violent slander, there was only one person who stood with me through it all. One person who refused to listen to rumors, who was not afraid to speak the truth to those who lied, the only one who openly stood as a friend in a time when it was very unpopular to be associated with me, the one person I could say was like a sister to me.

On December 30, 2011—my thirty-fifth birthday—that one person, my closest friend in South Africa, drowned. And another close friend of ours also drowned trying to save her. Words cannot describe the force of this grief and loss. Losing her was like losing ten people. At that time, she was the sum total of true community for me. We spent about three full days driving around the city delivering the horrible news to her family and her closest friends.

One week after that, my husband and I were assaulted at gunpoint by seven cops for no identifiable reason. It was a terrifying twenty-minute ordeal. I was left wondering, What kind of a wilderness have I come to where those threatening my life are the very ones I'm supposed to trust?

This is merely a "list" of events that we've suffered, but the internal turmoil and suffering is incalculable; immeasurable; indescribable. In one of the darkest moments, the Lord drew near. After months of crying out to Him and wondering why He felt so far in the darkest moments, He drew near in a way that I could sense and feel. I was reading Isaiah 53: "He was despised and forsaken of men, a man of sorrows and acquainted with grief; and like one from whom men hide their face He was despised. . . . He poured out Himself to death, and was numbered with the transgressors."

In some sense, my God "left" the comfort and glory of heaven to put Himself on earth in the weakness of human flesh. That, in and of itself, is unbelievable. But that wasn't all. He put Himself on earth, laying aside His privileges of being God (Phil 2) for the sake of saving fallen mankind, the single most selfless act in human history . . . only to be "despised and forsaken of men"; to become "a man of sorrows and acquainted with grief"; to be numbered with the transgressors. My holy, righteous, omnipresent, omnipotent God who spoke all of creation into being at the sound of His voice was regarded as a transgressor. Though He was perfect and innocent, regarded as a transgressor. For the first time in three years, I felt deeply His nearness. I, too, left everything, coming to South Africa as a brown girl longing to love and serve. I, too, was to be numbered with hatred as something that I am not, as a white oppressor with the scores of injustices perpetrated. Though I am far too fallible to be compared with our glorious Savior, I saw His story in mine. I somehow felt for the first time in so long a sense of redemptive purpose in the midst of unspeakable suffering.

I saw it was the gospel message. Although there are seasons of the Lord's discipline, I saw that suffering is the inextricable base-color thread woven through the fabric of the gospel. It is the canvas upon which salvation has been painted. Somehow in modern-day Christian circles, we tend to see God's faithfulness as saving us from suffering. And yes, sometimes, in His great mercy, He does save us from suffering. But that is not the mark of His faithfulness. We see in Scripture that many of those He loved deeply are also those who suffered greatly.

This great moment of nearness with my Father didn't remove the pain or the unspeakable grief, but it filled it with purpose and redemption. By the end of 2012, my health was steadily improving and my relationship with the Lord is steadily being restored. It has taken months of drawing near to Him, but I am now standing on my feet again. Still healing, but definitely standing. I see the fruit of suffering. And I see His story in mine.

NINE

Learning to Walk

We do not receive wisdom, we must discover it for ourselves, after a journey through the wilderness which no one can make for us, which no one can spare us.

Marcel Proust[296]

What about Our Glory?

We must not waste our sorrows, and according to the Bible, one set of purposes and uses for suffering has to do with the glory of God. Suffering reveals, communicates, and imparts God's glory as nothing else does. God's glory of course is perfect and therefore it cannot be increased. But it can, as the psalmists so often say, be "magnified." If God is treated as God during suffering, then suffering can reveal and present him in all his greatness.

But Paul says that suffering also prepares a glory for us. "For our light and momentary troubles are achieving for us an eternal glory that far outweighs them all" (2 Cor 4:17). And so we ask, How does suffering benefit us? Before we can answer that question, we must consider what the Bible teaches us about the whole issue of what today is called self-improvement. There is a principle at the heart of the Christian life that is expressed by two famous sayings of Jesus Christ:

> "Blessed are those who hunger and thirst for righteousness, for they will be filled" (Matt 5:6).

"Whoever finds their life will lose it, but whoever loses their
life for my sake will find it" (Matt 10:39).

In the first Jesus is saying, "Happy is the one who seeks not happiness
but righteousness." Happiness is a by-product of wanting something
more than happiness—to be rightly related to God and our neighbor. If
you seek God as the nonnegotiable good of your life, you will get happiness thrown in. If, however, you aim mainly at personal happiness, you
will get neither. The same principle is conveyed in the second saying. If
you are willing to lose your life for his sake—if you are willing to set
aside personal safety, comfort, and satisfaction in order to obey and
follow Jesus—then in the end you will find yourself. You will discover
who you really are in Christ and finally come to be at peace. If instead
you try to achieve personal comfort and satisfaction without centering
your life on God in Christ, you will find that you are left with a fatal lack
of self-knowledge and inner emptiness.

This could not be more contradictory to our Western culture of expressive individualism. And it applies directly to how Christians face
suffering. As we have seen, we should trust God because he is God and
not our personal assistant or life coach. We should trust him because it
is his due, he is worthy of it, not because it will get us something. If we
love and obey God for his own sake, not ours, it begins to turn us into
something strong and great and wise. If we don't seek to find ourselves
but to find God, we will eventually find both God and ourselves. "Aim
at heaven and you get earth 'thrown in'—aim [only] at earth and you
get neither."[297]

How does Jesus' principle work? Seeing and embracing God as he
truly is makes us wise, for it gets us in touch with reality. Just as turning
the lights on in a dark room enables you to walk without bumping into
things, seeing the justice, greatness, sovereignty, wisdom, and love of
God prevents you from stumbling through life in bitterness, pride, anxiety, and discouragement. If, then, we seek not our own benefit but
God's glory, it will lead paradoxically to a development of our own
glory, that is, of our character, humility, hope, love, joy, and peace.

Suffering, as we will see, can lead to personal growth, training, and transformation, but we must never see it as primarily a way to improve ourselves. That view could lead us to a form of masochism, an enjoyment of ache, because we only feel virtuous when we are in pain. Even without such perspective, suffering tends to make you self-absorbed. If it is seen as mainly about you and your own growth, it will strangle you truly. Instead, we must look at suffering—whatever the proximate causes—as primarily a way to know God better, as an opening for serving, resembling, and drawing near to him as never before.

It is only if we make God's glory primary in suffering that it will achieve our own. And yet sorrows and difficulties can do just that. We are called not to waste our sorrows but to grow through them into grace and glory.

Productive Suffering

Within the Western secular view of things, suffering is seen as an interruption of the freedom to live as makes you happiest. The circumstances that cause suffering and the negative emotions that go with it must be removed or minimized and managed. Psychologist James Davies knows he will get resistance when he talks instead of "productive suffering." Like Richard Shweder, he points to the many anthropological studies that show how non-Western cultures believe "suffering helps us apprehend new portions of reality."[298] In his book *The Importance of Suffering,* he critiques what he believes is the majority position among Western therapists, namely that suffering should be treated by helping the patient remove or manage the negative feelings that adversity brings. He writes, however, "It is a clinical mistake to interpret a patient who suffers from 'low self-esteem' or a 'sense of incompetence' or 'feelings of worthlessness' as simply suffering from . . . 'distorted thinking patterns' or 'thinking errors.' "[299]

Then how should suffering be approached? Davies goes on to make a radical suggestion. What if your negative thoughts about yourself are actually right? "The feeling of being 'cowardly,' " he writes, "may be less a symptom of 'faulty thinking' than an accurate appraisal of part of us that *is cowardly.* This makes the distress that accompanies our self-appraisal not only a perfectly natural response to encountering our cowardice, but also a necessary prerequisite for changing it."[300] So suffering can lead us to see a significant lack of courage in our character.

Or suffering may also show us a streak of selfishness. Davies points out studies that show "low self-esteem" is far from a universal problem. He points to the research of psychologists demonstrating that many people, instead of being plagued with low self-esteem, "are so infected with self-love that they are unable to love others . . . [and] cannot see beyond the horizon of their own needs and concerns. They are therefore unable to put themselves to one side and empathize with the needs and pains of others—their reality is best so all should adapt to it."[301]

With an even more countercultural impulse, Davies claims that people who have been through depression can become wiser and more realistic about life than those who have not. He presents a number of studies that show that people who have never been depressed tend to overestimate the amount of control they have over their lives. While severely depressed people are debilitated, in general an experience of depression can give you a more accurate appraisal of your own limitations and how much influence you can have over your circumstances. Quoting one of the researchers, Dr. Paul Keedwell, he writes:

> The prevailing view is . . . that the depressed person tends to distort reality in a negative way. . . . [But recent research has] turned this received wisdom on its head, providing evidence that it is not the depressive who distorts reality but the so-called healthy population. . . . Even if depression does distort reality in a negative way . . . the fact remains that *it removes the positive self-biases that are seen in the non-depressed.* . . . With recovery [from depression], and with the lifting of the mood, a new kind of truth could emerge.[302]

Davies, Jonathan Haidt, and others who argue for the benefits of adversity, are quick to point out that suffering does not automatically improve your life. Haidt speaks of two basic ways to cope with it—what he calls "active coping and reappraisal" and "avoidance coping and denial." [303] The latter strategy can lead to disaster, for it includes "working to blunt one's emotional reactions by denying or avoiding the events, or by drinking, drugs, and other distractions." The former strategy can lead to real gains, as it combines doing the hard inner work of learning and growing with seeking to change the painful external circumstances. Put another way, Haidt and Davies distinguish steadily walking through suffering from standing still, lying down, or just running away from it.

The stakes are high here. Suffering will either leave you a much better person or a much worse one than you were before. Haidt explains that those who work harder to manage their pain than to confront and learn from their suffering can become bitter and hopeless. Concluding that the world is completely unjust, that life is totally uncontrollable, and that things usually work out for the worst, "they weave this lesson into their life story where it contaminates the narrative."[304] So the wrong strategy will usually mean that one's character becomes weaker and less integrated while the right approach to suffering can lead to remarkable growth. Trials and troubles in life, which are inevitable, will either make you or break you. But either way, you will not remain the same.

How God Uses Suffering

The Bible explains and confirms the findings of psychologists such as Haidt and Davies. In a host of New Testament passages—Hebrews 12:1–17; Romans 8:18–30; 2 Corinthians 1:3–12, and 4:7–5:5, 11:24–12:10, as well as nearly all of 1 Peter—the Bible teaches us that God uses suffering to remove our weaknesses and build us up.

First, suffering transforms our attitude toward ourselves. It humbles us and removes unrealistic self-regard and pride. It shows us how fragile we are. As Davies points out, average people in Western society have extremely unrealistic ideas of how much control they have over how their lives go. Suffering removes the blinders. It does not so much make us helpless and out of control as it shows us we have *always* been vulnerable and dependent on God. Suffering merely helps us wake up to that fact and live in accordance with it.

Suffering also leads us to examine ourselves and see weaknesses, because it brings out the worst in us. Our weak faith, sharp tongues, laziness, insensitivity to people, worry, bitter spirit, and other weaknesses in character will become evident to us (and others) in hard times. Some of us are too abrasive, critical, and ungenerous. Some are impulsive and impatient. Others are argumentative, stubborn, and poor listeners. Many people have a great need to control every situation. Some are simply too fragile and self-pitying when discomfited over anything. Suffering will throw these inner flaws into relief during times of stress in a way that enables us to get out of denial and to begin working on them.

Second, suffering will profoundly change our relationship to the good things in our lives. We will see that some things have become too important to us. When we are devastated by a career reversal, there is real loss and grief. But we may also come to see that the magnitude of our suffering is due to the excessive weight we put on our job status or other achievements for our own self-worth. The reversal can be a unique opportunity to invest more of our hope and meaning in God and family and others. This effectively fortifies us against being too cast down by future reversals. It also brings us new sources of joy we were not tapping before.

Third, and most of all, suffering can strengthen our relationship to God as nothing else can. C. S. Lewis's famous dictum is true, that in prosperity God whispers to us but in adversity he shouts to us. Suffering is indeed a test of our connection to God. It can certainly tempt us to be so angry at God and at life that we have no desire to pray. Yet it also has the resources to greatly deepen our divine friendship. It starts with analysis. When times are good, how do you know if you love God or just love the things he is giving you or doing for you? You don't, really. In times of health and prosperity, it is easy to think you have a loving relationship to God. You pray and do your religious duties since it is comforting and seems to be paying off. But it is only in suffering that we can hear God "shouting" a set of questions at us: "Were things all right between us as long as I waited on you hand and foot? Did you get into this relationship for me to serve you or for you to serve me? Were you loving me before, or only loving the things I was giving you?" Suffering reveals the impurities or perhaps the falseness of our faith in God. In a sense, it is only in suffering that faith and trust in God can be known to be *in God,* and therefore it is only in suffering that our love relationship with God can become more and more genuine.

Suffering drives us toward God to pray as we never would otherwise. At first this experience of prayer is usually dry and painful. But if we are not daunted and we cling to him, we will often find greater depths of experience and, yes, of divine love and joy than we thought possible. As pastor John Newton wrote to a grieving woman, "Above all, keep close to the throne of grace [in prayer]. If we seem to get no good by attempting to draw near him, we may be sure we shall get none by keeping away from him."[305]

Finally, suffering is almost a prerequisite if we are going to be of much use to other people, especially when they go through their own trials. Adversity makes us far more compassionate than we would have been otherwise. Before, when we saw others in grief, we may have secretly wondered what all the blubbering was about, why people can't just suck it up and go on. Then it comes to us—and ever after, we understand. When we have suffered, we become more tenderhearted and able to help others in suffering. Suffering creates wisdom in people, if they handle it and it doesn't make them hard. It gives us a range of insights that are useful to many other people we meet. In 2 Corinthians, Paul writes:

> Blessed be the God and Father of our Lord Jesus Christ, the Father of mercies and God of all comfort, who comforts us in all our affliction, so that we may be able to comfort those who are in any affliction, with the comfort with which we ourselves are comforted by God. For as we share abundantly in Christ's sufferings, so through Christ we share abundantly in comfort too. If we are afflicted, it is for your comfort and salvation; and if we are comforted, it is for your comfort, which you experience when you patiently endure the same sufferings that we suffer. Our hope for you is unshaken, for

we know that as you share in our sufferings, you will also share in our comfort (2 Cor 1:3–7).

See the dynamics at work here. Paul's sufferings drive him into God and his unfathomable comforts. We have been looking at many of those in this volume—deeper views of God's glory, a heart-changing appreciation of Christ's suffering, new experiences of his love and joy, self-knowledge and growth, insights into life and human nature. What does Paul do with those insights? He shares them with others in affliction, who then through their suffering find the deeper comforts too. The implication is that these sufferers in turn become comforters to others—and on and on it goes. The church becomes a community of profound consolation, a place where you get enormous support for suffering and where people find themselves growing, through their troubles, into the persons God wants them to become.

Christian author George MacDonald put it like this:

> The Son of God suffered unto the death, not that men might not suffer, but that their sufferings might be like His.[306]

God's Gymnasium

We have mentioned the biblical metaphor of suffering as a refiner's furnace, and we will return to that image later. A less well known but similar biblical image is suffering as a "gymnasium."[307] Like 1 Peter, the book of Hebrews was written to a group of Christians facing many trials and afflictions. In Hebrews 12, the author says that such an experience is "painful," but "later on, however, it produces a harvest of righteousness and peace for those who are being trained by it." And the Greek word for "trained" is *gymnazdo,* from which we get our word *gymnasium.* The word literally meant to be "stripped naked"—to "exercise naked, to train." It meant to undergo a regimen of exercises deliberately aimed at strengthening weak parts of the body and further enhancing the strong ones.

Think of what happens in a gym. First, you have to strip out of your ordinary clothes. Why? Ordinary clothing would prevent us from doing the more strenuous physical moves. But there is another reason. The gym exposes deficiencies in our bodies' strength and stamina—and appearance. You can wear all kinds of daytime clothes that hide or minimize aspects of your body that you would like to be less visible to the eye. But in the gym, you cannot hide them. There you and your coach (and unfortunately everyone around you) can see where you bulge where you shouldn't. It's an incentive to get to work.

And so this metaphor tells us that when life is going along just fine, the flaws in our character can be masked and hidden from others and from ourselves. But when troubles and difficulties hit, we are suddenly in "God's gymnasium"—we are exposed. Our inner anxieties, our hair-trigger temper, our unrealistic regard of our own talents, our tendency to lie or shade the truth, our lack of self-discipline—all of these things come out. Perhaps the trouble was brought on by the presence of these negative qualities. Or maybe the new situation demands a certain response, and it reveals the absence of the positive qualities we need. Either way, the gymnasium shows you who you really are, inescapably.

But then what do you do? A good coach puts you through exercises, and what are they? They are ways to cause stress or put pressure on various parts of your body. Bicep curls with weights put pressure on the biceps. Forearm curls do the same. Running does many things, including taxing the respiratory and circulatory systems. A good coach will not put too much pressure on your body. To lift too much or run too much would cause your body to break down. But if, on the other hand, you exercise too little—if you put no pressure on your body and simply go through life doing ordinary life tasks—your body will also break down and age faster. What you need is exactly the right amount of pressure and just the right amount of discomfort and pain.

The biblical author is right when he says that suffering is painful "at the time" but later yields a harvest. That is exactly how exercise works. When you are actually doing your bicep curls, your arms feel as if they are getting weaker and weaker. But later they will come back stronger for the experience. In the gym, you *feel* you are getting weaker, and you may leave barely able to walk up the steps. And yet the experience of weakness, if your coach has been skillful, will lead to increasing strength.

Obviously, an unskillful coach could do us a lot of harm—but we have the perfect coach, the Great Coach. "No trial has overtaken you that is not common to mankind. And God is faithful. He will not let you be tempted beyond what you can endure" (1 Cor 10:13). This means that everything that happens to us in life has both a limit and a purpose. There's a limit. We must not say when things come upon us, "He's trying to crush me!" Remember how weak, exhausted, and spent you expect to feel in the gym. But there is also a purpose. "All things work together for good to them that love God" (Rom 8:28). We must not say, "I could run my life a lot better than this."

None of this is meant to see suffering as a game, as if God is up in heaven playing with us. We must set this teaching alongside everything else we have seen about evil as a disruption, as the enemy of God. He is the God who is grieved when we are grieved.

> In all their affliction he was afflicted,
> and the angel of his presence saved them;
> in his love and in his pity he redeemed them;
> he lifted them up and carried them all the days of old (Isa 63:9 ESV).

As our divine coach is guiding us through life with this balance, we should respond with the same careful moderation. The Hebrews writer says earlier in the chapter that we should neither "despise" the Lord's discipline nor "faint" under it (Heb 5). This means we should neither be stoics who just grit our teeth and refuse to see the suffering as God's training, nor should we become "faint," by giving up, despairing, and walking away from God. We must neither lie down nor run away, but rather we must move forward through the exercises. And we must remember God's own suffering. Indeed, Hebrews 12 begins with a call to "fix your eyes on Jesus . . . who endured the cross . . . its shame . . . who endured such opposition . . . so that you will not grow weary and lose heart" (Heb 12:2–3).

It is looking to Jesus that enables you to function in God's gymnasium. It takes away self-pity, as we consider what he endured for us without complaining. If he endured infinite suffering and loss for us, we should be able to endure finite grief and loss, knowing that God is working behind the hateful evil to bring out some good in our lives. If we keep our eyes "fixed" on Jesus, we will come through the pain and experience with the deeper peace that can be the result.

The common themes that tie together the metaphors of the furnace and the gymnasium are striking. Both are places of danger. Wrong responses could bring disaster. But right responses can bring beauty and strength. They must not—and, really, cannot—be avoided, nor should we panic when we find ourselves within their confines. Instead we look to the one who has passed through the ultimate furnace and race course when he went to the cross, and who now stands and walks beside us in our suffering.

Preparing the Mind for Suffering

So suffering does not automatically or naturally lead to growth and good outcomes. It must be handled properly or faced patiently and faithfully. But what does that mean? It is time to begin laying out exactly *how* we are to walk through pain and suffering. We have to be prepared in our mind and heart before suffering strikes so that we are not surprised by suffering. And when suffering does strike, we have to be sensitive to the varieties of suffering so that we do not apply the specific strategies in a wooden, one-size-fits-all way.

How do we prepare?

Preparation, if it is to be effective, should happen before we are actually experiencing the searing pain. As we have seen already in this book, most of the central truths and themes of biblical theology can serve as very powerful comforts and resources to sufferers. But the more deeply you know and grasp those teachings before the adversity comes, the more comfort they will be. Once you are in a crisis, there is no time to sit down to give substantive study and attention to parts of the Bible. As a working pastor for nearly four decades, I have often sat beside people who were going through terrible troubles and silently wished they had taken the time to learn more about their faith before the tidal wave of trouble had engulfed them. As we have seen, the main "reasons of the heart" that help us endure suffering are the foundational doctrines of the faith—creation and fall, atonement and resurrection. These are profound and rich truths we need to grasp before we suffer, or we will be unprepared for it. And many of these lessons are very difficult to learn "on the job" when we are in the midst of adversity.

A great deal of preparation for suffering is simple but crucial. It means developing a deep enough knowledge of the Bible and a strong and vital enough prayer life that you will neither be surprised by nor overthrown by affliction. Theologian Michael Horton writes:

> Understanding who God is, who we are, and God's ways in creation, providence, and redemption—at least as much as Scripture reveals to us—is to the trials of life what preparing for the LSAT is to the practice of law. Theology is the most serious business. Preparing for this exam is not just a head game. . . . It's a matter of life and death. . . . It's about living, and dying, well.[308]

By the term *theology*, Horton means more than mere data. The Bible speaks of the Word of God as a living power (Rom 1:16; Heb 4:12), as a supernatural seed that brings slow but steady transformation from within (1 Pet 1:23), as something that unfolds and enlightens as we believe, digest, practice, and store it in our hearts (Ps 119:11, 130), and as something that should "dwell richly" in us (Col 3:16).

One of the simplest theological truths is often missed. "Dear friends," writes St. Peter, "do not be surprised at the painful trial you are suffering, as though something strange were happening to you. But rejoice that you participate in the sufferings of Christ" (1 Pet 4:12–13). Some people have the naïve view that because they are fairly savvy people, or self-disciplined, or morally decent, or good Christians—that really, really *bad* things simply can't happen to them. That is nothing but bad theology. And so many people's misery and distress in suffering is doubled and trebled, coming not from the trouble itself but from the shock that they *are* suffering at all.

Surprise can be dealt with if we do some theological reflection. We may have an unexamined feeling that God will not let really bad things happen to good people. But Jesus Christ himself disproves that. If God allowed a perfect man to suffer terribly (but for an ultimate good), why should we think that something like that could never happen to us? We won't ever suffer as badly as Jesus did, because none of us will ever be used to accomplish salvation. But something like that could happen on a much smaller scale to us. And, as we have seen, Romans 8:19–23 and Genesis 3:16–18 show us that the world is filled with disease, death, and natural disasters because of sin in general. It is the curse on the human race. We are all subject to it—because we are all human beings.

Other theological points can also help us here. Because of God's infinite majesty and wisdom, we *expect* to not understand all his ways. It wouldn't make sense that everything he does would make sense. How could an infinite, beginningless being always manage our lives in a way that makes sense to us? We don't even understand other human beings fully, so how could we expect to understand everything God does? Because of our sin and his holiness, the life we have even with its adversities is better than we deserve. If we ever asked God to be completely fair and just and he complied, we would all be instantly destroyed.

In this—and in many other ways—growth in biblical knowledge and maturity in theological reflection is irreplaceable preparation for the onset of darkness and trouble.

Preparing the Heart for Suffering

But, as we have shown, suffering is not just an intellectual issue—"Why is there so much evil and suffering in life?"—but a personal problem—"How will I get through this?" This second question is in a different universe from the first. And therefore, we must prepare not only the mind for suffering but also the heart, and that means developing a consistent, vibrant, theologically deep yet existentially rich prayer life.

Philosopher Simone Weil writes that a soul in affliction finds it difficult to love anything. It must therefore almost force itself to keep loving God and others "or at least wanting to love, though it may only be with an infinitesimal part of itself." If, during affliction, "the soul stops loving it falls, even in this life, into something almost equivalent to hell."[309] So when suffering comes in, God, love, and hope seem unreal. But if they were already abstract and unreal to you to begin with, then there is almost no way to do what Weil urges. Suffering will be like a river that sweeps us into despair. However, if our understanding and experience of God's love was strong to begin with, they can serve as anchors that keep us from being sucked into the whirlpool.

If the mind is well prepared, the coming of adversity will not be a complete shock. But when suffering first hits you, the gap between what you know with the mind and what you can use out of your store of knowledge in your heart can be surprisingly large. When troubles come, you will need God's help to find the particular insights, consoling thoughts, and wisdom you will need to get you through. Some of these you may have already known intellectually, but God will have to make them real and relevant in a new way. Others you will not have seen before and will have to learn. But that is how you survive. If you are going to get through it all, you will need God being with you, helping you pick your way through by learning, grasping, and cherishing many ideas and truths that become powerful and consoling to you.

Here is a story of someone who was startled by the gap between his mind and his heart. Alvin Plantinga wrote:

> In the presence of his own suffering or that of someone near him [the believer in God] may find it difficult to maintain what he takes to be the proper attitude toward God. Faced with great personal suffering or misfortune, he may be tempted to rebel against God, to shake his fist in God's face, or even to give up belief in God altogether. But this is a problem of a different dimension. Such a problem calls, not for philosophical enlightenment, but for pastoral care.[310]

John S. Feinberg was a theological student when he first read Plantinga's statement, but he did not fully understand it. Feinberg wrote, "I thought that as long as one had intellectual answers that explained why God allowed evil in the world . . . the sufferer would be satisfied."[311] He sometimes saw Christians who had experienced a tragedy struggling with their relationship with God, and, he admits, he was impatient with them. But later, after he had become a teacher of theology at the graduate level, he learned that his wife had Huntington's chorea, a progressive neurodegenerative disorder that leads not only to the loss of all voluntary bodily movement but to memory loss, depression, and various forms of dementia including hallucinations and paranoia. He was told also that, since the disease is genetically transmitted, each of his children had a 50-50 chance of getting the disease, though symptoms do not show up until age thirty at the earliest.[312]

After a time of denial, it sunk in. "In one fell stroke, we learned that my whole family was under this cloud of doom."[313] With his mind, he knew the sound theological response to this situation:

> Anyway, who was I, the creature, to contest the Creator? As Paul says (Rom 9:19–21), the creature has no right to haul the Creator into the courtroom of human moral judgments and put him on trial as though he has done something wrong. God has total power and authority over me. I felt God had somehow misled me, even tricked me.[314]

It is striking how the last sentence follows on immediately from the previous sentence, without so much as a *nevertheless* or a *yet*. Feinberg knew the biblically and theologically sound response to his situation— that God has the right to do what he wants. He recited it, but then he admits that even as he knew with this mind that God could do no wrong, he felt in his heart that God had grievously wronged him. Ironically, he had written his master's thesis on the book of Job, and his doctoral dissertation at the University of Chicago focused on the problem of evil. "I had all these intellectual answers, but none of them made any difference in how I felt."[315]

Here was a man who with his intellect had worked out biblically based, rational answers to the problem of suffering, and he had done so at a high, scholarly level. Yet when suffering actually came into his life, he experienced such hopelessness that he wasn't able to function. He knew all sorts of biblical truths about evil and suffering, but now that he was in the actual furnace, they did not help him. He did not know how to existentially access them. He was filled with anger. And along with this came a sense of abandonment and the absence of God.

Did this mean that these biblical themes and reasonings were wrong, or simply useless? No. Feinberg relates how, eventually, he was able to regain his equilibrium only through revisiting many of the truths he had known in the abstract but that he had never connected to lived experience, or to the actual affections and functions of his heart. In other words, he found that biblical and theological reasoning can and does become important to the sufferer, but only after a great deal of hard inner heart work. But he concluded, "Many of those [biblical] answers won't help with a particular problem, and . . . others that do won't help at all stages in the sufferer's experience."[316] Theologian Don Carson explains this important insight well:

> There are millions of ordinary Christians who . . . do not feel there *is* a problem [of suffering]. They have theological answers that satisfy them: suffering is the result of sin; free will means that God has to leave people to make their own mistakes; heaven and hell will set the record straight. . . . And then something takes place in their own life that jolts them to the cores. . . . That is not to say, however, that the set of beliefs is irrelevant. It is to say that . . . the Christian, to find comfort in them, must learn how to *use* them.[317]

The Bible says a great deal about suffering, but it is one thing to have these things stored in the "warehouse of the mind."[318] It is quite another to know how to apply them to your own heart, life, and experience in such a way that they produce wisdom, endurance, joy, self-knowledge, courage, and humility. It is one thing to believe in God but it is quite another thing to trust God. It is one thing to have an intellectual explanation for why God allows suffering; it is another thing to actually find a path through suffering so that, instead of becoming more bitter, cynical, despondent, and broken, you become more wise, grounded, humble, strong, and even content.

So we must not ignore either the mind or the heart. By itself mere intellectual reasoning will fall short of what we require for life in this world, and it is cruel to shower a person currently in pain with theological arguments about how God is not responsible for evil and why his wisdom is beyond searching out. As one of the biblical proverbs says, "Like one who takes away a garment on a cold day, or like vinegar poured on a wound, is one who sings songs to a heavy heart" (Prov 25:20 NIV).

And yet—the theoretical and the practical are intertwined. The experience of suffering automatically raises more philosophical questions in the mind. "Why? What kind of God would allow this?" So using the intellect to make some sense out of suffering is important, but it must be accompanied not merely with knowing about God, but with knowing *God*.

Life Story: The Sweetness of Life with God

by Mark and Martha

MARTHA: As my husband, Mark, sits in his wheelchair unable to move anything but his eyes, and that being increasingly difficult, we are approaching the ten-year point in our journey.

It began with a small muscle twitch when Mark was forty-eight years old, and within a month, our doctor diagnosed the cause as the terminal illness ALS, or Lou Gehrig's disease. We had been married twenty-five years and had four children. We had always been an active family, so Mark's quick physical demise was devastating.

When Mark got sick, I fell into a black hole of despair. I didn't know how I was going to live through the pain of the coming days. I asked all my friends to pray that the fear of tomorrow would not rob me of the joy of today, because I was struggling. I wondered, "Who am I if I am not Mark's wife?"

Today, I understand the idolatry in that statement and why the despair was so deep. I had identified most deeply with Mark as my husband and provider. In my eyes, I had put him before God. How I moved out of despair is a mystery. I had no awareness of being "called forth," yet I experienced a sense of resurrection. During those early days, Mark and I quoted every verse we could think of about God's care. We attempted to find ways to beat into our hearts the love and faithfulness of God. We planted our feet in the truth we understood even though everything in our lives seemed otherwise.

MARK *(writing at a computer that captures eye movements)*: I played sports in my younger years, and I always hated sitting on the bench. One day just after my diagnosis, I cried out to God that I thought I was being pulled out of the game when I still had something to offer. His response was, "You have been on the sidelines for some time; you are just now going in the game." Hanging on to the truth that God is doing much that I can't see and that in His economy it is worth the suffering, but it is also a daily exercise of faith.

The "Body of Christ" moved into our lives in very tangible ways. Friends helped with meals, gave gift cards, did yard work, planned birthday parties for our kids, came and were just present. Even ten years into the journey, we still have many people reaching out to us with support and strength and love.

MARTHA: There were so many things at the beginning that I didn't think I could live through emotionally. One of those was picking a place to bury Mark. My daughters and I went one day to find a place. There was a tenderness between us and even laughter. I sensed God saying to me, "I'm here. In all those places you don't think you will be able to face, I will be there." It was a day of significance in sensing His presence with me, not just that day but for everything that lay ahead.

MARK: I have found that singing hymns and African-American spirituals in my head, because I have not been able to speak for the last eight years, has been helpful. Many hymns are about suffering and speak deeply to my need for a sense of his presence with me in the midst of my pain. These hymns are treasures that modern Christian music doesn't even approach, some of the best reminders that this world and its troubles is not our true home. Recently, I have been diagnosed with a terminal liver disease. Sometimes I say that I am unfairly suffering, but the only one who went through suffering unfairly was Jesus. His separation from the father on the cross is far beyond anything I could ever experience. How can I complain when he went through that cosmic pain for me? I remember Tim Keller relating the story of a man who was terminally ill and who told him that the sweetness of his life with God as a result of his illness he wouldn't trade for more years. I have found that to be true in my life as well.

MARTHA: We have found meaning, purpose, joy, growth, and wholeness in our loss. How much I would have missed if I had opted out of this season. God has had so much to give me in the midst of it. I see how intense sorrow and intense sweetness are mingled together. The depth and richness of life has come in suffering. How much I have learned and how much sweeter Jesus is to me now.

TEN

The Varieties of Suffering

Life is *pain, Highness. Anyone who says differently is selling something.*

The Princess Bride (1987)

Suffering is an important way to grow. People who have not suffered much are often shallow, unacquainted with both their weaknesses and strengths, naïve about human nature and life, and almost always fragile and unresilient. But we know that suffering does not deepen and enrich us automatically. Both images—of a furnace and of a gymnasium—reveal this. Fire in the furnaces can kill, and gymnasiums can severely injure. An old saying goes, "The same sun that melts wax hardens clay," and so the same traumatic experience can ruin one person and make another person stronger and even happier. How can we be prepared to handle suffering in such a way that it leads to growth?

Diversities of Suffering

Among the other measures we have already addressed, it is critical to recognize the remarkable variety in the Bible's teaching on pain and adversity. One man is suffering from drug addiction in prison because he attacked and maimed someone in a fit of rage. Another man's whole life changes when he accidentally kills a seven-year-old boy who suddenly runs out into his car's path. A young mother with three little children at home is dying of a brain tumor. A family with teenage children is devastated when their father commits suicide. Finally, there are the young parents who just gave birth to a severely impaired child. All of these people are suffering, but the causes and shapes of their pain and anguish are wildly divergent.

The Bible accordingly shows us the many kinds of suffering and points to just as great a range of possible responses. A one-size-fits-all prescription for handling suffering is bound to fail, because not only does suffering come in so many different forms but sufferers themselves come with so many different kinds of temperaments and spiritual conditions. The Bible forbids us to use a single template for handling pain and grief, but modern people tend to be more reductionist. We live in a technological society and we want simple "how to" formulations. Yet there is nothing less practical for sufferers than to think there is just one set of practical steps for "fixing" their situation.

In the early days of my pastoral ministry, I visited a woman going through a divorce. I lent her a book of sermons by a pastor that gave her an enormous boost. "That book saved my life!" she said to me. Confident that I had a great tool for pastoral care, a year later I gave the same book to another woman who was going through a divorce in what looked to me like the same circumstances. Her response was completely different—some of the volume confused her and some of it upset her. I learned not to assume that every sufferer needed the very same medicine.

Not long after I had gone through surgery and treatment for thyroid cancer, I met a woman who had breast cancer. "I'm a cancer survivor too," she said to me, and proceeded to tell me how she had gotten through it. I was uncomfortable during the entire conversation. She considered me a fellow sufferer, and indeed we both had had the tremendous shock of hearing a doctor say, "You have a malignancy." But I had not faced the radical surgery and permanent changes to my body that she had, nor did I face the same percentage likelihood of future reoccurrence. And as she related her experience I was struck not only by how different our sufferings had been but also by what different kinds of ideas and thoughts had comforted and strengthened each of us. I realized that many of the things that had gotten me through my cancer would not have been as relevant to her, and many of the ideas and help that fortified her were not effective for me.

So we will not be able to face our suffering well—or help others face it—unless we recognize the varieties of it. Let us look at four kinds of suffering that the Bible speaks of, each with its own cause and set of peculiar challenges.

Jonah, David, and the Suffering We Bring on Ourselves

One kind of suffering is directly caused by our own failures. A woman seeks to be successful in business by being ruthless and cruel throughout her career. But as time goes on, she finds herself with fewer and fewer friends and allies. When she makes a decision that leads to some losses for her company, she discovers that she has no support from her team. As a result she is summarily dismissed, and her reputation sustains great damage because many of her enemies gladly exaggerate her errors on the grapevine. Her career ruined, she slowly realizes it was due to her own hard-knuckled and foolish behavior. Here is another example. A married man has a very brief one-night stand on a business trip and is later found out. His marriage swiftly falls apart and he discovers himself permanently alienated from his children. Suffering accompanied with shame and guilt brings a unique kind of inner torment.

This first kind of suffering is seen in the lives the biblical figures Jonah and David. Within the short book of Jonah, the prophet endured two very different but traumatic experiences. First, God sent a massive, life-threatening storm at sea. Later, when Jonah was enjoying the shade and beauty of a particular climbing vine, God sent a "worm" and an "east wind" to destroy the plant, which deeply discouraged him. Why? Jonah had refused God's original call to go preach to the Assyrians of Nineveh. Later he was furious that God did not destroy them. Jonah was filled with a racist hatred of these people, and God was using adverse circumstances to show him the evil of his own heart. That is why everything went wrong for him. A storm almost drowned him. His mortal enemies escaped the noose. A hot east wind even destroyed his comfortable, shady dwelling. But God was trying to reveal something to Jonah—he was trying to wake him up.

Similarly, when King David's life fell apart, there was also a specific sin that caused it. And God was sending a specific message through the suffering. David had violated the law of God by having an affair with Bathsheba, another man's wife, and by arranging to have her husband killed. Then the new young son of David and Bathsheba became sick and died. And David realized that God was saying to him that he had to change his ways or lose his kingship and his life.

Was God "punishing" David and Jonah for their sins? Not exactly. Romans 8:1 says that there is "no condemnation" for a believer. That means, simply, that if Jesus has received our punishment and made payment for our sins, God can not then receive a second payment out of us as well. God does not exact "retribution" from a believer, because of Jesus and because, if he really punished us for our sins, we'd all have been dead long ago.[319] But God often appoints some aspect of the brokenness of the world (caused by sin in general: Gen. 3; Rom 8:18ff) to come into our lives to wake us up and turn us to him. The severity of this depends on our heart's need.

It is quite important to distinguish between a "David" experience of suffering and a "Job" type experience—namely, suffering not brought on directly by anything you've been doing. A Christian man who develops lymphoma should not think he is being punished for a sin, though he must not, on the other hand, miss this opportunity to put his roots down into God and discover a dimension of spiritual growth and wisdom he would never otherwise have had access to.

Now think through this illustration. Imagine that a man becomes engaged five times in a row, and each time he breaks up with his fiancée. Because each fiancée exhibits some personal flaw, he assigns the blame in every case to her faults. But actually, his own perfectionism and attitude of moral superiority are the main causes of the relationship failures. It is a huge blind spot for him. It may be, then, that one particularly brutal break-up might shake him to the core, and finally show him what he has been contributing to all this misery. His suffering and distress is a wake-up call to change something very particular in his life. Suffering could be the only way for such a man to be humbled and to wake up to his own shortcomings. The psalmist says, in Psalm 25: "Cleanse me from hidden faults." In general, it is only troubles and difficulties that can reveal such things to us.

Paul, Jeremiah, and the Suffering of Betrayal

So there is suffering caused by bad behavior. But, then, there is the suffering caused by good and brave behavior. Such behavior may be the occasion of betrayal or attacks from others. In the Bible, most of St. Paul's suffering was caused by this, as was the suffering of the prophet Jeremiah. Paul was constantly being beaten, imprisoned, or attacked by his own people as well as by Gentiles. At one place in his letters, Paul gives us a nonexhaustive list of what he has gone through as a messenger of God:

> I have worked much harder, been in prison more frequently, been flogged more severely, and been exposed to death again and again. Five times I received from the Jews the forty lashes minus one. Three times I was beaten with rods, once I was pelted with stones, three times I was shipwrecked, I spent a night and a day in the open sea, I have been constantly on the move. I have been in danger from rivers, in danger from bandits, in danger from my fellow Jews, in danger from Gentiles; in danger in the city, in danger in the country, in danger at sea; and in danger from false believers. I have labored and toiled and have often gone without sleep; I have known hunger and thirst and have often gone without food; I have been cold and naked. Besides everything else, I face daily the pressure of my concern for all the churches. Who is weak, and I do not feel weak? (2 Cor 11:23–29).

Jeremiah also was put in stocks and imprisoned for simply "speaking the truth to power" (Jer 20:1–6). In many parts of the world today, public criticism of the government or of the dominant religious or cultural institutions can get you beaten, imprisoned, or killed. In our culture, it is very possible to become the object of a political attack within your company or neighborhood if you are open about your commitment to an unpopular cause. But it is even more likely that this kind of betrayal happens simply through a personal relationship going sour. When someone perceives that they have been wronged by you, they may embark on a program of trying to hurt you or damage your reputation. Often someone you thought you knew well can turn on you and attack you because it furthers their career or interests. Personal betrayals are particularly horrific, and this sort of trial can tempt you to give in to debilitating anger and bitterness.

While the first kind of suffering requires that you learn repentance, this kind of suffering will entail that you wrestle with the issues of forgiveness. The temptation will be to become bitter and to hide your growing hardness and cruelty under the self-image of being a noble victim. Often confrontation and the pursuit of justice is indeed required, but it must be carried out without the spirit of vengefulness that will allow the experience to turn you into a worse person rather than a better one.

Mary, Martha, and the Suffering of Loss

While some suffering can overwhelm you with anger and resentment, there is another kind that can crush you with grief. Some have called this kind of suffering "universal" because it eventually comes to everyone, no matter your behavior, good or bad. It is grief and loss in the face of mortality, decay, and death. In the Bible we see this when Jesus comforts Mary and Martha, who have just lost their brother and are mourning for him.

Everyone comes to know this kind of suffering, yet even within this category there are almost endless variations. It is one thing to face the death of a spouse after fifty years of marriage, another to do so when

young children are left behind. It is one thing to face your own imminent death from disease when you are eighty, another when you are
thirty. It is one kind of grief to lose a relative that you had a good relationship with, another when there were unresolved issues and your grief
is shot through with guilt and resentment. And then there are different
modes of decay and death. There is the slow but sure decay of aging,
and the swift deaths of automobile accidents, floods, and landslides.

Decay and death—losses of home and loved ones—are inevitable to
all and so can be said to be a kind of universal suffering. There may be
some issues around these losses that require self-examination and repentance, or confrontation and forgiveness. But mainly, when facing grief
Christians must learn to direct their minds and hearts to the various
forms of comfort and hope that their faith offers them. Paul directs a
group of bereaved believers to not "grieve like the rest of men, who have
no hope" (1 Thess 4:13) and "We do not lose heart. . . . For our light
and momentary troubles are achieving an eternal glory that far outweighs them all. So we fix our eyes not on what is seen, but on what is
unseen" (2 Cor 16–18).

Job and the Suffering of Mystery

Finally, there is a kind of suffering that is "none of the above" though it
may overlap with one or more of the others. This is the mysterious,
unlooked for, and horrendous suffering that people most often call
"senseless." It can be argued that it is this kind of suffering that the Bible
pays particular attention to. In Psalm 44 the authors, "the Sons of
Korah," look at a devastated country and ask God:

> All this has come upon us, though we have not forgotten you,
> and we have not been false to your covenant. Our heart has not
> turned back nor have our steps departed from your way; yet
> you have broken us in the place of jackals and covered us with
> the shadow of death. . . . Why do your hide your face? Why do
> you forget our affliction and oppression? (Ps 44:17–19, 24).

Such cries fill the pages of the Psalms, as well as those of prophets such as Habakkuk and Jeremiah. And then there is Job. The Bible relates the stories of David, Paul, Mary, and Martha—all persons who suffered grievously. But the Bible gives greater focused attention to the suffering of Job than to all of these others. The other kinds of affliction have causes easy to identify—moral failure, persecution and betrayal, and the inevitability of death. And in each case, the entailed emotions of guilt, anger, and grief are difficult to handle, yet straightforward. But then there is truly "Job-type" suffering. Job's sufferings were extraordinary. All of his children were killed at once. All of his wealth was wiped out in an instant. These are not the more universally experienced sorrows of human life, nor were they caused by Job's moral lapses or by persecution and betrayal. When people experience horrendous, unusually severe suffering, it leaves the sufferer not so much filled with guilt, or resentment toward others, or pure grief—but with anger toward life and God himself.

When Job's life fell apart, at first he looked for a specific sin for which he was being chastised. Or, at least, he sought a clear lesson from God that he was supposed to be learning. In short, he wanted to know what there was in his life that had caused all this. Job's friends also looked for sins and things for Job to work on. But there was no one thing in his life that God was after. In fact, that *was* the point of Job's suffering. He was being led to the place where he would obey God simply for the sake of who God is, not in order to receive something or to get something done.

Job's suffering, then, was not a chastisement or a lesson aimed at changing a particular flaw in Job's life. But that didn't mean it wasn't a powerful vehicle both for Job's personal growth and for God's glory. Job had looked in vain for a specific "lesson," but the lesson was really a revelation about the whole tenor of his life, and his need to base it fully, with all his heart, on God. However, it was a long, long journey from the beginning to the end of the book of Job, where Job began to see this. And when this kind of mysterious, inexplicable suffering comes upon us, our journey is also a long one. It certainly may entail repentance, forgiveness, and fixing our eyes on our hopes. But Job-type suffering requires a process of honest prayer and crying, the hard work of deliberate trust in God, and what St. Augustine called a re-ordering of our loves.

Diversities of Temperament

The diversity of suffering does not consist only in external factors, however, but also in the internal—the different personalities and temperaments of those experiencing the adversity.

One of the best efforts to break down the experience of suffering into its different facets is Simone Weil's classic essay "The Love of God and Affliction."[320] The French philosopher and activist calls the inner pain caused by suffering *malheur*. There is no exact English synonym for this French word. It includes a sense of doom and hopelessness. The closest English word is perhaps *affliction*. Affliction, Weil writes "is an uprooting of life, a more or less attenuated equivalent of death. . . . A kind of horror submerges the whole soul."[321] Weil distinguishes between suffering, the external circumstances in the world, and affliction, which is the internal experience of pain and sorrow. Weil then seeks to outline what she considers the various aspects of this experience.

Weil observes that one of the marks of affliction is *isolation*.[322] A barrier goes up between us and even our closest friends. One reason is that you the sufferer suddenly sense a new gulf between yourself and almost anyone who has not experienced what you are going through. People who, you once felt, shared a common experience with you no longer do. Andrew Solomon, in his study of parents who bear children who are deaf, autistic, schizophrenic, or otherwise disabled, argues that they experience a shift in identity.[323] This in some ways is true of anyone in severe adversity. Severe suffering turns you into a different person and some of the people that you once felt affinity for no longer look the same to you. But isolation is also caused by friends who simply stay away. Why do we so often avoid a person in affliction?[324] It may be as simple as the feeling of incompetence—we don't know what to say or do. It may also be the sheer fear of being drawn into and drowning in the sufferer's pain. Others stay away because, like Job's friends, we need to believe that the afflicted person somehow brought this on or wasn't wise enough to avoid it. That way we can assure ourselves that it could never happen to *us*. The afflicted person challenges us to admit what we would rather deny—that such severe difficulty can come upon anyone, anytime.

A second aspect of affliction we can call *implosion*. Intense physical pain makes you unavoidably self-absorbed. You cannot think about anyone else or anything else—there is just the hurt and the need to have it stop. In the same way, inner pain can virtually suck us down into ourselves, so that we can hardly notice what is happening in anyone around us. In *The Lord of the Rings* the effect of the One, ruling ring was to magnify the ego. So when Samwise puts on the ring, "All things around him were not dark but vague; while he himself was there in a grey hazy world, alone, like a small black solid rock."[325] Suffering can do that too; it can make you and your needs the only solid, real thing, and all other concerns vague, hazy, and unimportant. This self-absorption can make you unable to give, receive, or feel love. There is a numbness, a fixation on what is happening to you. You may be unable to "get out of yourself" and think of, serve, or love others, or even feel loved by others. Beneath all of this, Weil says, is a loss of any sense of God. "Affliction makes God appear to be absent for a time, more absent than a dead man, more absent than light in the utter darkness of a cell. . . . During this absence there is nothing to love."[326] We may know intellectually that someone loves us, or even believe that God loves us, but it doesn't seem real to our hearts.

A third mark of affliction is a sense of doom, of hopelessness, and of *condemnation*. This comes in part from a hard-to-define, barely conscious shame. "Affliction hardens and discourages us because, like a red hot iron it stamps the soul to its very depth with the scorn, the disgust, even the self-hatred and sense of guilt and defilement that crime logically should produce but actually does not."[327] In other words, while we should feel guilty when we do wrong, we usually don't. It is not until great suffering comes upon us that we feel we are perhaps being punished and so we look around and begin to admit the wrongdoing in our lives. And it is not hard to find. Even though the things we have done wrong may not have any direct connection to the affliction, the affliction makes us keenly aware of our flaws and our fragility. This sense of condemnation is even persistent in Western cultures, in which all efforts are made to see sufferers as victims and not responsible for it in any way.

A fourth aspect of affliction is usually *anger*. Depending on the cause and context, the anger may be more or less directed at various objects. There might be anger at oneself, or deep bitterness against people who have wronged you or let you down, or specific anger at God, or general anger against the injustice and emptiness of life.

Weil adds a final toxic effect of affliction that often occurs. It is *temptation*—the temptation toward complicity. Suffering can "little by little, turn the soul into its accomplice, by injecting a poison of inertia into it." We become complicit with the affliction, comfortable with our discomfort, content with our discontent. "This complicity impedes all the efforts he might make to improve his lot; it goes so far as to prevent him from seeking a way of deliverance, sometimes even . . . from wishing for deliverance."[328] It can make you feel noble, and the self-pity can be sweet and addicting. Or affliction can become a great excuse for all sorts of behavior or patterns of life you could not otherwise justify. Or perhaps, at some subconscious level, you may feel you need to pay for your sins, and the suffering is the way to do it.

As a pastor and a sufferer, I find Simone Weil's analysis of affliction to be incisive. It also explains how infinitely complex and variegated a condition affliction can be. These factors—isolation, self-implosion and numbness, anger, condemnation and shame, and the temptation to embrace suffering—are like elements in a chemical compound. It could be argued that they are nearly all present to some degree in any affliction, depending not only on the causal circumstances but on our individual temperaments. People of different personalities, genders, and cultures process emotions differently. They also have different internal values and commitments. A father, for example, may love his children deeply but identify personally more with his career. His wife may be quite dedicated to her vocation but identify her worth more closely with how her children are faring. And so, if there is a career reversal, the husband may be more "overthrown" and despondent, while if one of their children gets seriously injured, the mother may be more disconsolate than the father.

Same trouble, different responses, because there is a different identity structure within the heart.

And so these elements that Weil names may exist in very different proportions and maintain sharply different, complex interrelationships to one another within each case.

Diversities of Pathways

Every affliction, then, is virtually unique. And it means that every sufferer will need to find a somewhat different path through it. When John Feinberg discovered his family's dire physical condition, it cast him into a time of darkness. He recounts that friends came by to see him and tried to give him thoughts and ideas that would help him get through the difficult time. Most were reflections on theological truths. To recount his experience, he gives us two lists.

One list was of things that were said that he admitted with his mind were basically true—yet were irritating or downright discouraging to him at the time. Job's friends say many things about God that are true in the abstract. They say, "In the end all evil will be judged" and "God is pleased with the righteous" and "God is not unjust or unfair" and "We can't understand God's ways—they are beyond our puny minds." Yes—all true statements. And yet Job calls them "miserable comforters" (Job 16:2), and in the end, God condemns the friends for how they respond to Job. Why? They gave true statements but applied these truths inappropriately. Biblical scholar Don Carson writes about Job's friends:

> There is a way of using theology and theological arguments that wounds rather than heals. This is not the fault of theology and theological arguments; it is the fault of the "miserable comforter" who fastens on an inappropriate fragment of truth, or whose timing is off, or whose attitude is condescending, or whose application is insensitive, or whose true theology is couched in such culture-laden clichés that they grate rather than comfort.[329]

Feinberg mentions some of the "miserable comforts" he received. Some friends said that God often uses one problem to spare us from some other problems we'll never see. He knew that could be true in the abstract, but it only made him feel worse. What possible problem could be worse than seeing his wife die by inches over the years? Another person said, "Well, everyone is going to die from something. You just know in advance what it is in your wife's case." Feinberg replied, very sensibly, that while this is true, most people would *not* want to know this information. Other people opened up about some very terrible things that had happened to them in order to say "I understand how you feel." Feinberg responded, "What helps is not knowing you feel like I do but knowing that you care!"[330]

Perhaps the most typical and unhelpful "help" he received was a set of nodding statements that "we know all things are for the best and we have to trust God." John Feinberg was a professor of systematic theology in a graduate school. He already believed that. He had written whole treatises on that. But the more he heard this from people, the more guilt he felt. He wasn't being allowed to lament or wail or cry out like David in the Psalms or Job. He was being implicitly told that if he was not already experiencing peace in his heart, knowing the wisdom and goodness of God, he was a spiritually immature man.[331]

It is important to see that the list of "Things That Didn't Help" consisted of real truths—applied poorly. They either were expressed unskillfully or were offered at the wrong time, in an "unseasonable" manner. When he turned to a list of "Things That Helped" and began to heal, we see a set of truths applied in the right order, in the right way. One of his friends one day was talking to Feinberg about an idea that made him feel so guilty—about "rejoicing in his sufferings." The friend pointed out that it didn't mean he was rejoicing *for* the sufferings—that would be masochistic. "You have to learn to live with this, but you don't have to like it," he said. The point was that Feinberg would have to learn to rejoice more in God and his love, but the evil was evil and would always be painful.[332] A "penny dropped" for him in that conversation. Other help came from his father, who comforted him by pointing out that he shouldn't expect to feel God's grace and strength now for the whole ordeal ahead. He was petrified that he would have to face the death of one or more of his immediate family and that it would be more than he could bear. But, his father said, he was not facing it now, and so he shouldn't expect to feel strong enough now for something that had not yet happened. "God never promised to give you tomorrow's grace for today. He only promised today's grace for today, and that's all you need" (Matt 6:34). Another penny dropped.

After some of these small but important rays of light broke through, Feinberg began to sense God's love and presence again in a growing way. And he began to go back to the things he already knew—about where evil and suffering came from, and the wisdom and sovereignty of God, and the sacrificial suffering of Jesus on the cross for him. Bit by bit he reappropriated each truth, thinking it through from his new perspective and applying it to his heart and to the world as he now knew them. And it began to light things up for him in a fresh way.

Feinberg's story is helpful for anyone. But for me as a pastor, the two lists were quite striking. I recognized some things on his "discouraging" list were things that I had seen help suffering people greatly, and some items on his "encouraging" list were ideas that I had seen irritate and anger them. This reveals the remarkable diversity of suffering.

As the years went on, I came to realize that most books on and for sufferers, though usually speaking universally (e.g., "When you go through suffering, you should think this") were in reality singling out a particular kind of affliction or person to address. Some people in suffering are tempted toward self-pity and pride, toward feeling like a noble martyr. They need gentle opposition. Others are tempted toward shame and self-hatred. They need assurance.

Some books on suffering take the direct approach, telling you to "make use" of your sorrow, to learn from it. And indeed, some need to use such times to make obvious, needed changes in their lives. For example, a man who has put too much emphasis on having and spending lots of money, when he faces the trauma of a major business failure, needs to confront himself about his greed and his internal identification of net worth with self-worth. It is also right to talk about God's sovereign plan for our lives, how he uses pain and difficulty to get our attention, and how he brings good things out of the bad circumstances. But what about the young parents who have just lost their five-year-old daughter, who was run over by a car? Should the first things you say to them be "God's trying to get your attention. Be sure to learn from this! What changes should you be making?" The parents, with warranted vehemence, would say, "What kind of God would sacrifice an innocent little girl to teach us 'spiritual lessons'!?"[333]

We should not overlook the importance of grasping truths in the right order. So it is important to know that nothing that happens, not even the most horrendous events, are outside God's wise purposes and control, and that he promises to overrule and weave even the worst circumstances into a plan for ultimate good. This important teaching might be important to bring soon to the attention of a person who has had a business failure through his own greed. But it should not be the first thing to say to bereaved parents of a dead infant, even if ultimately, in order to be healed, they need to circle around and use it on their hearts.

We have seen that, when it comes to suffering, there are diversities of shape, temperaments, and pathways. There are multiple truths that the Bible teaches about suffering, and these different truths need to be applied in a different order depending on circumstance, stage, and temperament. But there is also a diversity of expression of those truths and ideas. When my wife, Kathy, has had her darkest periods, she finds that other than the Bible, nothing can speak to her heart better than the pastoral letters of eighteenth-century ex–slave trader and hymn writer John Newton. His prose is stately and somewhat archaic, and many people in pain would not be able to read hundreds of pages of his letters, as Kathy has, with deep satisfaction. For example, the principle "God is in control" can sound cold or even threatening. But when Kathy or I come across John Newton's aphorism "Everything is needful that he sends; nothing can be needful that he withholds"—we are both challenged and comforted. Often the expression that helps us in dark times is a particular poem, or story, or quote, or Bible verse, or song or argument, or hymn. A line or two becomes "radioactive" and we meditate on it and find it brings illumination, comfort, assurance, and healing, shrinking the tumors of anger and despair.

"When I walk through the valley of the shadow of death, I will fear no evil, for thou art with me" (Ps 23:4). As it turns out, there is more than one path in that valley. And the Lord, the perfect Guide, will help you find the best way through.

Life Story: Surrender Does Not Mean Defeat

by Gloria

Most of my life has been without tumultuous events. Growing up in a Christian family, I learned my first prayer from my maternal grandmother. By God's grace, I was called to Christ at age sixteen, and I was baptized the same year. I have been blessed with a fine education, a consistent career, opportunities to travel the world, and good health.

At age sixty-seven, I planned to retire in August 2013. My goal was to enjoy many spiritual activities that I couldn't while working. However, my retirement plans did not include the lung cancer found in a CT scan. Further tests confirmed tumors in both lungs, and metastases in my brain and lymph nodes. My final diagnosis is gene mutation lung cancer for nonsmokers. I was scheduled for chemotherapy with no expectation of cure or eradication.

Where has God been during this dark episode? First, He was with me in the chance detection of cancer, since I had no symptoms. Second, He has strengthened my faith in His plans for me without fear. Lung cancer is a silent invader. It attacks without warning through physical damage, but also in the fear of an unexpected shortening of life. But Jesus, the Healing Shepherd, has granted me a quiet peace through His gracious love.

Throughout, I have clung to the prayer my grandmother taught me: "Thank you, Heavenly Father, for food and drink, for peace and joy. Thy will be done." I had no need to ask "why me?" and "why now?" I prayed not for the miracle of healing but to keep my faith in Jesus as sovereign Lord. I also submitted to His power not only to grant miraculous recovery from illness, but as the Son of God to give life—eternal life. I knew that Jesus would carry me through the valleys I was about to enter.

Since the initial chemotherapy led to a total shrinkage of brain tumors early on, I began to yearn for the same result in my lungs. But after nine months of additional treatment, there is no sign of shrinkage in the tumors in my lungs. Containment is now the strategy. Waiting for the results of a CT scan every three months will become my new normal.

However, instead of seeing the tumor stability as good news, I began to feel defeated and blamed myself for not requesting a more aggressive treatment. I became discouraged and could not feel Jesus' peace in my daily quiet time. What I experienced was not physical pain but misery in the soul, which was totally self-inflicted. But, once again, God reached out to me with an invitation from Proverbs 3:5: "Trust in the Lord with all your heart, and lean not unto your own understanding." That trust in Jesus required a further total and absolute surrender to His will on a continual basis. Because of God's profound mercy, I began to see my submission in terms of a greater participation with Christ in His suffering on the cross and His absolute submission of self to the Most High. I continue to pray for God's grace to accept and guide my surrendering.

Now I have found freedom in anchoring my days and nights with Jesus' spirit. To live one day at a time without fretting over tomorrow frees me and soothes my suffering. With renewed trust in Jesus comes renewed love, hope, and faith. My focus turns from my pain to His love. I have discovered a new treasure—the gift of pain is the gift of God Himself. In the end, He alone is truly my delight and comfort. I have learned the meaning of Psalm 119:71: "It was good for me to be afflicted so that I might learn your decrees."

Psalm 27:4 will now guide my journey till the end. "One thing I ask of my Lord, this is what I seek: that I may dwell in the House of the Lord all the days of my life, to gaze upon the beauty of the Lord, and to seek Him in His temple."

PART THREE

Walking with God in the Furnace

ELEVEN

Walking

When through fiery trials thy pathways shall lie,
My grace, all sufficient, shall be thy supply;
The flame shall not hurt thee; I only design
Thy dross to consume, and thy gold to refine.

John Rippon, "How Firm a Foundation"

We have looked at how to prepare for suffering. It is time to ask: How can we actually, practically, face and get through the suffering that has come upon us?

Most books and resources for sufferers today no longer talk about enduring affliction but instead use a vocabulary drawn from business and psychology to enable people to manage, reduce, and cope with stress, strain, or trauma. Sufferers are counseled to avoid negative thoughts; to buffer themselves with time off, exercise, and supportive relationships; to problem solve; and to "learn to accept things we can't change." But all the focus is on controlling your immediate emotional responses and environment. For centuries, however, Christianity has gone both higher and deeper in order to furnish believers with the resources to face tribulation.

Walking with God in Suffering

A famous hymn speaks of Jesus "treading" through the same griefs and troubles that we walk through.

Crown Him the Son of God, before the worlds began,
And ye who tread where He hath trod, crown Him the Son of Man;
Who every grief hath known that wrings the human breast,
And takes and bears them for His own, that all in Him may rest.[334]

As we have observed, one of the main metaphors that the Bible gives us for facing affliction is *walking*—walking through something difficult, perilous, and potentially fatal. Sometimes it is characterized as walking in darkness. "Even though I walk through the darkest valley, I will fear no evil, for you are with me" (Ps 23:4 NIV; cf. Isa 50:10, 59:9; Lam 3:2). Another image is that of passing through deep waters. "I sink in the miry depths, where there is no foothold. I have come into the deep waters" (Ps 69:2; cf. Ps 69:15; 88:17; 124:4; Job 22:11; Ex 15:19). There is also the hint of walking carefully on slippery and dangerous mountain paths (Ps 73:2). What ties all these metaphors together is the insistence that suffering is something that must be walked through.

The walking metaphor points to the idea of progress. Many ancients saw adversity as merely something to withstand and endure without flinching, or even feeling, until it goes away. Modern Western people see suffering as something like adverse weather, something you avoid or insulate yourself from until it passes by. The unusual balance of the Christian faith is seen in the metaphor of walking—through darkness, swirling waters, or fire. We are not to lose our footing and just let the suffering have its way with us. But we are also not to think we can somehow avoid it or be completely impervious to it either. We are to meet and move through suffering without shock and surprise, without denial of our sorrow and weakness, without resentment or paralyzing fear, yet also without acquiescence or capitulation, without surrender or despair.

Let's consider particularly the metaphor of walking through fire. Fire, of course, destroys and can deliver an agonizing death. It was a very common image for adversity and judgment in Jewish, Greek, and Roman literature.[335] Also in many passages in the Bible, affliction is likened to fire (Ps 66:10; Prov 17:3, 27:21; Zech 13:9; Mal 3:3). It is not surprising, then, that adversity and sorrow in general came to be characterized as being plunged into the fire (Job 18:14–16; Ps 66:12). The most famous of all biblical passages that uses this symbol is Isaiah 43, in which God himself speaks to his people, saying,

> When you pass through the waters, I will be with you; and when you pass through the rivers, they will not sweep over you. When you walk through the fire, you will not be burned; the flames will not set you ablaze. For I am the Lord your God, the Holy One of Israel, your Savior. . . . Do not be afraid, for I am with you (Isa 43:2–3, 5).

Floods and fire are "terms of extreme hardship."[336] And notice that, just as in the famous Psalm 23, there is no promise to believers of exemption from trouble. God does not say, "*If* you go through the fire" and flood and dark valleys but *when* you go. The promise is not that he will remove us from the experience of suffering. No, the promise is that God will be with us, walking beside us in it. Isaiah takes the metaphor one step further and says that, while God's people will experience the heat, it will not "set them ablaze." That seems to mean that while they will be in the heat, the heat will not be in *them*. That is, it won't enter and poison their souls, harden their hearts, or bring them to despair.

1 Peter speaks of suffering, proportionately, more than any other book in the Bible.[337] The apostle Peter has Isaiah 43 in mind when he tells his readers that suffering is like a refiner's fire, like a forge or furnace. Peter is speaking to people who are facing suffering. He says they are now in a period in which they are "suffering grief in all kinds of trials" (v. 6). The Greek word for "trials" is a word that means "an attempt to learn the nature or character of something. A test."[338] "Their . . . faith was being slandered and maligned. Their social status, family relationships, and possibly even their livelihood were threatened."[339] This is the fire of which Peter speaks, but he extends the metaphor and depicts suffering not just as fire but as a forge or furnace, which can obliterate or improve, depending on the object thrust into the fire and the manner in which it is treated. So Peter adds,

> Trials . . . have come so that the proven genuineness of your faith—of greater worth than gold, which perishes even though refined by fire—may result in praise, glory and honor when Jesus Christ is revealed (1 Pet 1:7).

We looked at this image briefly in the Introduction—adversity is like a fire that, rather than destroying you, can refine, strengthen, and beautify you, as a forge does with metal ore. How does it do that? How can it do that?

Gold is a precious metal, and if you put it through fire it may soften or melt but it will not kindle and go to ashes.[340] However, gold can be filled with impurities that indeed can be destroyed. If put through the fire they burn off or rise to the surface to be skimmed off by the goldsmith. In a sense, the fire "tries" to destroy the metal put into the fire but only succeeds in making it more pure and beautiful.

Now Peter likens Christians with saving faith in Jesus Christ to gold filled with impurities. Mixed in with our faith in God are all sorts of competing commitments to comfort, power, pride, pleasure, and self. Our faith is largely abstract and intellectual and not very heartfelt. We may believe cognitively that we are sinners saved by God's grace, but our hearts actually function on the premise that we are doing well because we are more decent or open-minded or hardworking or loving or sophisticated than others. We have many blemishes in our character. We are too fragile under criticism or too harsh in giving it. We are bad listeners, or ungenerous to people we think foolish, or too impulsive, or too timid and cowardly, or too controlling, or unreliable. But we are largely blind to these things, even though they darken our own lives and harm other people.

Then suffering comes along. Timidity and cowardice, selfishness and self-pity, tendencies toward bitterness and dishonesty—all of these "impurities" of soul are revealed and drawn out by trials and suffering just as a furnace draws the impurities out of unrefined metal ore. Finally we can see who we really are. Like fire working on gold, suffering can destroy some things within us and can purify and strengthen other things.

Or not. It depends on our response. Peter urges his readers in various ways not to be shocked by suffering (1 Pet 4:12), not to give up hope. While suffering, they should "commit themselves to their faithful Creator and continue to do good" (1 Pet 4:19), promising that "the God of all grace . . . after you have suffered a little while, will himself restore you and make you strong" (1 Pet 5:10). Peter is saying that the fiery furnace does not automatically make us better. We must recognize, depend on, speak with, and believe in God while in the fire. God himself says in Isaiah 43 that he will be *with* us, walking beside us in the fire. Knowing him personally while in our affliction is the key to becoming stronger rather than weaker in it.

Three in the Furnace

This promise of Isaiah 43:2–3 became literally true in the story of three Jewish exiles in Babylon under the rule of King Nebuchadnezzar, recounted in the third chapter of the book of Daniel.[341] The account tells how the king had made an enormous golden statue and set it up in a public place. The identity of the statue is never specified, but that may have been deliberate. It could then be seen as representing the king himself, or the king's god, or the empire itself, or all three at once. Babylon, like most of the Near East, was a religiously pluralistic society. Every city and region had its own god, and all were free to pay homage to additional gods as well. But Nebuchadnezzar demanded that whenever his musicians struck up their instruments every person bow down to the image, and "whoever does not fall down and worship will immediately be thrown into a fiery furnace" (Dan 3:6). The king's purpose was clear. People were free to serve various gods or not as they chose, but the one object to which all people *had* to pay homage was the power of the state.

The story tells us that the vast majority of people willingly complied, except for three Jewish men who worked in civil service. Their Babylonian names were Shadrach, Meshach, and Abednego. They knew that to obey the king would be a violation of their faith in the God of Israel, who revealed himself as not *a* god but *the* God of the whole world. They refused to bow down at the appointed time, and so word reached the king. They were summoned into his presence and threatened with a swift and painful death if they did not obey.

> And Nebuchadnezzar said to them, "Is it true, Shadrach, Meshach and Abednego, that you do not serve my gods or worship the image of gold I have set up? . . . If you do not worship it, you will be thrown immediately into a blazing furnace. Then what god will be able to rescue you from my hand?" (Dan 3:14–15).

These three men found themselves in the same predicament as millions of people past and present who refused to conform their religious faith and practice to the demands of a totalitarian regime. And in many ways, the three young men also represent all people who suddenly find a painful affliction falling on them unlooked for, through no fault of their own. In response to his order, Nebuchadnezzar received a famously unconditional refusal. The three said to the king:

> "We have no need to answer you in this matter. . . . Our God whom we serve is able to deliver us from the burning fiery furnace, and he will deliver us out of your hand, O king. *But if not,* be it known to you, O king, that we will not serve your gods or worship the golden image that you set up" (Dan 3:17–18 ESV).

There is an almost paradoxical balance of confidence and humility in this response. Their statement combines elements that we would consider antithetical to one another. On the one hand, they express a strong belief that God not only is able to rescue them but actually *will* rescue them (v. 17). But then we are puzzled by their next sentence, beginning "*But if not.*" If they are confident in God, why would they even admit the possibility of not being delivered?

The answer is that their confidence was actually in God, not in their limited understanding of what they thought he would do. They had inner assurance that God would rescue them. However, they were not so arrogant as to be sure they were "reading God right." They knew that God was under no obligation to operate according to their limited wisdom. In other words, their confidence was in God himself, not in some agenda that they wanted God to promote. They trusted in God, and that included trust that he knew better than they what should happen. So they were essentially saying this: "Even if our God does not rescue us—and that is right—we will serve him and not you. We will serve him whether he conforms to our wisdom or not. We do not defy you because we think we are going to live—we defy you because our God *is* God."

I often hear people say, "If God is going to bless us, we must believe fervently without any doubts that God *will* bless us. We must claim our blessing with full assurance that we will get it." But we don't see that here, nor do we see that attitude in other places in the Bible. Think of all the greatest servants, from Abraham to Joseph to David to Jesus himself, who often prayed and did *not* get the answer they sought. If we say, "I *know* you will answer this prayer, God. You *can't not* answer it"— then our confidence is not really in God's wisdom but in our own. As a pastor, I have heard countless people say, "I trusted God, and I prayed so hard for X, but he never gave it to me. He let me down!" But to be more precise, their deepest faith and hope was actually set on an agenda they had devised for their lives, and God was just a means they were deploying to get to that end. At best, they were trusting in God-plus-my-plan-for-my-life. But these three men trusted in God *period*.

The "I just know he will rescue us" kind of approach may seem confident on the surface, but underneath, it is filled with anxiety and insecurity. We are scared that maybe he *won't* answer the prayer for deliverance. But Shadrach, Meshach, and Abednego really believed "all the way down" to God. So they were not nervous at all. They were already spiritually fireproofed. They were ready for deliverance or death— either way, they knew God would be glorified and they would be with him. They knew God would deliver them *from* death or *through* death.

Their greatest joy was to honor God, not to use God to get what they wanted in life. And as a result, they were fearless. Nothing could overthrow them.

Four in the Furnace

When he received this defiant response, Nebuchadnezzar was filled with even greater fury. He had the fire of the furnace execution chamber fueled seven times hotter. He had the three tied up and thrown into the furnace. The flames were so hot that the heat killed the soldiers who cast them in (v. 22). But when the king looked into the fire, what he saw shook him to the roots.

> Then King Nebuchadnezzar leaped to his feet in amazement and asked his advisers, "Weren't there three men that we tied up and threw into the fire?" They replied, "Certainly, O king." He said, "Look! I see four men walking around in the fire, unbound and unharmed, and the fourth looks like a son of the gods" (Dan 3:24–25 NIV).

Instead of hearing cries of agony and seeing three bodies writhing in pain, the king saw *four* figures walking about calmly in the fire, unbound and unharmed. But it was the fourth man who caught his attention. "The fourth looks like a son of the gods." Evidently, even through the smoke and flame, this figure appeared to be a being of enormous power. He looked in some way superhuman, divine. It is obvious that the reason the three men were walking in the fire without catching fire was because of this fourth person walking beside them. And we notice that he does not come out with the other three.

Who was it? In the Old Testament, there is a mysterious figure called simply "the angel of the Lord"—not just *an* angel but *the* angel—and later Nebuchadnezzar actually says that the Lord "sent his angel and rescued them" (v. 28). Who was this? He is not like other angels who appear elsewhere in the Bible. When he appears and speaks in the burning bush to Moses, his words are said to be God's words; his speaking is God speaking (Ex 3:2–6). When the angel appears, he is given worship (Joshua 5:15) in a way that other angels refuse (Rev 19:10). To see this angel was to see God (Judges 13:16–22). The angel is mysterious because he seems to be God in a visual form. And indeed, Christians have understood for centuries who he was. Old Testament scholar Alec Motyer sums it all up well:

> "The Angel is revealed as a merciful 'accommodation' or 'condescension' of God, whereby the Lord can be present among a sinful people when, were he to go with them himself, his presence would consume them. . . . He is that mode of deity whereby the holy God can keep company with sinners. There is only one other in the Bible who is both identical with and yet distinct from the Lord. One who, without abandoning the full essence and prerogatives of deity . . . is able to accommodate himself to the company of sinners . . . Jesus Christ."[342]

And so this text looks backward and forward in powerful ways. The fiery, divine friend is a vivid commentary on Isaiah 43:3, 5—"When you walk through the fire, you will not be burned; the flames shall not set you ablaze. . . . Do not be afraid for I will be with you." Who would have ever expected how concretely God was speaking when he said, "I will be *with* you in the fire?" Do you see the infinite lengths to which he went to be with us? When we remember that Jesus had been living in unimaginable glory and bliss for all eternity, we realize that his entire life was, for him, like walking in a furnace.

At the birth of Jesus Christ, he came to be with us in our finite, weak humanity. All of his life he was under stress, often attacked by people seeking to kill him (Luke 4:29), constantly misunderstood, rejected. But it was supremely at the end of his life, on the cross, when he truly entered our furnace. Like Shadrach, Meschach, and Abednego, he was condemned unjustly to a painful death by a totalitarian regime.

But when it came time for Jesus to enter the furnace of affliction, there was no one to walk through that furnace beside him. He was in it all by himself. No divine personage stood beside him, for he cried out on the cross, "My God, my God, why hast thou forsaken me?" "When the fire of God's wrath burned him to the core and blazed unchecked over him, he was entirely alone."[343] Why? Why would God be with these three Jewish exiles but not his only begotten Son? The answer is that on the cross Jesus was suffering not only with us but *for* us. Shadrach, Meshach, and Abednego were good men, but they were still flawed human beings. David said that if anyone were to keep a record of our sins of hand and heart, no one could stand before God (Ps 130:3). These three did not then deserve the Lord's deliverance because of the perfect purity of their lives. God could walk through the fire with them because he came to earth in Jesus Christ and went through the fire of punishment they and we all deserve. That is why he can forgive and accept those who trust in his mercy. And that is why he can be with us flawed, undeserving people in the fire.

Lessons of the Furnace

What do we learn? If you believe in Jesus and you rest in him, then suffering will relate to your character like fire relates to gold. Think of four things that we want. Do you want to know who you are, your strengths and weaknesses? Do you want to be a compassionate person who skillfully helps people who are hurting? Do you want to have such a profound trust in God that you are fortified against the disappointments of life? Do you want simply to be wise about how life goes? Those are four crucial things to have—but none of them are readily achievable without suffering. There is no way to know who you really are until you are tested. There is no way to really empathize and sympathize with other suffering people unless you have suffered yourself. There is no way to really learn how to trust in God until you are drowning.

But we also learn from this story that God is with us in the fire. That is a metaphor that means he knows what it's like to live through the miseries of this world—he understands. It means he is near, available to be known and depended upon within the hardship. He walks with us, but the real question is—will we walk with *him*? If we have created a false God-of-my-program, then when life falls apart we will simply assume he has abandoned us and we won't seek him.

This is important to consider, because we all know that suffering does not only refine, it can also harden and consume. Plenty of people have been broken by suffering, terribly broken. So what do you have to do in order to grow instead of being destroyed by your suffering? The answer is that you must walk with God. And what is that?

It means we must treat God *as* God and *as there*. Of course that means to speak to him, to pour out your heart to him in prayer. It means to trust him. But preeminently, it means to see with the eyes of your heart how Jesus plunged into the fire for you when he went to the cross. This is what you need to know so you will trust him, stick with him, and thus turn into purer gold in the heat. If you remember with grateful amazement that Jesus was thrown into the ultimate furnace *for* you, you can begin to sense him in your smaller furnaces *with* you.

This means remembering the gospel. He was thrown into the ultimate fire, the fire that we deserve. And that is how we are saved: If we believe in him, then none of that wrath comes to us. What if, however, you believe that God saves only those who live a very good life? If that is your belief when suffering hits, you are going to hate either God or yourself. Either you will say, "I lived a good enough life. I deserve better. God has done me wrong." Or you will say, "Oh, I must have failed to live as I should. I am a loser." Either way, you go into despair. A heart, then, forgetting the gospel, will be torn between anger and guilt.

If you go into the furnace without the gospel, it will not be possible to find God in there. You will be sure he has done terrible wrong or you have and you will feel all alone. Going into the fire without the gospel is the most dangerous thing anyone can do. You will be mad at God, or mad at yourself, or mad at both.

But if you say to yourself when you get thrown into the furnace, "This is my furnace. I am not being punished for my sins, because Jesus was thrown into that ultimate fire for me. And so if he went through that greatest fire steadfastly for me, I can go through this smaller furnace steadfastly for him. And I also know it means that if I trust in him, this furnace will only make me better."

The hymn writer John Rippon gave this classic expression:

When through the deep waters I call thee to go,
The rivers of woe shall not thee overflow;
For I will be with thee, thy troubles to bless,
And sanctify to thee thy deepest distress.

When through fiery trials thy pathways shall lie,
My grace, all sufficient, shall be thy supply;
The flame shall not hurt thee; I only design
Thy dross to consume, and thy gold to refine.

The soul that on Jesus has leaned for repose,
I will not, I will not desert to its foes; ———
That soul, though all hell should endeavor to shake,
I'll never, no never, no never forsake.

Ways to Walk with God

Walking with God through suffering means treating God as God and as there, as present. Walking is something nondramatic, rhythmic—it consists of steady, repeated actions you can keep up in a sustained way for a long time. God did not tell Abraham in Genesis 17:1 to "somersault before me" or even "run before me" because no one can keep such behavior up day in and day out. There are many people who think of spiritual growth as something like high diving. They say, "I am going to give my life to the Lord! I am going to change all these terrible habits, and I am really going to transform! Give me another six months, and I am going to be a new man or new woman!" That is not what a walk is. A walk is day in and day out praying; day in and day out Bible and Psalms reading; day in and day out obeying, talking to Christian friends, and going to corporate worship, committing yourself to and fully participating in the life of a church. It is rhythmic, on and on and on. To walk with God is a metaphor that symbolizes slow and steady progress.

So walking with God through suffering means that, in general, you will not experience some kind of instant deliverance from your questions, your sorrow, your fears. There can be, as we shall see, times in which you receive a surprising, inexplicable "peace that passes understanding." There will be days in which some new insight comes to you like a ray of light in a dark room. There will certainly be progress—that is part of the metaphor of walking—but in general it will be slow and steady progress that comes only if you stick to the regular, daily activities of the walking itself. "The path of the righteous is like the [earliest] morning sun, shining ever brighter till the full light of day" (Prov 4:18).

So what are those regular, daily activities? What specific means do we use so that we maintain fellowship with God and grow stronger rather than weaker during our difficult times? Throughout the Bible, we see many different actions and ways that sufferers face their suffering. We are called to walk, to grieve and weep, to trust and pray, to think, thank, and love, and to hope. For the remainder of this book, we will explore each one of these in its own chapter.

These activities are complementary strategies, none of which can be left out, but some of which may be more important depending on which type of suffering it is, as well as on the person's temperament and other unique circumstances. And so the several strategies or ways of dealing with suffering we will now discuss must not be seen as a set of steps, nor should we think of them as all equally important for every person. As we have said, no two paths through suffering are identical. And yet none of the things the Bible calls sufferers to do can be ignored.

Life Story: Gold

by Mary Jane

I'm sixty-two years old and a four-year-old Christian.

Two weeks ago, I was listening to the AA testimony of a woman whose suffering was beyond scary. I got that overwhelmed feeling, and suddenly was reliving what I felt when I was raped as a ten-year-old. Terror, sickening danger, paralysis. Then the speaker said something that hit my heart and I rushed to write it down because it is my truth. It is the answer.

She said, "Our suffering is our gold," and with that I understood what Jesus was doing with my suffering.

There was a rush of something outside me; powerful, complete, holding me up as I relived the old terror. As if he wanted me to stay right there and not be distracted. I get it—I am not the Lamb. He is, and always has been, for me. Although listening to that testimony feels raw, He holds me safe, even strong. His own suffering is mixed up with his God-size love.

I buried that rape deep inside. I learned how things work: Don't ask for help, it won't come. Keep quiet. You don't deserve rescuing. Be vigilant—life is unsafe.

In college I was in an abusive relationship. The man punished me because I was "guilty" of a great "betrayal"—I was not a virgin. Eventually, I tried suicide. By God's grace, I was found and spent two weeks in the hospital. When I came out, I was raped on the same day by two men—the abusive ex-boyfriend and the medical student intern in that psychiatric ward.

Again, the lesson: Don't expect help. It won't come. You don't deserve rescuing.

The middle part of my life—age twenty-five through fifty-nine—could have these chapters: "Fun," "Fun with Problems," and "Just Problems."

"Fun" was getting married, living in four European capitals, having cute kids, adventures, chasing careers, hobnobbing, learning all those languages.

"Fun with Problems": Without a career to justify me, who was I? I needed a perfect me and a perfect life. Instead, there was pesky depression, loneliness, neediness. People just wouldn't behave! Friends who were not perfect, an inappropriate father-in-law, an angry mother-in-law, "difficult" school administrators who didn't understand.

"Just Problems": Back in the USA, over the next twelve years, our teen and young-adult children faced bullying, addictions, eating disorders, brushes with the law, and finally, brushes with death. Despite therapy, yoga, Zen, and Al-Anon. It was crushing to be confronted with this fact: Not only had I not helped them, but I had been a part of their biggest problems. I learned something from Al-Anon, but it felt humiliating: "I can't help them; God can; and I will let Him."

Indeed, God did help. My atheist son, like a thunderbolt out of a blue sky, became a Christian. This son, whom I so loved, appeared to be a new person; he was asking how he could pray for us—as he deployed to Afghanistan with his special ops rescue unit. Yet we were suffering. We had seen his life dangle by a thread. There was a rawness in our hearts that defied words.

God's mission of salvation is the biggest, loudest thing in the room. He has taken ownership of me. I see how the fierceness of suffering turns into something like God's fierce love. As if he is saying, "You are mine now. Now you are free to love me as deeply as you used to fear. Now you really know what the point is—to love me and serve me in my mission of salvation—with the strength I have now given you." I know in my own heart that Jesus' power is in fact with me wherever I am. All I had to do was turn toward him, to trust him all the way with my suffering, and he does the rest. Our suffering becomes his gold. "Nothing shall hurt you" (Luke 10:19).

So He was always there with me.

God is moving powerfully to strip me of my self-centeredness. It is that refiner's fire Isaiah wrote about. It's fierce. If I can just remember every day to turn to him, entrust my whole life, he will do all the rest.

TWELVE

Weeping

I live to show his power, who once did bring
My joys to weep, and now my griefs to sing.

George Herbert, "Joseph's Coat"

If we understand the more general principles, it is now safe to treat each of the individual ways or strategies that the Bible lays out for walking through suffering. None of them is sufficient in itself, nor should we interpret them as a series of discrete "steps" that can be followed like a recipe. They overlap and inter-penetrate one another. And, depending on causes and temperaments and other factors, they will be followed in different ways.

The Disappearance of Lament

Ronald Rittgers's magisterial book *The Reformation of Suffering* traces how Luther and the German Reformers sought to recover a more biblical approach to suffering. They believed that the medieval church, with its assumption that patience under suffering could merit salvation, had fallen into a new, paganlike stoicism. Lutherans argued forcefully that Jesus bore all our punishment for sin. Therefore we do not need to earn Christ's help and attention but can be assured that he is lovingly present with us in our affliction.

But, Rittgers argues, the Lutheran church nevertheless seemed to follow the medieval church in one respect—by ignoring the significant biblical witness of "lament" as a valid response to troubles and misery. A great number of the psalms are called "Psalms of Lament." They are poignant cries of distress and grief. Often the psalmist is complaining about the actions of others, or is even troubled by his own thoughts and actions. But some of the Psalms are expressions of frustration with God himself.[344] Psalm 44:23 reads "Rouse yourself! Why do you sleep, O Lord?" and Psalm 89:49 says "Lord, where is your steadfast love of old, which by your faithfulness you swore to David?" Of course, the book of Job is filled with cries of lament, as are some of the prophetic utterances of Jeremiah. Jeremiah even likens God to a watercourse that looks permanent but runs dry. "Why is my pain unending and my wound grievous and incurable?" cries the prophet to the Lord. "You are to me like a deceptive brook, like a spring that fails" (Jer 15:18).

Rittgers says that the Lutherans, in their concern that Christians not doubt the love of Christ, minimized the legitimacy of lament. He argues that the early Reformers created a culture in which the expression of doubts or complaints was frowned upon. Christians were taught not to weep or cry but to show God their faith through unflinching, joyful acceptance of his will. Rittgers cites early Lutheran authors who were embarrassed that the book of Job was even in the Bible, since questioning God—as Job did—was a terrible sin. One theologian explained the book's inclusion by saying that God wanted to show us he could still forgive and have mercy on someone with faith as weak as Job's.[345]

This certainly is partly true. Job did not exercise his faith as he should have, and in the final chapter he admits as much, saying to God, "My ears had heard of you but now my eyes have seen you. Therefore I despise myself and repent in dust and ashes" (Job 42:5–6). Nevertheless, the assertion that Job's outbursts, cries, and laments were completely illegitimate does not square with the biblical text.

In the first chapter, for example, when Job first gets all the bad news about the deaths of his children and the loss of his estate, we are told that "Job got up and tore his robe" and then he "fell to the ground" (Job 1:20), but then the author adds, "In all this Job sinned not" (Job 1:22). Here is a man already behaving in a way that many pious Christians would consider at least unseemly or showing a lack of faith. He rips his clothes, falls to the ground, cries out. He does not show any stoical patience. But the biblical text says, "In all this Job sinned not." By the middle of the book, Job is cursing the day he is born and comes very close to charging God with injustice in his angry questions. And yet God's final verdict on Job is surprisingly positive. At the end of the book, God turns to Eliphaz, the first of Job's friends, and says:

> "I am angry with you and your two friends, because you have not spoken the truth about me, as my servant Job has. So now take seven bulls and seven rams and go to my servant Job and sacrifice a burnt offering for yourselves. My servant Job will pray for you, and I will accept his prayer and not deal with you according to your folly. You have not spoken the truth about me, as my servant Job has." So Eliphaz the Temanite, Bildad the Shuhite and Zophar the Naamathite did what the Lord told them; and the Lord accepted Job's prayer (Job 42:7–9).

Job's grief was expressed with powerful emotion and soaring rhetoric. He did not "make nice" with God, praying politely. He was brutally honest about his feelings. And while God did—as we will see later—forcefully call Job to acknowledge his unfathomable wisdom and majesty, nevertheless God ultimately vindicated him.

A Bruised Reed He Will Not Break

It is not right, therefore, for us to simply say to a person in grief and sorrow that they need to pull themselves together. We should be more gentle and patient with them. And that means we should also be gentle and patient with ourselves. We should not assume that if we are trusting in God we won't weep, or feel anger, or feel hopeless.

Isaiah 42 describes the mysterious Suffering Servant who, Isaiah 53 reveals, will have the guilt of our transgressions put upon him so that, by his suffering, our condemnation will be taken away. In Isaiah 42:3, it says about the Servant that "a bruised reed he will not break, and a smoldering wick he will not snuff out until in faithfulness he brings forth justice." The Hebrew word translated as "bruise" does not mean a minor injury. It denotes a deep contusion that destroys a vital internal organ—in other words, a deathblow. If applied to a person, it means an injury that doesn't show on the surface but that is nonetheless fatal. When it refers to a bruised reed, it means a stalk of grain that has been broken at an angle, not into two pieces. But because it has been thus broken, it is never going to produce grain. And yet this servant does what no one else can do. He can heal it so it produces grain again.

Who is this Servant? The Christian church has since its very beginning understood this to be Jesus Christ himself (Acts 8:32–33) and in Matthew 12:20, it is said that Jesus will not break the bruised reed or snuff out the dying candle. It means Jesus Christ the servant is attracted to hopeless cases. He cares for the fragile. He loves people who are beaten and battered and bruised. They may not show it on the outside, but inside they are dying. Jesus sees all the way into the heart and he knows what to do. The Lord binds up the brokenhearted and heals our wounds (Ps 147:3; Isa 61:1).

Let me give you an example. In 1 Kings 18–19, we read about the ministry of Elijah. Elijah is a mighty prophet, a great man of God, but he is cracking under the pressure of his ministry. The people have turned against him and his message. Though he speaks in the name of the Lord, they are not listening. Elijah is a great prophet but a human being can take only so much disappointment, opposition, and difficulty. He is despondent; he is suicidal. He travels out into the wilderness and says to God, "Take away my life. I don't even want to live" (1 Kings 19:4). Then he lies down under a bush and falls into a troubled sleep.

Now here is a despondent man, a bruised man. Here is someone flickering, his candle ready to go out. And he is not handling his suffering and stress all that well. He is not saying, "I'm just rejoicing in the Lord!" No, he wants to die. So God sends him an angel. And do you know the first thing the angel does? The angel cooks him a meal.

An angel touched him and said, "Get up and eat." He looked around, and there by his head was some bread baked over hot coals, and a jar of water. He ate and drank and then lay down again. The angel of the Lord came back a second time and touched him and said, "Get up and eat, for the journey is too much for you." So he got up and ate and drank. Strengthened by that food, he traveled forty days and forty nights until he reached Horeb, the mountain of God (1 Kings 19:4–8).

God sends an angel to this suffering man, and does the angel say, "Repent! How dare you lose hope in me!"? No. Does the angel, on the other hand, say, "Rejoice! I bring good tidings!"? No. Does the angel ask him any probing questions? No. The angel touches him. He does not shake him; he touches him in the way you touch someone in greeting, or in tenderness. And then he cooks him something and speaks encouragement: "You need more strength for the journey." And after letting Elijah sleep some more, he cooks for him again.

If you read the narrative, you know this is not all that Elijah needs. Eventually, God comes to him and challenges him out of despair. God asks him questions, gets him talking, and challenges his interpretation of things, showing him it is not as hopeless as he thinks. And God reveals that he still has a plan for Israel (1 Kings 19:9–17).

But reasoning and explaining are not the first things God does with Elijah. He knows the prophet is also a physical being—he is exhausted, spent. He needs rest and food. He needs touch and gentleness. Later, he talks to him. The balance is striking. Some today conceive of depression as *all* physical, simply a matter of brain chemistry, and so they just need medicine and rest. Others, often Christians, may instead come upon a depressed person and tell him to buck up, to repent and get right with God, to pull himself together and do the right thing. But God here shows us that we are complex creatures—with bodies and souls. To oversimplify treatment would be to break the bruised reed—to put out the smoldering wick. God does not do that. At the right time, a despondent person may need a confrontation, to be challenged. But she also may need a walk by the sea and a great meal.

Isaiah 42 means that Jesus is gentle with the bruised and never mistreats them. Richard Sibbes, the great seventeenth-century British Puritan minister, wrote a classic work called *The Bruised Reed and a Smoking Flax*, and in it he said,

> But to see Christ's mercy to bruised reeds, consider his borrowed names, from the mildest creatures, as Lamb, or Hen (Luke 13:34). Consider that Jesus will heal the brokenhearted (Isaiah 61:1), that at his baptism, the Holy Spirit sat on him in the shape of a dove, to show that he should be a dove-like gentle mediator. Hear his invitation to "Come unto me, all ye who are weary and heavy laden" (Matt 11:28). He is a physician good at all diseases. He died that he might heal our souls with the medicine of his own blood. Never fear to go to God, since we have such a mediator with him, that is not only our friend, but our brother and husband. Let this keep us when we feel ourself bruised. Think. . . . "if Christ be so merciful as to not break me, I will not break myself by despair. . . ."[346]

The point is this—suffering people need to be able to weep and pour out their hearts, and not to immediately be shut down by being told what to do. Nor should we do that to ourselves, if we are grieving. A man who lost three sons at various times in his life wrote about grief in *The View from a Hearse*:

> I was sitting, torn by grief. Someone came and talked to me of God's dealings, of why it happened, of hope beyond the grave. He talked constantly, he said things I knew were true.
>
> I was unmoved, except to wish he'd go away. He finally did.
>
> Another came and sat beside me. He didn't talk. He didn't ask leading questions. He just sat beside me for an hour or more, listened when I said something, answered briefly, prayed simply, left.
>
> I was moved. I was comforted. I hated to see him go.[347]

My younger brother, Billy, was a gay man who had AIDS. My parents were Christians who held to the church's historic teaching that homosexuality is a sin. When Billy took a turn for the worst and was moved into a hospice, my parents, then in their seventies, moved nearly a thousand miles, slept at nights on a pullout couch in a relative's den, and for seven months stayed beside Billy and cared for him fourteen hours a day. They did not confront him about or even bring up their differences. They fed him sips of juice and spoonfuls of yogurt. They served his most basic needs. Eventually, he himself brought up the issues that had divided the family for many years. He was able to do so because my parents had created a climate of care in which such a frank discussion felt safe to have. We talked them through with truth and tears, and many relational and spiritual issues were resolved.

Weeping in the Dark

There is seldom a place provided for lamentation in the church, and down to the present day, many do not give sufferers the freedom to weep and cry out, "Where are you, Lord? Why are you not helping me?" John Feinberg felt the sting of being told—directly and indirectly—that he shouldn't grieve *too* much, that he needed to quickly get on to "rejoicing in tribulations." But Feinberg felt dead inside; he wanted to do that but could not. Reading and praying the Psalms of lament back to God would have been good counsel, but no one offered it to him.

Psalm 88 is a lamentation Psalm, but even within the category of the Psalter's "sad songs," it stands out. Most Psalms of lament end on a note of praise, or at least some positive expectation. But this one and one other, Psalm 39, are famous for ending without any note of hope at all. Old Testament scholar Derek Kidner says of Psalm 88, "There is no sadder prayer in the Psalter."[348] The Psalm was composed, according to the title, by Heman the Ezrahite. The last word of the Psalm in Hebrew means "darkness," saying that darkness is *my closest friend*. It is a forceful way of saying bluntly to God—and *you* aren't! Yet when read in light of the whole Bible, the text is a great resource and even encouragement. Heman writes:

Lord, you are the God who saves me;
day and night I cry out to you.
May my prayer come before you;
turn your ear to my cry.
I am overwhelmed with troubles
and my life draws near to death.
I am counted among those who go down to the pit;
I am like one without strength.
I am set apart with the dead,
like the slain who lie in the grave,
whom you remember no more,
who are cut off from your care.
Do you show your wonders to the dead?
Do their spirits rise up and praise you?
Is your love declared in the grave,
your faithfulness in Destruction?
Are your wonders known in the place of darkness,
or your righteous deeds in the land of oblivion?
I cry to you for help, Lord;
in the morning my prayer comes before you.
Why, Lord, do you reject me
and hide your face from me?
From my youth I have suffered and been close to death;
I have borne your terrors and am in despair.
Your wrath has swept over me;
your terrors have destroyed me.
All day long they surround me like a flood;
they have completely engulfed me.
You have taken from me friend and neighbor—
darkness is my closest friend (Psalm 88:1–6; 10–18).

As we read this we learn, first, that believers can stay in darkness for
a long time. Three times in the Psalm the word *darkness* occurs (v. 7, 12,
18). The effect is to say it is possible to pray and pray and endure and
things not really get any better. The Psalm ends without a note of hope,

and so its teaching is that a believer can live right and still remain in darkness. Darkness may symbolize either outside difficult circumstances or an inner spiritual state of pain. That is the very realistic, tough message at the center of this Psalm. Things don't have to quickly work themselves out, nor does it always become clear why this or that happened. One commentator wrote: "Whoever devises from the Scriptures a philosophy in which everything turns out right has to begin by tearing this page out of the volume."[349]

Second, we learn that times of darkness—while they continue—can reveal God's grace in new depths. Heman is angry. He is essentially cross-examining God, saying, "I *want* to praise you. I *want* to declare your love and faithfulness to others." There is no "I'm sure you will bring good out of this, God." Finally, at the end, Heman is virtually saying, "You've never really been there for me." He does not keep control of his temper nor does he speak reverently to God. And yet Derek Kidner says: "The very presence of such prayers in Scripture is a witness to His understanding. He knows how men speak when they are desperate."[350] Kidner's point is this: If we believe that God through the Holy Spirit inspired and assembled the Scriptures for us, then we see that God has not "censored" out prayers like this. God does not say, "Oh! Real believers don't talk like that! I don't want anything like *that* in my Bible." As in the case of Job, this does not mean that Heman's attitude is blameless. Nevertheless, neither at the end of the book of Job nor here do we see God saying that all cries of agony are illegitimate. God understands. Or, put another way, it shows that God remains this man's God not because the man puts on a happy face and controls all his emotions, but because of grace. God is patient and gracious with us—he is present with us in all our mixed motives. Salvation is by grace.

Heman is not praising God—he's weak and falling apart—yet here is his prayer in the Psalter. It's an encouragement to be candid about our inner turmoil, to pour it out and express it honestly.

Third, we learn that it is perhaps when we are still in unrelenting darkness that we have the greatest opportunity to defeat the forces of evil. In the darkness we have a choice that is not really there in better times. We can choose to serve God just because he is God. In the darkest moments we feel we are getting absolutely nothing out of God or out of our relationship to him. But what if *then*—when it does not seem to be paying or benefiting you at all—you continue to obey, pray to, and seek God, as well as continue to do your duties of love to others? If we do that—we are finally learning to love God for himself, and not for his benefits.

And when the darkness lifts or lessens, we will find that our dependence on other things besides God for our happiness has shrunk, and that we have new strength and contentment in God himself. We'll find a new fortitude, unflappability, poise, and peace in the face of difficulty. The coal is becoming diamond. J. R. R. Tolkien describes one of his characters in *The Lord of the Rings,* Sam Gamgee, who has a similar trial of faith and comes through it.

> But even as hope died in Sam, or seemed to die, it was turned to a new strength . . . and he felt through all his limbs a thrill, as if he was turning into some creature of stone and steel that neither despair nor weariness nor endless barren miles could subdue.[351]

That's what can happen to us. As we noted, we know little about Heman, but we still have a hint of what happened in his life. Kidner says:

> If there is hardly a spark of hope in the psalm itself, however, the title supplies it, for this supposedly God-forsaken author seems to have been one of the pioneers of the singing guilds set up by David, to which we owe the Korahite psalms, one of the richest veins in the Psalter. Burdened and despondent as he was, his [life] was far from pointless. If it was a living death, in God's hands it was to bear much fruit.[352]

The Darkness of Jesus

The last thing this Psalm points us to is that our darkness can be relativized by Jesus' darkness. Heman's darkness was used by God—his darkness evidently turned him into a great artist. And so the rejection was not total, as Heman felt it was at the time. It never is. We may feel he has abandoned us, but if we have put our faith in Christ, there is "no condemnation" (Rom 8:1) and so we are wrong. We may feel he has no plan for what is happening, but we are told he is working "all things" out for good (Rom 8:28) and so we are wrong.

But, you may ask, how can I be sure this is true for me? How can I be sure he's present and filled with goodwill toward me, even when I sense nothing but darkness? Here's how.

Psalm 39—the other "hopeless Psalm"—ends with the psalmist saying, "Turn your face from me" (Ps 39:13). But the only person who sought God and truly *did* lose God's face and truly *did* experience total darkness—was Jesus. He really was abandoned by God. At the moment he died, everyone had betrayed, denied, rejected, or forsaken him, even his Father. Total darkness was indeed Jesus' only friend.

> From noon until three in the afternoon darkness came over all the land. About three in the afternoon Jesus cried out in a loud voice, *"Eli, Eli, lama sabachthani?"* (which means "My God, my God, why have you forsaken me?") (Matt 27:45–46).

It was Jesus who truly experienced the ultimate darkness—the cosmic rejection we deserved—so that we can know the Lord will never leave or forsake us (Heb 13:5). Because he was truly abandoned by God, we only *seem* to be or *feel* to be abandoned by him. But we aren't, despite our failures. Amy Carmichael, Irish missionary to India in the early twentieth century and the author of many books, wrote the poem "These Strange Ashes" as a dialogue between a soul and God.

"But these strange ashes, Lord, this nothingness,
This baffling sense of loss?"
Son, was the anguish of my stripping less
Upon the torturing cross?[353]

When Jesus was suffering in Gethsemane, he could have aborted the mission. He could have said, "Why should I go literally to hell for these disciples of mine who don't understand me, won't stand by me, and can't even stay awake with me in my hour of greatest need?" No, he didn't do that. He went into suffering for us. He did not abandon us despite all his own suffering. Do you think he will abandon you now in the midst of yours? Bible commentator Michael Wilcock imagines Jesus is speaking to us through the Psalm:

> It is true that Christ himself came down [into darkness] in this way, and was lifted out again. But here he is concerned to reach back, through his word and through the servants who know his word, to the soul that is stuck in the depths. "This can happen to a believer," he says. "It does not mean you are lost. This can happen to someone who does not deserve it [after all, it happened to me!]. It doesn't mean you have strayed. It can happen at any time, as long as this world lasts; only in the next will such things be done away. And it can happen without your knowing why. There are answers, there is a purpose, and one day you will know."[354]

Because of Jesus—there is always hope, even in the darkest moments of your life.

Grieving and Rejoicing

We should end with a final note on what it means to "rejoice in suffering." This is not the last time we will treat this subject, but it should now be clear that we should not conceive of this biblical exhortation in purely subjective, emotional terms. Rejoicing cannot strictly mean "have happy emotions." Nor can it mean that Christians are to simply keep a stiff upper lip and say defiantly, "I won't let this defeat me!" That is a self-absorbed and self-sufficient response, acting as if you have the strength you need when it will be found only in God. It is unrealistic and even dangerous. Suffering creates inner sorrow, it *does* make you weak. To deny your hurt—to tell yourself you are just fine, thank you—means you will likely pay a price later. You may find yourself blowing up, or breaking down, or falling apart suddenly. Then you will realize you were kidding yourself. You hurt more than you thought you did.

In 1 Peter 1:6–7 Peter says that his readers see God's salvation in Christ and "in this you greatly rejoice," but then adds "though now . . . you have had to suffer grief in all kinds of trials." It is remarkable that both statements are made in the present tense. They *are* rejoicing in their salvation even as they *are*—again, present tense—suffering deep grief, hurt, and sadness. The Greek word here for "suffer" is a form of *lupeo,* which means "severe mental or emotional distress." Significantly, it was used of Jesus in the Garden of Gethsemane, describing how "he began to be sorrowful [*lupeo*] and troubled. Then he said, 'My soul is overwhelmed with sorrow to the point of death'" (Matt 25:37–38). So Peter says many of his readers are in deep trouble and sorrowful—yet at the same time they are rejoicing. Two present tenses.

Notice that Peter does not say, "You used to rejoice in Christ, but now you are in a time of pain and suffering. But don't worry, you will rejoice again." Nor does he say, "It's good to see that during these trials and tribulations, you are not sad or filled with grief, but you are rejoicing in Jesus." Peter does not pit these things against each other. He does not say that we can either rejoice in Christ *or* wail and cry out in pain, but that we can't do both. No, not only can we do both, we *must* do both if we are to grow through our suffering rather than be wrecked by it.[355]

This is a difficult concept for modern Western people, since we think of our feelings as almost holy, sovereign things. We either feel happy or we don't, and, we think, we can't force our feelings. And that is right;

we must not deny or try to create feelings. But we must remember that in the Bible, the "heart" is not identical to emotions. The heart is understood as the place of your deepest commitments, trusts, and hopes. From those commitments flow our emotions, thoughts, and actions. To "rejoice" in God means to dwell on and remind ourselves of who God is, who we are, and what he has done for us. Sometimes our emotions respond and follow when we do this, and sometimes they do not. But therefore we must not define *rejoicing* as something that precludes feelings of grief, or doubt, weakness, and pain. Rejoicing in suffering happens *within* sorrow.

Here is how it works. The grief and sorrow drive you more into God. It is just as when it gets colder outside, the temperature kicks the furnace higher through the thermostat. Similarly, the sorrow and the grief drive you into God and show you the resources you never had. Yes, *feel* the grief. There is a tendency for us to say, "I am afraid of the grief, I am afraid of the sorrow. I don't want to feel that way. I want to rejoice in the Lord." But look at Jesus. He was perfect, right? And yet he goes around crying all the time. He is always weeping, a man of sorrows. Do you know why? Because he is *perfect*. Because when you are not all absorbed in yourself, you can feel the sadness of the world. And therefore, what you actually have is that the joy of the Lord happens inside the sorrow. It doesn't come after the sorrow. It doesn't come after the uncontrollable weeping. The weeping drives you into the joy, it enhances the joy, and then the joy enables you to actually feel your grief without its sinking you. In other words, you are finally emotionally healthy.

D. M. Lloyd-Jones, in a sermon on these verses in 1 Peter, makes the same point. He says that we are not to expect that God will exempt Christians from suffering and inner darkness, nor that he will simply lift us out of the darkness as soon as we pray. Rather than expecting God to remove the sorrow and replace it with happiness, we should look for a "glory"—a taste and conviction and increasing sense of God's presence—that helps us rise above the darkness. He says:

> What we are really saying . . . is that the Christian is not one
> who has become immune to what is happening around him.

We need to emphasize this truth because there are certain people whose whole notion and conception of the Christian life makes the Christian quite unnatural. Grief and sorrow are something to which the Christian is subject . . . and the absence of a feeling of grief . . . is unnatural, goes beyond the New Testament, it savors more of the stoic or psychological states produced by a cult than of Christianity. . . . [The Christian] has something that enables him to rise above these things, but the glory of the Christian life is that you rise above them though you feel them. It is not an absence of feeling. This is an important dividing line.[356]

THIRTEEN

Trusting

"If God were small enough to be understood, he wouldn't be big enough to be worshipped."

—Evelyn Underhill[357]

Having looked at the importance of honest grieving and realistic "lamenting" in handling suffering, it is important to look also at the call to trust God in it nonetheless. Some Christian writers point emphatically to the complaints of Job, the criticisms of Jeremiah, and the Psalms of lamentation as the right way for believers to process their pain. Other writers of a more conservative and traditional temper argue from other passages in the Bible that we must always trust God's unfathomable wisdom and sovereignty. The fact is that both sets of texts are in the Bible and they are both important. We should not interpret one group in such a way that it contradicts or weakens the claims and assertions of the other.

Trusting the Lord in all things is a difficult assignment. Thankfully, the Bible does not help us do that only with commands and directives. It also gives us stories. On this subject, there is none better than the story of Joseph and his brothers in the last chapters of Genesis.

Joseph's Story

Joseph was the eleventh of Jacob's twelve sons. But as the oldest child of Jacob's favorite wife, the deceased Rachel, he was by far his father's favorite. Jacob had made for Joseph an extremely expensive and ornate robe for him to wear (Gen 37:3), and when the brothers saw "that their father loved him more than any of them, they hated him and could not speak a kind word to him" (Gen 37:4). When the biblical account begins, Joseph is already an older teenager and the toxic effects of Jacob's favoritism had begun to show its effects.

Joseph had two vivid dreams, each of which obviously meant that all of his brothers would eventually bow down to and serve him. Now, often dreams make concrete and vivid a desire we have been harboring secretly or subconsciously. Joseph's eager announcement of the dreams shows that he had a growing sense of his own superiority. He was fast becoming a very arrogant young man, a narcissist with unrealistic views of himself, who would eventually have an inability to empathize with and love others. He was headed for the unhappy marriages and broken relationships and all-around miserable life that such people have.

But Joseph was also blind to the toxins in the family system. His dreams only made his brothers more furious at him (Gen 37:11), poisoning their hearts with more bitterness. They craved their father's love but didn't get it. They hated Joseph and competed with one another. The interlude chapter 38, the story of Judah and Tamar, shows the effect all this had on the characters of Jacob's sons. They were becoming callous, selfish, and capable of real cruelty. The future was dim for everyone. A lifetime of fear, jealousy, disappointment, violence, and family breakdown was ahead of them all.

But then a terrible thing happened to Joseph. In fact, a long string of terrible things happened to him. His brothers were tending their father's flocks in a remote place, and Jacob sent Joseph out to them to see how they were doing and bring back word. When Joseph arrived at the location, he found his brothers were gone, but a stranger he met there told him where his brothers were. This new, even more isolated location called Dothan gave his bitter brothers their chance to do away with Joseph without being found out. When he arrived they seized him and threw him into an empty cistern, where they kept him prisoner as they debated what to do with him. While some wanted to kill him, others advised that they sell him for silver to slave traders. And that is what they did. Then they told their father that an animal had attacked and eaten Joseph.

The helpless Joseph was taken in bonds to distant Egypt, where he became a house slave. There he worked diligently with the hope of pleasing his master and improving his lot, but he was falsely accused by a frustrated would-be lover, his master's wife. As a result, he was thrown into prison with no hope of ever emerging.

The narrative through these chapters does not say much directly about Joseph's spiritual life. We know he cried out from the cistern to his brothers for his life (Gen 42:21), and certainly he would have also called to the God of his fathers Abraham, Isaac, and Jacob. He would have asked God to deliver him—but there was just silence. Then, in Egypt, he may have prayed that he could escape his slavery, or at least be permitted to work himself out of it. Not only did that not happen— instead he became a hopeless prisoner in the dungeons of the Pharaoh. So Joseph probably prayed for years and years for help from God—and never received a single answer.

But then the turn. While in prison, Joseph met a man from Pharaoh's court who had been sent there because he fell out of favor with the king. The man, Pharaoh's cup bearer, had a dream that Joseph interpreted correctly with the help of God's Spirit. The man was reinstated in Pharaoh's court but forgot about Joseph until the Pharaoh himself had two puzzling dreams. Then the cup bearer brought Joseph to the palace and there God helped Joseph again. Joseph showed the Pharaoh the meaning of the dreams. They were warnings from God about a coming seven years of famine that would be of unprecedented severity. In addition, Joseph outlined a plan of public policies that would not only prepare and save Egypt from starvation but would also increase Egypt's power and influence throughout that part of the world.

Pharaoh immediately recognized Joseph's brilliance and the divine Spirit that was with him. He promoted Joseph to a high government position, giving him the authority to carry out the program he had outlined. Joseph used his new power to set up a massive and effective government hunger relief program that kept everyone in the country alive during the years of famine. Soon, indeed, people from that entire region of the world began coming to Egypt for food. And so it was that one day, ten tired and dusty Hebrew men appeared at Joseph's door, eager to purchase grain in order to keep their families alive.

They were Joseph's brothers, of course, but when they saw him, they did not recognize him, now grown up and wearing the garments of Egyptian royalty. Joseph, however, recognized them, and he was cut to the heart. Nonetheless, he hid his emotions and decided to also hide his identity from his brothers. Then, over the course of several meetings with them, he tested them by first wining and dining them, and then by threatening and scaring them. Derek Kidner, in his commentary on Genesis, writes: "Just how well-judged was [Joseph's] policy can be seen in the growth of quite new attitudes in the brothers, as the alternating sun and frost broke them open to God."[358]

This comment by Kidner summarizes Joseph's strategy. On the one hand, there was "frost," mild "tastes of retribution." He accuses them of being spies—which they deny—but he keeps one of their number, Simeon, in custody as a guarantee of their sincerity. All of this reminds the brothers poignantly of their former sins. Joseph continually arranges things so that they are forced to relive their past.

Then Joseph makes his final move. He insists that the brothers bring their youngest brother, Benjamin, to Egypt if they are to receive any more food. Benjamin now is their father's favorite, the last child of his wife Rachel. They are loath to ask their father and it nearly kills Jacob to send Benjamin, but they feel they have no choice if they do not wish to starve. They return to Egypt with Benjamin, but Joseph arranges it so that Benjamin appears to have stolen a valuable cup. And he gives the brothers his ultimatum. He tells them that they can go home free if they just let him keep Benjamin for punishment.

In short, he sets things up so that the brothers have every opportunity to do to Benjamin what they had done to Joseph. He gives them the opportunity, once more, to rid themselves of their father's favorite, and sacrifice him in order to secure their own lives and freedom (Gen 44:17). Kidner writes:

"Joseph's strategy . . . now produces its master-stroke. Like the judgment of Solomon, the sudden threat to Benjamin was a thrust to the heart: in a moment the brothers stood revealed . . . all the conditions were present for another betrayal. . . . The response, by its unanimity (13), frankness (16), and constancy (for the offer was repeated v. 17), showed how well the chastening had done its work."[359]

Then one of the brothers, Judah, steps forward. He had taken the lead before in selling Joseph into slavery. But now he makes not simply a plea for mercy but an offer of substitutionary suffering (Gen 44:33–34). He begs the Egyptian lord to take him instead of Benjamin. He offers his life to pay the penalty of the theft, so that Benjamin can go free. He says to the man he doesn't think he knows:

"Now then, please let your servant remain here as my lord's slave in place of the boy, and let the boy return with his brothers. How can I go back to my father if the boy is not with me? No! Do not let me see the misery that would come on my father."

When Joseph hears this, he cannot control himself any longer. Bursting into tears, he says to the stupefied amazement of his brothers, "I am Joseph! . . . I am your brother Joseph, the one you sold into Egypt! And now, do not be distressed and do not be angry with yourselves for selling me here, because it was to save lives that God sent me ahead of you" (Gen 45:3–5). Soon, Joseph is reunited with his entire family, including their father, and they live together in peace and prosperity within the realm of Egypt until both Jacob and Joseph die, old and full of years.

The Hidden God

What does this have to do with how we face disappointment, pain, and suffering? Everything.

Standing where we do, we can look back and ask whether God was really "missing in action" all of those years when he seemed to be absent from Joseph's life. When Joseph prayed for his life in that cistern, did God really not hear him? And all those years when absolutely everything seemed to go wrong for Joseph, was God not there? No, he was there, and he was working. He was hidden, but he was also in complete control.

Some people have counted all the "accidents" and "coincidences" and other things that had to happen in order for Joseph to become a slave in Egypt. Jacob had to decide to send Joseph to see how his sons were doing grazing their sheep (Gen 37:13). Jacob had to believe that his sons were grazing at Shechem (Gen 37:12). If he had known that they were in Dothan (v. 17b), which was farther away and much less populated, he would likely not have sent him. When Joseph comes to Shechem, he had to "accidentally" run into a stranger who knew where his brothers had gone and who was friendly enough to initiate a conversation (v. 15). The stranger says he knew about the brothers' whereabouts only because he had just "happened" to overhear a conversation by men in a field (v. 17a). If Joseph had not met the stranger, or the stranger had not overheard the conversation, Joseph would never had gone to Egypt. It is only because they were in such a remote place that they were able to get away with Joseph's "disposal," and the story of an animal attack in that region was plausible (v. 19–20). The oldest brother, Reuben, was against the mistreatment of Joseph, and he just happened to be away (v. 29) when the traders came by, enabling Judah and the others to sell Joseph into slavery (v. 26–28).

Then there was another string of coincidences that brought Joseph into Pharaoh's court. Joseph had to be sent to the estate of a man who had a wife who fell in love with Joseph. If Joseph had not been falsely accused, he would not have ended up in prison. If the Pharaoh had not become angry at his cup bearer, he may never have ended up in prison either, and the cup bearer would not have met Joseph (Gen 40:1–3).

How many "coincidences" was that? We begin to lose count. But here's what we know: Unless every one of these little events had happened just as they did—and so many of them were bad, terrible things—

Joseph would have never been sent to Egypt. But think how things would have gone if he had not gotten to Egypt. Enormous numbers of people would have died. His own family would have died of starvation. And spiritually, his family would have been a disaster. Joseph would have been corrupted by his pride, the brothers by their anger, and Jacob by his addictive, idolatrous love of his youngest sons.

Now, we have looked at the theology of this before. According to the Bible, God is sovereign and in control, and at the same time, human beings have free will and are responsible for their choices. There it is as a theological proposition, but how much more vivid and powerful it is when seen in an actual story. If the brothers had not betrayed Joseph and sold him into slavery, the family (and Joseph) would not have been saved from disaster and death. It was obviously part of God's plan. God was present at every point, and was working even in the smallest details of the daily lives and schedules and choices of everyone. So this shows that "all things work according to the counsel of his will" (Eph 1:10–11; Rom 8:28).

So was it all right that they did what they did? Not at all. What they did was wrong—no one forced them to do it. And the shame and inner guilt crushed them. They needed a painful process by which they relived their evil behavior and were able to renounce it and get freedom and forgiveness.

How did all this come? It came through suffering. Suffering for the brothers and Jacob, terrible suffering for Joseph too. The terrible years of crushing slavery for Joseph, the terrible years of debilitating guilt for the brothers, and the terrible years of grief and depression for Jacob, were all brought about by God's plan. Yet how else could they have been saved physically and spiritually? He "disciplines us for our good." After the pain, comes a "harvest of righteousness and peace" (Heb 12:10–11).

British shepherds often take sheep and rams, one by one, and throw them into a dipping trough, a huge vat filled with an antiseptic liquid. The shepherd must completely submerge each animal, holding its ears, eyes, and nose under the surface. It is of course horribly frightening for the sheep. And if any of the sheep try to climb out of the trough too soon, the sheepdogs bark and snap and force them back in. But as terrifying an experience as it is for the sheep, without the periodic treatment, they would become the victims of parasites and disease. It is for their good. One Christian writer witnessing this process couldn't help but remember that Jesus is called our Good Shepherd and we are his sheep. She wrote:

> I've had some experiences in my life which have made me feel very sympathetic to those poor rams—I couldn't figure out any reason for the treatment I was getting from the Shepherd I trusted. And he didn't give me a hint of explanation. As I watched the struggling sheep I thought, "If only there were some way to explain! But such knowledge is too wonderful for them—it is high, they cannot attain unto it" (Ps 139:6).[360]

We too have a Good Shepherd who is committed to his sheep, though he often does things to us that frighten us and that we cannot, at the moment, understand.

Trusting the Hidden God

It is perhaps most striking of all to realize that if God had given Joseph the things he was likely asking for in prayer, it would have been terrible for him. And we must realize that it was likely that God essentially said no relentlessly, over and over, to nearly all Joseph's specific requests for a period of about twenty years. Most people I know would have given up and said, "If God is going to shut the door in my face *every time* I pray, year in and year out, then I give up." But if Joseph had given up, everything would have been lost. In the dungeon, Joseph turns to God for help in interpreting the dream. Despite all the years of unanswered prayer, Joseph was still trusting God.

The point is this—God *was* hearing and responding to Joseph's prayers for deliverance, rescue, and salvation, but not in the ways or forms or times Joseph asked for it. During all this time in which God seemed hidden, Joseph trusted God nonetheless. As we saw, in the dungeon, Joseph immediately turned to God for help to interpret the dream. He had an intact relationship with the Lord—he had not turned away from him.

We must do the same thing. Now, we must remember we may be more like Job than Joseph. Joseph eventually got to see what God's plan was. Things came together and he could look back and see God working all along. More of us, however, never get to see that much of God's plan for our lives. We are often like Job, who even at the end of the ordeal never is told what the reader knows, that Job's trial was seen by the heavenly council and became the subject of one of the great literary works of the ages. Most of us are neither like Joseph—who saw many of God's reasons behind his suffering—nor like Job—who saw almost none of them. It is likely we will see some, and perhaps a few more as the years go by. But regardless of how much we are able to discern, like Joseph, we must trust God regardless.

It is interesting to contrast another event that happened in Dothan many years later, when it was no longer a remote spot but a city. The prophet Elisha and his servant were trapped in the city, besieged by Syrian troops. Elisha's servant was very afraid, but the prophet prayed to God that his eyes would be opened, and then he saw "chariots of fire"— God's angelic hosts—surrounding the city, protecting them all. The city was later delivered when the entire Syrian army was struck blind by God (2 Kings 6:8–23).

Now think of these two divine acts of deliverance at Dothan. In the first incident, Joseph cries out to God for deliverance and rescue. But instead, God appears to do nothing at all. In the second incident at Dothan, God answers Elisha's prayer for deliverance with an immediate massive miracle. On the surface, it appears that God ignores Joseph and responds to Elisha. But that is not so. "It would turn out that God had been as watchful in his hiddenness as in any miracle. The two extremes of His methods meet in fact in Dothan, for it was here, where Joseph cried in vain (Genesis 42:21), that Elisha would find himself visibly encircled by God's chariots."[361]

God was just as present and active in the slow answers to Joseph as in the swift answer to Elisha. He was as lovingly involved in the silence of that cistern as he was in the noisy, spectacular answer to Elisha's prayer. And indeed, it could be argued that Joseph's salvation, while less supernatural and dramatic, was greater in depth and breadth and effect. The Joseph story tells us that very often God does not give us exactly what we ask for. Instead he gives us what we would have asked for if we had known everything he knows.

We must never assume that we know enough to mistrust God's ways or be bitter against what he has allowed. We must also never think we have really ruined our lives, or have ruined God's good purposes for us. The brothers surely must have felt, at one point, that they had permanently ruined their standing with God and their father's life and their family. But God worked through it. This is no inducement to sin. The pain and misery that resulted in their lives from this action were very great. Yet God used it redemptively. You cannot destroy his good purposes for us. He is too great, and will weave even great sins into a fabric that makes us into something useful and valuable.

Ultimately, we must trust God's love. After Jacob dies, the brothers fear that Joseph may harbor residual resentment toward them and now take his revenge. Joseph, however, assembled them and said:

> "Don't be afraid. Am I in the place of God? You intended to harm me, but God intended it for good to accomplish what is now being done, the saving of many lives. So then, don't be afraid. I will provide for you and your children." And he reassured them and spoke kindly to them (Gen 50:19–21).

This little speech holds enormous resources for anyone facing confusing dark times and betrayal at the hands of others. First, Joseph assumes that behind everything that happened was the goodness and love of God. Even though what the brothers did was evil and wrong, God purposed to use it for good. This is the Old Testament version of Romans 8:28—"All things work together for good to them who love God." Paul then adds a set of powerful questions and declarations and run-on sentences concluding that nothing "in all creation" can "separate us from the love of God that is in Christ Jesus our Lord" (Rom 8:31–38).

Paul and Joseph are saying that, no matter how bad things get, believers can be assured that God loves them. In verses 38–39, Paul says that he is *absolutely* certain of this. He bursts the limits of language to say that neither death nor life, not heaven or hell, nothing can separate you from the love of God which is in Christ Jesus our Lord. Nothing. All the powers of evil inside of you and all the powers of evil outside of you cannot separate you from the love of God. Once you give yourself to God through Christ, he is yours and you are his. Nothing can ever change that.

Everything Hangs Together

The story of Joseph shows us that everything that happens is part of God's plan, even the little things and the bad things. Let me give you just one personal example of this.

I sometimes ask people at my church in New York City, Redeemer Presbyterian, if they are glad the church exists. They are (thankfully!). Then I point out an interesting string of Joseph-like "coincidences" that brought it all about. Redeemer exists to a great degree because my wife, Kathy, and I were sent to New York City to start this as a new church. Why were we sent? It was because we joined a Presbyterian denomination that encouraged church planting and that sent us out. But why did we join a Presbyterian denomination? We joined it because in the very last semester of my last year at seminary, I had two courses under a particular professor who convinced me to adopt the doctrines and beliefs of Presbyterianism. But why was that professor at the seminary at that time? He was there only because, after a long period of waiting, he was finally able to get his visa as a citizen of Great Britain to come and teach in the United States.

This professor had been hired by my U.S. seminary but had been having a great deal of trouble getting a visa. For various reasons at the time the process was very clogged and there was an enormous backlog of applications. What was it that broke through all the red tape so he could get his visa and come in time to teach me that last semester? I was told that his visa process was facilitated because one of the students at our seminary at the time was able to give the school administration an unusually high-level form of help. The student was the son of the sitting president of the United States at the time. Why was his father president? It was because the former president, Richard Nixon, had to resign as a result of the Watergate scandal. But why did the Watergate scandal even occur? I understand that it was because a night watchman noticed an unlatched door.

What if the security guard had not noticed that door? What if he had simply looked in a different direction? In that case—nothing else in that long string of "coincidences" would have ever occurred. And there would be no Redeemer Presbyterian Church in the city. Do you think all that happened by accident? I don't. If that did not all happen by accident, nothing happens by accident. I like to say to people at Redeemer: If you are glad for this church, then even Watergate happened for you.

Very seldom do we glimpse even a millionth of the ways that God is working all things together for good for those who love God. But he is, and therefore you can be assured he will not abandon you. It is against the background of Joseph's story that this classic pastoral letter by the eighteenth-century Anglican minister and author John Newton to a grieving sister makes great and powerful sense:

> Your sister is much upon my mind. Her illness grieves me: were it in my power I would quickly remove it: the Lord can, and I hope will, when it has answered the end for which he sent it. . . . I wish you may be enabled to leave her, and your-self, and all your concerns, in his hands. He has a sovereign right to do with us as he pleases; and if we consider what we are, surely we shall confess we have no reason to complain: and to those who seek him, his sovereignty is exercised in a way of grace. All shall work together for good; everything is needful that he sends; nothing can be needful that he with-holds. . . .

You have need of patience, and if you ask, the Lord will give it. But there can be no settled peace till our will is in a measure subdued. Hide yourself under the shadow of his wings; rely upon his care and power; look upon him as a physician who has graciously undertaken to heal your soul of the worst of sicknesses, sin. Yield to his prescriptions, and fight against every thought that would represent it as desirable to be permitted to choose for yourself.

When you cannot see your way, be satisfied that he is your leader. When your spirit is overwhelmed within you, he knows your path: he will not leave you to sink. He has appointed seasons of refreshment, and you shall find that he does not forget you. Above all, keep close to the throne of grace. If we seem to get no good by attempting to draw near him, we may be sure we shall get none by keeping away from him.[362]

Newton's statement—"everything is needful [necessary] that he sends, nothing can be needful [necessary] that he withholds"—puts an ocean of biblical theology into a thimble. If the story of Joseph and the whole of the Bible is true, then anything that comes into your life is something that, as painful as it is, you need in some way. And anything you pray for that does not come from him, even if you are sure you cannot live without it, you do not really need.

The Ultimate Joseph

Joseph says to his brothers, as it were, "You tried to destroy me, but God used this cup of evil and suffering given to me to save many lives, including yours. And because I see God's redemptive love behind it all, now God has promoted me to the right hand of the throne of power; I forgive you and use my might to restore and protect you." Joseph's ability to see God's hand behind even the bad things in his life enabled him to forgive. But Joseph, as great as he is, is just a forerunner. Kidner writes:

This biblical realism, to see clearly the two aspects of every event—on the one hand, human mishandling (and the blind work of nature), on the other the perfect will of God . . . was to be supremely exemplified in Gethsemane, where Jesus accepted his betrayal as "the cup which the Father has given me."[363]

Centuries after Joseph, another came who was rejected by his own (John 1:11) and was sold for silver coins (Matt 26:14–16). He was denied and betrayed by his brethren, and was unjustly put into chains and sentenced to death. He too prayed fervently, asking the Father if the cup of suffering and death he was about to experience could pass from him. But when we look at Jesus' prayer, we see that he, like Joseph, says that this is "the *Father's* cup" (John 18:11). The suffering is part of God's good plan. As he says to Pilate, "You would have no power over me if it were not given to you from above" (John 19:11). Jesus finally says to the Father, "Thy will be done" (Matt 27:42). He dies for his enemies, forgiving them as he does, because he knows that the Father's redemptive loving purposes are behind it all. His enemies meant it for evil, but God overruled it and used it for the saving of many lives. Now raised to the right hand of God, he rules history for our sake, watching over us and protecting us.

Imagine you have been an avid follower of Jesus. You've seen his power to heal and do miracles. You've heard the unsurpassed wisdom of his speech and the quality of his character. You are thrilled by the prospect of his leadership. More and more people are flocking to hear him. There's no one like him. You imagine that he will bring about a golden age for Israel if everyone listens to him and follows his lead.

But then, there you are at the cross with the few of his disciples who have the stomach to watch. And you hear people say, "I've had it with this God. How could he abandon the best man we have ever seen? *I don't see how God could bring any good out of this.*" What would you say? You would likely agree. And yet you are standing there looking at the greatest, most brilliant thing God could ever do for the human race. On the cross, both justice and love are being satisfied—evil, sin, and death are being defeated. You are looking at an absolute beauty, but because you cannot fit it into your own limited understanding, you are in danger of walking away from God.

Don't do it. Do what Jesus did—trust God. Do what Joseph did—trust God even in the dungeon. It takes the entire Bible to help us understand all the reasons that Jesus' death on the cross was not just a failure and a tragedy but was consummate wisdom. It takes a major part of Genesis to help us understand God's purposes in Joseph's tribulations. Sometimes we may wish that God would send us *our* book—a full explanation! But even though we cannot know all the particular reasons for our crosses, we can look at *the* cross and know God is working things out. And so you can sing to others:

> *Ye fearful saints, fresh courage take;*
> *The clouds ye so much dread*
> *Are big with mercy and shall break*
> *In blessings on your head.*

Again and again in the Bible, God shows that he is going to get his salvation done through weakness, not strength, because Jesus will triumph through defeat, will win by losing, he will come down in order to go up. In the same way, we get God's saving power in our life only through the weakness of repentance and trust. And, so often, the grace of God grows more through our difficulties than our triumphs.

FOURTEEN

Praying

Though dark be my way, since He is my Guide,
'Tis mine to obey, 'tis His to provide. . . .
By prayer let me wrestle, and He will perform.
With Christ in the vessel I smile at the storm.

—John Newton, "Begone Unbelief," *Olney Hymns*

The Uniqueness of Job

No one can understand what the Bible tells us about suffering without coming to grips with the Old Testament book of Job. It is here that we see writ large that famous saying of Rabbi Abraham Heschel, "God is not nice. God is not an uncle. God is an earthquake."[364] Philosopher Peter Kreeft says, "Job is a mystery. A mystery satisfies something in us, but not our reason. The rationalist is repelled by Job, as Job's three rationalist friends were repelled by Job. But something deeper in us is satisfied by Job, and is nourished. . . . It puts iron in your blood."[365]

No other book in the Bible or, to my mind, in all of ancient literature, faces the questions of evil and suffering with such emotional and dramatic realism yet also with such intellectual and philosophical deftness.[366] Obviously, the main theme is that of innocent suffering—why do so many very good people have a disproportionate number of afflictions and tragedies, while many dishonest, selfish, and greedy people have comfortable lives? The book of Job is uniquely balanced in its treatment of this theme. It treats it neither abstractly nor just viscerally. The problem of evil is examined through one man's vividly described agony. His cries are poignant and provocative. Nevertheless, the long speeches of Job are filled with profound, thoughtful reflection. This perfectly conveys that the problem of horrendous suffering is both a great philosophical *and* a great personal problem. To treat it as only one or the other is inadequate.

Another way the book of Job is unique is in its implicit critique of nearly all the common answers to the problem of evil. When suffering comes upon us, we wonder why it is happening to us. The traditional religious answer to this question is: *You must have done something wrong or bad.* The secular answer to the question is: *There is no good reason. A good God wouldn't allow this—so he doesn't exist or he's cruel.* One of the main messages of the book of Job is that both the religious and the ir-religious, the moralistic and the nihilistic answers are wrong. Both are, in the end, pat answers that can be stated in a sentence or two. But neither the author of Job nor Job himself will go for such easy solutions. Both classic answers are given withering critiques in the book, and that is largely what creates the dramatic tension and makes the book so in-triguing. The religious answer expressed by Job's friends is revealed to be slanderously wrong: Job's difficulties come upon him not despite his goodness but because of it. But the nihilistic view, which Job veers toward at times, is also a grave mistake.

My Servant Job

The first two chapters of Job are in prose, not verse, and they prepare us for the confrontation between Job, his friends, and God himself.

Job was a good and godly man, "blameless and upright" (Job 1:1), meaning that he was beyond reproach. No one could make a charge against him in any area of his life. He was a caring father and husband, deeply devoted to God, just and compassionate in all his dealings, and successful and wealthy on top of it all. He is said to have been "the greatest man" in the East (Job 1:3). Each of his children had their own home, which was highly unusual, and were engaged in constant feasting. It was a sign of their family's prosperity.

But suddenly, this very good man is inexplicably overtaken by a series of disasters in which he loses his wealth, family, and health. Why? The readers are given a view of things that neither Job nor any of his friends ever see. In Job 1:6–8, we are shown a great heavenly council with God and the angels, and with Satan present. The first response of modern readers to this is confusion. What in the world is Satan doing in the heavenly court? Wasn't he cast out of heaven? But the biblical authors are notoriously selective in what they tell us. We have a similar kind of dialogue in Luke 16, Jesus' parable of the rich man and Lazarus. In that story, a man in hell has a dialogue with Abraham, who is in heaven. Why would people in heaven be talking to people from hell?

The best response to this question is to accept the narrator's restrictions. The purpose of the author is to give us enough details to understand the actions within the story. The Bible gives us very little in the way of details about heaven, angels, and the supernatural world, so let's not press the details. It is interesting, however, that in the Job narrative Satan never shows any deference to God—never addressing him as Lord nor bowing or showing any respect. That fits in with what we would expect from other things that Scripture tells us. Nevertheless, if the purpose of the author was to inform us about such things, he would have given us more specifics. Instead of speculating about matters that are not in view, we should just read the story and see the remarkable way this dialogue teaches the "asymmetrical" relationship of God to suffering and evil.

God points to Job as his finest servant. "There is no one like him on earth . . . a man who fears God and shuns evil" (Job 1:8). Satan—and his name means "Accuser"—immediately charges Job with a kind of hypocrisy. He seems to bristle when God calls Job his servant. "Does Job fear God for nothing?" he hisses. "You have blessed the work of his hands, so that his flocks and herds are spread throughout the land. But now stretch out your hand and strike everything he has, and he will surely curse you to your face" (Job 1:9–11). Satan is saying, quite simply, that Job is in his relationship with God merely for the benefits. "He doesn't serve and love *you*," Satan is arguing. "He is only loving himself, serving himself, and using you to do it. You are just an instrument, a means to an end. I'll prove it to you and to this council. Make things unprofitable for him, stop blessing him—and you will see. He'll drop you like a hot iron."

Satan is saying that, for Job, obeying God is just an exercise in self-love and self-salvation. If the earthly benefits of serving God were removed, then Job would be revealed for what he is. But ultimately this is an attack on God. Job, you see, is the best servant God has. If he is indeed a phony, then it means God has completely failed to make any men or women into his loving servants. Satan hates the good, and he hates God. And so his motives are completely evil. He enjoys inflicting pain and he wants to see people suffer. And he knows the heart of love God has for the human race, so he wants to defeat God's purpose to turn them into joy-filled, great and good worshippers of him. He wants to frustrate the great desire of God's heart.

Becoming "Free Lovers" of God

God allows Satan to test Job. Why? I believe it meant that God knew Job already loved him. And yet there was still a need for Job's love to be refined—in a way that would do enormous good down through the ages. The suffering was allowed to bring Job to a level of greatness.

But that means Satan had a point. There is a difference between external religiosity and internal heart love and devotion to God. That gap is to some degree in us all, and it is one of the reasons we don't have the intimacy with God and the peace and joy in him that we should. What is a real servant of God? Well, think of any love relationship. What if you fell in love with someone who seemed to love you back, but then when you had a financial reversal, he or she broke off the relationship? Wouldn't you feel used? Wouldn't you think the person loved the things you could give him rather than loving you for you yourself? It's no different with God. We should love God for himself alone, not for the benefits he brings.

How do you develop a love like that? Let's say you initially fall in love with a person, and, if you are honest, it was partly because of some of the person's "assets"—his or her looks or connections, for instance. But as the relationship progresses, you begin to love the person for himself alone, and then when some of the assets go away, you don't mind. We call that growth in love and character. Now, what if you grew in your love for God like that? What if you could grow in your love for him so that he became increasingly satisfying in himself to you? That would mean that circumstances wouldn't rattle you as much, since you had God and his love enriching and nourishing you regardless of the circumstances of life.

How can you get there—how can you move from loving God in a mercenary way toward loving God himself? I'm afraid the primary way is to have hardship come into your life. Suffering first helps you assess yourself and see the mercenary nature of your love for God. When your most cherished things are taken from you, you may be tempted to angrily reject him. But then suffering gives you an opportunity. Instead of giving up on God and moving away from him you could adjust and focus on him in a way you had never done before. C. S. Lewis, in his satirical work *The Screwtape Letters,* depicts a senior devil writing advice to a junior devil still out on the tempting field. He tells him that Jesus—called the Enemy—uses difficulties and hardships to turn believers from mercenary employees into people who serve him out of love:

> The Enemy allows . . . disappointment to occur on the threshold of every human endeavor. It occurs when the boy who has been enchanted in the nursery by stories from the Odyssey buckles down to really learning Greek. It occurs when lovers have got married and begin the real task of learning to live together. In every department of life it marks the transition from dreaming aspiration to laborious doing. The Enemy takes this risk because He has a curious fantasy of making all these disgusting little human vermin into what He calls His "free" lovers and servants—"sons" is the word He uses, with His inveterate love of degrading the whole spiritual world by unnatural liaisons with the two-legged animals. Desiring their freedom, He therefore refuses to carry them, by

their mere affections and habits, to any of the goals which He sets before them: He leaves them to "do it on their own." And there lies our opportunity. But also, remember, there lies our danger. If once they get through this initial dryness successfully, they become much less dependent on emotion and therefore much harder to tempt.

God knew that Satan was ultimately wrong about Job. But he also knew that Satan was penultimately right. Job was not fully the servant he should be, and could be, and God was going to enable him to attain that kind of greatness the only way it can be attained—through adversity and pain. Job would become more fully someone who serves God for nothing and loves God for himself alone. And so God willed to show the hosts of heaven as well as all the hundreds of millions of readers of the book of Job that he *can* make human beings into loving servants.

God and Evil

So God gives Satan permission to bring pain and suffering into Job's life. In chapter one, he says that Satan can take away Job's things but not touch his body (Job 1:12), while in the second chapter, he allows Satan to send Job painful diseases but not to take his life (Job 2:6). Modern readers cringe at God's granting these to Satan, but, again, we must not miss the main point of this narrative action. It conveys vividly the asymmetrical relationship of God to evil. There is profound philosophy here. In the book of Job, we do not have a dualistic view of the world, in which there are two equal and opposite forces of good and evil. In that view, life is truly a battlefield and a "crap shoot" because there is no single force in charge. History is just a struggle between equally balanced forces of good and evil. There is no being powerful enough to carry out a coherent plan for history. The Bible shows us no such world. God is completely in charge. He has total control over Satan. Satan can go so far, and no further. God is clearly sovereign.

But on the other hand, the book of Job does not depict God himself inflicting all these things on Job. This is a brilliant way to get across the truth that, while nothing happens outside of God's plan, God does not will evil things like he wills the good. God is not out of control of history, yet he does not enjoy seeing people suffer. Evil and suffering are not God's original intent for the world, and therefore only a temporary condition until its renewal.

The first disasters that come upon Job are the loss of his wealth and of his children. Job's response is to express great grief but nonetheless to bow and worship, saying famously, "The Lord gave and the Lord has taken away; may the name of the Lord be praised" (Job 1:21). Job's response is emotionally authentic. Job got up and tore his robe . . . and fell to the ground—he is not stoic. He shows proper gratitude ("the Lord gave") and appropriate deference ("the Lord has taken away"). And so, we might say, round 1 goes to Job. Satan loses.

But when Job loses his health as well, he cannot maintain that composure. Now Job loses his poise. In 3:23, he blames God for his troubles though he does not "curse God and die" as Job's wife counsels in 2:9. He does not turn away from God or contemplate suicide, but he also struggles enormously with what feels like grave injustice. A life of goodness can make affliction even harder for a person to take, since it makes it all seem so completely senseless and unfair.

The Speeches of Job and His Friends

The middle chapters of the book of Job consist of three long cycles of speeches by Job's friends—Eliphaz, Bildad, and Zophar—who come to "comfort" him. But their counsel to him wounds deeply. Chapter 4, a speech of Eliphaz, is a sample of their basic approach. "Consider now," he says, "who, being innocent, has ever perished? Where were the upright ever destroyed? As I have observed, those who plow evil and those who sow trouble reap it" (Job 4:7–9). The message of Job's friends is clear. Job wouldn't be suffering like this unless he had failed to pray, trust, and obey God in some way. God would never be so unjust as to let all this happen unless Job had done something to deserve it. So if Job wants to be restored, he simply needs to confess all his known sins and get his life straight.

Eliphaz's speech is uncomfortably close to conventional evangelical piety. He says many things that are, in the abstract, true biblical propositions. There *is* a moral order to the universe. It *is* true that bad behavior can lead to painful consequences, sooner or later. We *should* trust God and not always assume we are in the right. And if we come into times of trouble, we certainly should humble ourselves before God and examine ourselves. As we have noted before, we might be in the position of a David or a Jonah. Maybe God is trying to wake us up. Eliphaz says to Job in 5:17, "Blessed is the man that God corrects; do not despise the discipline of the Almighty." That again is true. But, as Old Testament commentator Frances I. Anderson says about these speeches by Job's friends, "True words can be thin medicine for a man in the depths."[367]

Even though Job's friends can piece together strings of technically true statements, their pastoral mistakes stem from an inadequate grasp of the grace of God. They have a moralistic theology. Eliphaz says, "Hardship does not spring from the soil, nor does trouble sprout from the ground" (Job 5:6). He means that suffering doesn't happen naturally—it only happens if you live wrongly and bring it on yourself. But here he shows an ignorance of the teaching of Genesis 3:16, where God says that, because of sin, thistles and thorns *will* come up out of the ground—now for everyone. In other words, the world is broken by sin, and bad things do happen to people regardless of how well they live. Job's friends therefore have a view of God that is very domesticated. There is never a mystery—if life goes well, it is because you are living rightly. If life does not go well, it must be your fault.

But Anderson shows that this puts God on a leash, as it were. "To bring God under obligation to a [human] morality . . . is a threat to His sovereignty."[368] In other words, a moralistic person like Eliphaz believes God can be managed with morality. His advice to Job is: Push the right buttons, confess all known sin, straighten up and fly right, and everything will be good again. Guaranteed.

Job does not take his friends' tone-deaf cruelty lying down. His response in chapter 6 is spine-tingling in its emotional realism. He knows his friends' domesticated view of God is wrong, yet neither will he simply curse and reject God as unjust. To go in either the traditional religious or irreligious direction would have been the easier ways to go, but he will not take either. As a result, his agony is enormous.

> If only my anguish could be weighed
> and all my misery be placed on the scales!
> It would surely outweigh the sand of the seas—
> no wonder my words have been impetuous.
> The arrows of the Almighty are in me,
> my spirit drinks in their poison;
> God's terrors are marshaled against me (Job 6:2–4).

He so fears that he will speak unworthily of his God that he imagines it might be better to die before he can do so.

> Oh, that I might have my request,
> that God would grant what I hope for,
> that God would be willing to crush me,
> to let loose his hand and cut off my life!
> Then I would still have this consolation—
> my joy in unrelenting pain—
> that I had not denied the words of the Holy One (Job 6:8–10).

But he is also brutally honest with his friends about what he thinks of their counsel.

> Anyone who withholds kindness from a friend
> forsakes the fear of the Almighty.
> But my brothers are as undependable as intermittent streams. . . .

> Teach me, and I will be quiet;
> show me where I have been wrong.
> How painful are honest words!

But what do your arguments prove?
Do you mean to correct what I say,
and treat my desperate words as wind?

Relent, do not be unjust;
reconsider, for my integrity is at stake
Is there any wickedness on my lips? (Job 6:14–15, 24–26, 28–29).

Job's sarcastic responses to his friends are classic: "Miserable comforters are you all!" (Job 16:2) he says, and "Doubtless you are the only people who matter, and wisdom will die with you!" (Job 12:2).

And so, for many chapters, Job and his three friends engage in a heated, extensive dialogue and debate about the meaning of Job's suffering. In Job's speeches, he not only debates with his friends but also cries out to God, asking the perennial questions of sufferers—Why this? and Why me? Eventually another figure appears, a younger man named Elihu, who criticizes both Job and the other friends (Job 32–38). Dramatic interest builds as it becomes clear that neither Job nor his friends seem to be "winning" or seeing the ways of God clearly. Many of the friends' speeches are extremely eloquent—but Job's speeches are often the same. Who is right? Who will win? And what does God think?

Both the prologue and middle chapters of the book of Job reveal to the reader that Job's sufferings are not punitive. They are not retribution for Job's personal sin. But they also are not corrective. They are not designed to wake Job up to a particular mistaken path, or to bring him back to faith from a wandering path. Francis Anderson says that slowly but surely it emerges that the purpose of Job's suffering is "enlarged life with God." This is the only other possible reason for it, once Job's devout life eliminates the other possibilities. Anderson writes:

> If there is a grain of truth in Eliphaz's teaching about "the [correction] of the Almighty" (5:17), it is not in the negative sense of training so a person is restrained from potential sin. Job had long since attained this. . . . The readers know what

Job does not know, namely that *Job's highest wisdom is to love God for Himself alone*. Hence Eliphaz's words, far from being a comfort, are a trap. The violence with which Job rejects them shows his recognition of the danger.[369]

Anderson means that if Job agreed with his friends that this was punishment or correction for some specific sin, he would have missed the real purpose and benefit of what he was going through. He was being called to live on a new plane. Job shows that he has an inkling of this. Through all the speeches and prayers, Job repeatedly states his desire to meet God and hear from him directly. At the end of the book, his desire is granted, but not in the way he expected. When God actually does appear to speak to Job in the final chapters of the book, there are four great shocks and surprises.

The Lord Appears—and Job Lives

The first surprise is that God does indeed show up, taking a terrible form—and yet he does not destroy Job. At first, the harsh words lead us to think God is about to judge Job severely. God thunders:

> Who is this that obscures my plans
> with words without knowledge?
> Brace yourself like a man;
> I will question you,
> and you shall answer me.
> Where were you when I laid the earth's foundation?
> Tell me, if you understand.
> Who marked off its dimensions? Surely you know!
> Who stretched a measuring line across it?
> On what were its footings set,
> or who laid its cornerstone—
> while the morning stars sang together
> and all the angels shouted for joy? (Job 38:2–7).

But despite this strong, challenging language, God has not come to judge or crush Job but rather to reach out to him in grace. The first indication of this is the sudden appearance of the Hebrew personal name Yahweh (translated into English as "the Lord"), which has been almost completely absent from the book of Job until now. Yahweh is the name God reveals to Moses in the burning bush when he calls him. It is the personal, intimate revelation of his name that God gives to those in a covenantal, love relationship with him. It is *Yahweh* who now speaks to Job.

Also, we are told that Yahweh *answered* Job out of the storm.[370] This phrase, as generic as it looks to us in English, is significant. Many readers, such as George Bernard Shaw, have understood God's speech to Job as a "sneer" and a "jeer."[371] But in Hebrew idiom, to "speak to" someone indicates a one-way communication of an authority to an inferior, while to "answer" or "reply to" expresses a dialogue between two parties. It is striking, then, that when God shows up, he enters into a dialogue—he does not come to simply denounce. In other words, God is inviting Job into a relationship. He even gives Job the final word! (Job 42:1–6) One commentator writes:

> This evidence of condescension and accommodation on the part of God gives the interaction between God and Job a different character than is commonly assumed. God is not the caustic, confrontational deity who seeks to rebuke Job and ridicule him. . . . Instead, God comes in his fullness and brings to Job an overwhelming experience of the reality of God. . . . Thus Job (and the reader) is put in his place—not by a rebuke, nor by a warning against questioning God, but by the gracious advent of God who allows himself to be seen inasmuch as that is humanly possible. As a result, the [appearance of God]—overwhelming as it must be—can only be understood as an act of grace.[372]

Nevertheless, despite the intimacy of the name Yahweh and the mode of address, God appears to Job in a *storm*—literally, a "storm-wind." Ancient people knew nothing more terrifying or destructive than a hurricane-force windstorm. Job's children had been destroyed by one (Job 1:19). Job was afraid that, if God actually did appear to him, "he would crush me with a storm" (Job 9:17) and indeed, when God shows up, he comes in the most fierce, overwhelming, majestic form possible—as the Storm King. Job and the readers of the Old Testament would expect that God in this form would immediately destroy him. But he does not. When God appears on Mt. Sinai, no one could approach or even touch the mountain lest they die. But here God's very presence appears before Job, and he lives.

The paradox, then, should not be missed. God comes both as a gracious, personal God and as an infinite, overwhelming force—at the very same time. He is both at once. How can this be? Only in Jesus Christ do we see how the untamable, infinite God can become a baby and a loving Savior. On the cross we see how both the love and the holiness of God can be fulfilled at once. God is so holy and just Jesus had to die for sins or we could not be forgiven. But he was so filled with love for us he laid down his life willingly. The gospel, then, explains how God can be both the God of love and of fury that Job meets on that dark and stormy day.

The Lord Does Not Answer—and Yet Does

The second surprise is that God's long speeches do not, at first glance, address any of the concerns of Job or his friends at all, even though the text says God "answers" Job. Job expected an *explanation* if God showed up. Job's friends expected a *condemnation* of Job if God showed up. They get neither. Instead, God gives us long poetic discourses about the wonders of the natural world.

Before looking at the speeches themselves, we must stop and weigh the significance of the fact that God gives Job no explanation for what happened to him. He says nothing about Satan or the heavenly council. He gives no reasons why he allowed Satan to bring suffering upon Job. It would not have been hard for God to do this. He could have said something like this: "Job, I know it has been painful. But you must realize that because of all this, you will become great and someday be an inspiration to hundreds of millions of sufferers until the very end of time. No one except my own Son will be better known for patience under affliction." If he had said that, Job might have said, "Oh, that's different. I guess if that is the outcome, it puts things in a different light." But no. God says nothing. Why not? Francis Anderson is again very insightful.

> It is one of the many excellences of the book that Job is brought to contentment without ever knowing all the facts of his case. . . . [T]he test would work only if Job did *not* know what it was for. God thrusts Job into an experience of dereliction to make it possible for Job to enter into a life of naked faith, to learn to love God for himself alone. God does not seem to give this privilege to many people, for they pay a terrible price of suffering for their discoveries. But part of the discovery is to see the suffering itself as one of God's most precious gifts. To withhold the full story from Job, even after the test was over, keeps him walking by faith, not by sight. He does not say in the end, "Now I see it all." He never sees it all. He sees God (Job 42:5). Perhaps it is better if God never tells any of us the whole of our life-story.[373]

The accusation of Satan was that Job did not actually love or serve God—he was loving and serving himself through compliance with God's will. And we have said that this is always partly true of even the best of God's followers. But it is because we don't fully love God just for his own sake that we are subject to such great ups and downs depending on how things go in our lives. We do not find our hearts fully satisfied with God unless other things are also going well, and therefore we are without sufficient roots, blown and beaten by the winds of changing circumstances. But to grow into a true "free lover" of God, who has the depth of joy unknown to the mercenary, conditional religious observer—we must ordinarily go through a stripping. We must feel that to obey God will bring us no benefits at all. It is at *that* point that seeking, praying to, and obeying God begin to change us.

And so the expanded life with God that Job eventually receives can come to him only by God's *not* telling him why he suffered. God would have been cooperating with Job's impulse for self-justification had he given him those reasons. Instead, the experience of suffering leads Job to the place where he loves and trusts him simply because he is God. Job becomes a person of enormous strength and joy, who does not need favorable circumstances in order to stand up straight spiritually. This makes the suffering—or, more accurately, the results of the suffering—a very great gift indeed, and it is doubtful that this level of reliance on the grace of God can ever be gotten any other way. As Anderson says, Job never sees the big picture, he sees only God. But that's what we really need—for all eternity.

And there is another crucial reason for God to not give Job any explanation for his suffering. Satan had charged that Job was a phony, that he lived morally and obeyed God only for the personal benefits. Satan wanted to not only bring pain on Job but to discredit him, to expose him as a fraud. But God allows Satan only enough space to accomplish the very opposite of what Satan had wanted. Modern readers may be upset when they see God giving Satan permission to attack Job, but we should keep in mind that Satan's attack in the end gave Job a name that will live forever, made him one of the most famous men in history. If you knew that 3,000 years later, millions of people would be reading about and discussing your words and deeds, you could consider yourself successful. And in afflicting Satan with suffering, God only created one of the great resources in the history of the world, which has inspired countless sufferers to face their adversity with endurance and patience.

God allows evil just enough space so it will defeat itself. The story of Job is a smaller version of what God is doing in your life and in the history of the world. God has now mapped out a plan for history that includes evil as part of it. This confuses and angers us, but then a book like Job pulls back the veil for just an instant and shows us that God will allow evil only to the degree that it brings about the very opposite of what it intends.

The Lord Is God—and You Are Not

In these final speeches the Lord calls Job to consider the creation of the world (Job 38:4–7) to make the point that human beings have only the most infinitesimal knowledge of all God has put into creation. "Surely you know!" God says ironically (Job 38:5). He depicts the great oceans of the world as just a helpless baby to him, bundled up in clouds by God as a midwife wraps a newborn in swaddling clothes! (v. 8–9) Next, God goes out to the edges of the world—to the sunrise and sunset (v. 12–15); to the depths of the earth, to the uttermost foundations of stone and sea (v. 16–18); and to the heights above the earth, to the storehouses of snow, hail, rain, and lightning (v. 19–30), and even to the constellations and the stars (v. 31–38). God has created and knows all about them. Does Job?

After looking at the physical world, God calls Job now to consider the lion (v. 39–40), raven (v. 41), mountain goats and birthing deer (39:1–4), the wild ass (v. 5–8) and ox (v. 9–12,) the ostrich (v. 13–18), the horse (v. 19–25,), and the hawk and falcon (v. 26–30). God does not draw moral lessons from the animals, as many religious authors over the years have done. There is no "be like the deer, who . . ." The animals are God's works of art, to be loved and enjoyed for their own sakes, and for what they show us about the wisdom, joy, power, and beauty of the Artist himself.

The catalogue of natural wonders is staggering. The point is simple: We are not God. His knowledge and power are infinitely beyond ours. This first speech ends in Job 40:2 with the Lord's question: "Will the one who contends with the Almighty correct him? Let him who accuses God answer him." A seven-year-old cannot question the mathematical calculations of a world-class physicist. Yet we question how God is running the world. Does that make sense?

In God's second speech (Job 40:6–41:34), God makes this argument directly. In Israelite society, the judge not only gave a verdict but enforced it. When a king sat as an adjudicator and found a plaintiff guiltless, he then proceeded to restore the man's place in society, putting things to rights. After telling Job in Job 40:8 that he has essentially put himself in the seat of Judge of the World, in order to justify himself, he then forcibly argues in v. 9–14:

> "Do you have an arm like God's, and can your voice thunder like his? Then . . . unleash the fury of your wrath . . . crush the wicked where they stand. Bury them all in the dust together; shroud their faces in the grave. Then I myself will admit to you that your own right hand can save you."

Now we see what God had been driving at as he pointed out the wonders of the created order. Since Job does not have the power to be judge, he does not have the right. Job says that he can run the universe better than God—but that is simply a fiction. Job is being told to drop his claim that he can do so. Anderson says that Job is being called to "hand the whole matter over completely to God more trustingly, less fretfully. And do it without insisting that God should first answer all his questions."[374]

This is the way of wisdom—to willingly, not begrudgingly, admit that God alone is God. The alternative is to become evil yourself. Anderson notes:

> Here, if we have rightly found the heart of the theology of the whole book, is a very great depth. There is a rebuke in it for any person who, by complaining about particular events in his life, implies that he could propose to God better ways of running the universe than those God currently uses. Men are eager to use force to combat evil and in their impatience they wish God would do the same more often. But by such destructive acts men do and become evil. [If Job were to do what is described in 40:8–14, he] would not only usurp the role of God, he would become another Satan. Only God can destroy creatively. Only God can transmute evil into good.[375]

Few people have expressed this idea better than Elisabeth Elliot, who, thinking back over her life, the deaths of two of her husbands, and countless inexplicable tragedies and troubles, reflected on the end of Job and wrote this:

> God is God. If He is God, He is worthy of my worship and my service. I will find rest nowhere but in His will, and that will is infinitely, immeasurably, unspeakably beyond my largest notions of what He is up to.[376]

Job Is in the Right—and You Are in the Wrong

Finally, there is the fourth surprise. We said that Job expected an explanation from God, but his friends expected a *condemnation* of Job as a sinner. Instead, when God is completely finished with his speeches, he turns to Eliphaz, Bildad, and Zophar, telling them that they and their legalistic, self-justifying, retribution theology has been in the wrong, and that Job "my servant" (!) has been in the right in his insistence that he is an innocent sufferer (Job 42:7–9). God then says that Job must pray for them if they are to escape divine punishment.

This part of the story leads many modern readers to wonder aloud. "But why would God be so affirming of Job? Job cursed the day he was born, challenged God's wisdom, cried out and complained bitterly, expressed deep doubts. It didn't seem that Job was a paragon of steady faith throughout. Why would God vindicate him like that?"

The first reason is that God is gracious and forgiving. But the crucial thing to notice is this: Through it all, Job never stopped praying. Yes, he complained, but he complained to *God*. He doubted, but he doubted to *God*. He screamed and yelled, but he did it in God's presence. No matter how much in agony he was, he continued to address God. He kept seeking him. And in the end, God said Job triumphed. How wonderful that our God sees the grief and anger and questioning, and is still willing to say "you triumphed"—not because it was all fine, not because Job's heart and motives were always right, but because Job's doggedness in seeking the face and presence of God meant that *the suffering did not drive him away from God but toward him.* And that made all the difference. As John Newton said, if we are not getting much out of going to God in prayer, we will certainly get nothing out of staying away.

Now, this is perhaps the single most concrete and practical thing sufferers can learn from the book of Job. The Bible says that God is "near to the brokenhearted" (Ps 34:18). "He upholds all who fall, and lifts up all who are bowed down" (Ps 145:14). Those are universals— God is near and cares about all sufferers. In addition he promises to help groaning Christians with his Spirit (Rom 8:26). And he says to believers in Christ "I will never leave you; I will *never* forsake you" (Heb 13:5). Jesus says that we are his sheep and "no one will snatch them out of my hand" (John 10:28).

All of this means that even if we cannot feel God in our darkest and most dry times, he is still there. And so there is no more basic way to face suffering than this: Like Job, you must seek him, go to him. Pray even if you are dry. Read the Scriptures even if it is an agony. Eventually, you will sense him again—the darkness won't last forever. The strength you need for suffering comes in the doing of the responsibilities and duties God requires. Shirk no commands of God. Read, pray, study, fellowship, serve, witness, obey. Do all your duties that you physically can and the God of peace will be with you.

There are other examples of this in the Bible. One of the most famous is Psalm 42, where the psalmist addresses himself.

> These things I remember
> as I pour out my soul:
> how I used to go to the house of God
> under the protection of the Mighty One
> with shouts of joy and praise
> among the festive throng.
> Why, my soul, are you downcast?
> Why so disturbed within me?

Put your hope in God,
for I will yet praise him,
my Savior and my God.
My soul is downcast within me;
therefore I will remember you (Psalm 42:4–6).

Psalm 42 is an intense, sustained, and eloquent prayer. He is "pouring out his soul" to God. What does that mean? First, to "pour out your soul" means to get into one's own heart. It is an ancient and healthier version of what is sometimes now called getting in touch with your feelings. It means to look honestly at your doubts, desires, fears, and hopes. But notice that this is not abstract self-examination but, rather, something he does before God. This man is not over in a corner looking at himself, he is exposing his inner being to God. This is crying, longing, reflecting, remembering—all before God. "Pouring out one's soul" means also simply calling to God. As we look through the psalm, we see many honest, direct statements of confusion and frustration. But nevertheless he prays—in a sustained, focused way.

The other thing to notice is that the psalmist is not merely listening to his heart but also talking to it. He is addressing himself when he says, "O my soul." This is something all people in the midst of suffering and trials must remember. Yes, we must listen to our hearts. We must learn what we can about ourselves by an honest look at our feelings. But we must not only listen to our hearts, we should also talk to them. We should listen for the premises of the heart's reasoning but we should challenge those premises where they are wrong, and they often are.

We may hear our heart say, "It's hopeless!" but we should argue back. We should say, "Well, that depends on what you were hoping *in.* Was that the right thing to put so much hope in?" Notice how the psalmist analyzes his own hopes—"*Why* are you so cast down, O my soul?" Notice that he admonishes himself. "Put your hope in God, for I *will* yet praise him." The psalmist is talking to his heart, telling it to go to God, looking to God. D. M. Lloyd-Jones, in a sermon on this text, says that the psalmist is downcast but is taking up an important strategy that you must use when you are discouraged.

The first thing we have to learn is what the Psalmist learned—we must learn to take ourselves in hand. . . . He is talking to himself, he is addressing himself. . . . [It is important to see that this is not the same as] morbidity and introspection. . . . We must talk to ourselves instead of allowing "ourselves" to talk to us. In spiritual depression we allow our self to talk to us instead of talking to our self. Am I being deliberately paradoxical? Far from it. This is the very essence of wisdom in this matter. Have you realized that so much of the unhappiness in your life is due to the fact you are listening to yourself instead of talking to yourself? . . . So this man stands up and says: "Self, listen for a moment. . . ." Then you must go on to remind yourself of who God is, and what God is and what God has done and what God has pledged himself to do. . . . Then end on this great note: defy yourself, and defy other people, and defy the devil and the whole world, and say with the man, "I *shall* yet praise Him . . . for he is my God."[377]

Lloyd-Jones is careful to say this is not forcing your emotions. It is the opposite. It means regularly spending time in prayer and Bible reading even when you are quite dry. John White, who was a Christian psychiatrist, wrote a book called *The Masks of Melancholy*. He said,

Years ago when I was seriously depressed, the thing that saved my sanity was a dry as dust grappling with Hosea's prophecy. I spent weeks, morning by morning, making meticulous notes, checking historical allusions in the text, and slowly I began to sense the ground under my feet growing steadily firmer. I knew without any doubt that healing was springing from my struggle to grasp the meaning of the passage. If sufferers have any ability to concentrate, they should do solid, inductive Bible study rather than devotional reading, because in most depressed people, devotional reading is stopped all together or degenerated into something unhealthy and unhelpful.[378]

White knew that when you are despondent an effort to read the Bible "devotionally"—that is, looking for inspiration and uplift—is not the answer. Instead, he counsels that you should study the Bible for content. Get the truth out of the text. Remind yourself of who God is, and who you are in Christ, and what he has done for you. Simone Weil says that it is important to at least *want* to love God. So do what you can to pray to him and ponder the truth. And wait. Wait like Job waited.

Many people who have done this work—this "dry meditation and prayer"—have especially used the Psalms to great profit. The Psalms are filled with teaching about God, of course, but they are also, in the main, prayers. And they are prayers that cover almost the entire range of human experience. They show us people processing their condition before God—they are "praying" their situation instead of merely thinking about it. We see psalmists praying their tears, their doubts, their fears, their griefs, their hopelessness—as well as their joys and blessings. There is no better place to wait for God than deep inside the Psalter.

"My Servant Job"—Again

Job gives his final reply to God in Job 42:2–6. It is clear from the grammar and the words that this is an act of worship, not a begrudging knuckling under, for Job calls God "wonderful" (v. 3). His opening lines are really an exclamation, almost an outburst: "You can do everything! None of your plans can be frustrated!" Job admits that his demands had not taken into consideration the wonder of who God is (v. 2–3). He also admits that God has plans behind everything that happens, even if those plans are hidden.

To what do we owe this new change of tone, this new sense of discovery? Job says that originally he had heard of God with the ears, but now "my eyes have seen you." This means that the abstract concepts of God's power, majesty, and might had not really gripped his heart. God's appearance and speeches had brought all this home to him, and had shaken him out of his desire for self-justification, his insistence on explanation and public vindication, and out of his belief that he knew better than God what needed to happen. So the change in Job is as much a matter of spiritual experience as deeper theology. It is both, really, not just one or the other.

And finally Job says, "Therefore I despise myself and repent in dust and ashes" (v. 6). This statement is not quite what it appears to be on the surface. The word *myself* is not in the Hebrew—it is an interpretive move by the NIV translators, and many commentators don't think it is the best one. The word *repent* can also mean "retract" and since this has been the point of the whole of God's speeches, it seems that is the best way to read it. Job is not here expressing a general repentance for all his depravity. That would defeat the whole purpose of the book, because that is what Job's friends have been trying to get him to do. Instead, he is doing what he was unwilling to do in Job 40:3–5. He abandons his self-justification project. He retracts his demand that God, because of Job's righteousness, must give him explanation and public vindication. He gives up trying to control God (that is to say, he stops mistrusting God) in any way. He bows before God and lets him be who he is. He serves God for himself alone.

The Other Innocent Sufferer

But we must notice something that is easily missed. Though God's long speeches are filled with strong words reminding Job of his finite humanness—they do not contain any statements about Job's sins. God never says anything about any sins bringing on Job's suffering. And so, though Job never learns the reasons for the tragedy, he also learns something crucial for his peace of mind. "The fact that God does not come forward (as the friends did) with a list of Job's sins was itself proof that this was not needed," writes Anderson.[379] God's appearance to Job in a terrifying storm, yet as *Yahweh,* without any accusations, means that God loves and accepts him, that his unusual suffering is *not* punishment for unusual sin. And so the very lack of condemnation means that Job is right with God. In effect God is saying, "This should be enough for you, Job." And it is.

God's great silence about Job's sin is a tremendous assurance of love. How do *we* get this assurance in the midst of our suffering? How can we be sure that no matter what it looks like to the world, we are loved and accepted by the only eyes that count? How can *we* trust God's grace, not our own righteousness, so we can refrain from being Judge of the World even when things are so confusing?

We don't need a voice out of the storm. Rather, we need to know that Jesus Christ bowed his head into the greatest storm—the storm of divine justice—for us, so we can hear a voice of love from the holy God. He took the condemnation we deserve so God can accept us. For Jesus is the ultimate Job, the only truly innocent sufferer. Jesus "was willing to live the life of Job to its ultimate conclusion. He was willing to die while considered by friend and foe alike to be a fool, a blasphemer, even a criminal—powerless to save himself."[380] As Job was "naked," penniless, and in physical pain (Job 1:21), so Jesus was homeless, stripped naked, and tortured on the cross. While Job was relatively innocent, Jesus was absolutely, perfectly innocent, and while Job felt God abandoning him, Jesus actually experienced the real absence of God, as well as the betrayal of his foolish friends and the loss of family. In the Garden of Gethsemane, Jesus saw that if he obeyed God fully, he'd be absolutely abandoned by God and, essentially, destroyed in hell. No one else has ever faced such a situation. Only Jesus truly "served God for nothing."

Far more than Job, Jesus was assaulted by Satan. But in the greatest reversal of all, Satan only brought about the achievement of God's salvation and grace. Francis Anderson says, "This is the final answer to Job and all the Jobs of humanity. As an innocent sufferer, Job is the companion of God."[381] In other words, when you suffer without relief, when you feel absolutely alone you can know that, because he bore your sin, he will be with you. You can know you are walking the same path Jesus walked, so you are *not* alone—and that path is only taking you to him.

FIFTEEN

Thinking, Thanking, Loving

The Son of God suffered unto the death, not that men might not suffer, but that their sufferings might be like His.

—George Macdonald, *Unspoken Sermons*, First Series[382]

If we were to make a list of the most prominent sufferers of the Bible, Paul would have to be among them. When Paul was called to the ministry, God said of him, "This man is my chosen instrument to proclaim my name to the Gentiles. . . . I will show him how much he must suffer for my name" (Acts 9:15–16). Not long afterward, we hear Paul preaching that it is only "through many tribulations that we may enter the kingdom of God" (Acts 14:22). Six times in his letters, Paul gives us catalogues of his afflictions (Rom 8:35; 1 Cor 4:9–3; 2 Cor 4:8–9; 6:4–5; 11:23–39; 12:10). Put together, they cover an enormous range of physical, emotional, and spiritual hardships, including hunger, imprisonment, and betrayals. Five times he was given the brutalizing punishment of flogging, the "forty lashes minus one" (2 Cor 12:24). Then he goes on with a list:

> Three times I was beaten with rods, once I was pelted with stones, three times I was shipwrecked, I spent a night and a day in the open sea, I have been constantly on the move. I have been in danger from rivers, in danger from bandits, in danger from my fellow Jews, in danger from Gentiles; in danger in the city, in danger in the country, in danger at sea; and

in danger from false believers. I have labored and toiled and have often gone without sleep; I have known hunger and thirst and have often gone without food; I have been cold and naked. Besides everything else, I face daily the pressure of my concern for all the churches. Who is weak, and I do not feel weak? (2 Cor 12:25–29).

The Peace That Passes Understanding

How did Paul handle it all? In 2 Corinthians 1, Paul writes about a recent severe trial. "The troubles we experienced," he said, were a "great pressure, far beyond our ability to endure, so that we despaired of life itself." But "this happened that we might not rely on ourselves but on God, who raises the dead" (2 Cor 1:8–9). In the same chapter, he observes that God "comforts us in all our troubles, so that we can comfort those in any trouble with the comfort we ourselves receive from God" (2 Cor 1:4). That means that if we want to discover how Paul himself faced all his adversity, we need only look at how he comforted others in trials and afflictions within his letters.

One of the places where Paul conveys a comfort to others that he received from God is in Philippians 4.

> Rejoice in the Lord always. I will say it again: Rejoice! Let your gentleness be evident to all. The Lord is near. Do not be anxious about anything, but in everything, by prayer and petition, with thanksgiving, present your requests to God. And the peace of God, which transcends all understanding, will guard your hearts and your minds in Christ Jesus. Finally, brothers, whatever is true, whatever is noble, whatever is right, whatever is pure, whatever is lovely, whatever is admirable—if anything is excellent or praiseworthy—think about such things. Whatever you have learned or received or heard from me, or seen in me—put it into practice. And the God of peace will be with you.

I rejoice greatly in the Lord that at last you have renewed your concern for me. Indeed, you have been concerned, but you had no opportunity to show it. I am not saying this because I am in need, for I have learned to be content whatever the circumstances. I know what it is to be in need, and I know what it is to have plenty. I have learned the secret of being content in any and every situation, whether well fed or hungry, whether living in plenty or in want (Phil 4:4–12).

What is this "peace of God"? There are two things Paul tells us about it. First, it is an inner calm and equilibrium. In verses 11–12 he says, "I have learned how to be content in whatever circumstance; I have learned the secret of being content in every situation," which is to say he is the same in one situation as in another. Realize how strong a claim this is. Remember Paul's circumstances. We all want inner peace, but you and I are trying to get inner peace to face what? Our bills, competition at work, a difficult boss, our big date or a lack of dates. But Paul was facing torture and death. He is in prison even as he writes, and yet he is saying, "I have learned the secret of being able to smile at that."

And look carefully. Does Paul say, "I can smile in the face of torture and death because I am just that kind of guy, I am tough"? No. That would be a peace that was just a natural kind of steely temperament. It would be a talent—and talent is something that you are born with or you aren't. It is like artistic or athletic talent—either you have it or you do not. But Paul does not say that. He says, "I have *learned* this." It means it is not natural to him. And the particular kind of inner peace of which he speaks is not natural to any of the rest of us either. He is saying, "I have learned it, so that I have this equilibrium in any situation."

The second thing Paul tells us is that this peace is not merely an absence—it is a presence. It is not just an absence of fear. It is a sense of being protected. That does not come out as well in the English translation. It says in verse 7, "the peace of God . . . will *guard* your hearts and your minds." The Greek word translated as "guard" means to completely surround and fortify a building or a city to protect it from invasion. If you have an army all around you protecting you, then you can sleep really well—that's the idea. And this is getting at something very important. Today, when you read books or websites on overcoming anxiety and handling fear, they usually talk about *removing* thoughts. They say: Do not think about that; do not think those negative thoughts. Control your thoughts, expel the negative ones. But here we see the peace of God is not the *absence* of negative thoughts, it is the *presence* of God himself. "The God of peace will be with you" (Phil 4:9).

Christian peace does not start with the ousting of negative thinking. If you do that, you may simply be refusing to face how bad things are. That is one way to calm yourself—by refusing to admit the facts. But it will be a short-lived peace! Christian peace doesn't start that way. It is not that you stop facing the facts, but you get a living power that comes into your life and enables you to face those realities, something that lifts you up over and through them.

Many believers have experienced this peace of God. It is not just positive thinking or willpower. It is a sense that no matter what happens, everything will ultimately be all right, even though it may not be at *all* right at the moment. In my experience, people usually break through to this kind of peace only in tragic situations, often in the valley of the shadow of death. Here is a metaphor for it. If you have ever been on a coast in a storm and seen the waves come in and hit the rocks, sometimes the waves are so large that they cover a particular rock, and you think, "That is the end of that rock." But when the waves recede, there it is still. It hasn't budged an inch. A person who feels the "peace that passes understanding" is like that. No matter what is thrown at you, you know it will not make you lose your footing. Paul of course is the classic example. He is beaten; he is stoned; he is flogged; he is shipwrecked; he is betrayed; his enemies are trying to kill him. There is wave after wave, and yet—there he is still. "I have found a way to be completely poised under any and all circumstances," he said. All the waves of life could not break him. And he says it isn't a natural talent of his—you and I can learn this.

That is the character of Christian peace. It is an inner calm and equilibrium but also a sense of God's presence and an almost reason-transcending sense of his protection.

If it is not natural—if it is something you learn—then how does one learn or find this? What are the disciplines by which you can develop this peace? Paul gives a lot of advice in this passage on how you can learn it. That doesn't mean he is giving us "four steps to guaranteed inner peace." The peace of God is not something that can be manipulated by technique. Nevertheless, Paul speaks of three sorts of disciplines in which to engage. Those who do these things more often find God's peace along the way. I will call these disciplines: a kind of thinking, of thanking, and of loving.

The Discipline of Thinking

In Philippians 4:8–9, Paul says, "Brothers, whatever is true, whatever is noble, whatever is right, whatever is pure . . . *think* about such things. . . . And the God of peace will be with you." Now, when we hear terms like "noble" and "right" we might think that Paul is merely recommending high and inspirational thoughts in general. But scholars of Pauline literature tell us that is not the case. He is not referring to general loftiness of mind but rather to the specific teaching of the Bible about God, sin, Christ, salvation, the world, human nature, and God's plans for the world—the plan of salvation. And Paul also uses the word *logizdomai* to describe how we are to think about these things. That is an accounting word, sometimes translated "to reckon" or "to count up."[383] Paul is saying if you want peace, think hard and long about the core doctrines of the Bible.

This is so completely different from what you will find if you walk into any bookstore and go to the section on anxiety, worry, and dealing with stress. Here is what you will never see: None of the books will ever say, "Are you stressed, unhappy, or anxious? Let's start dealing with that by asking the big questions: What is the meaning of life? What are you really here for? What is life all about? Where have you come from, and where are you going? What should human beings spend their time doing?" Never! Contemporary books go right to relaxation techniques and to the work-rest balance. For example, they will say that every so often you should go sit on a beach, look at the surf, and just bracket out worrying and thinking about things. Or they will give you thought-control techniques about dealing with negative thoughts and emotions, guilt thoughts, and so forth.

Why don't contemporary books on stress and anxiety tell you to respond to it by doing deep thinking about life? It is because our Western secular culture is perhaps the first society that operates without any answers to the big questions. If there is no God, we are here essentially by accident, and when we die, we are only remembered for a while. Eventually, in this view, the sun will die and all that has ever been done by human beings will come to nothing. If that is the nature of things, then it is no wonder that secular books for people under stress never ask them to think about questions such as "What are we here for?"[384] Instead, they advise you to not think so hard about everything but to relax and to find experiences that give you pleasure.

Paul is saying Christian peace operates in almost exactly the opposite way. Christian peace comes not from thinking less but from thinking more, and more intensely, about the big issues of life. Paul gives a specific example of this in Romans 8:18, where he uses the same word, *logizdomai,* and speaks directly to sufferers. He says, "I *reckon* that our present sufferings are not worth comparing to the glory that shall be revealed in us." To "reckon" is to count up accurately, not to whistle in the dark. It is not to get peace by jogging or shopping. It means "Think it out! Think about the glory coming until the joy begins to break in on you."

Someone reading this might say, "You are talking about doctrine but what I really need is comfort." But think! Is Jesus really the Son of God? Did he really come to earth, die for you, rise again, and pass through the heavens to the right hand of God? Did he endure infinite suffering for you, so that someday he could take you to himself and wipe away every tear from your eyes? If so, then there is all the comfort in the world. If not—if none of these things are true—then we may be stuck here living for seventy or eighty years until we perish, and the only happiness we will ever know is in this life. And if some trouble or suffering takes that happiness away, you have lost it forever. Either Jesus is on the throne ruling all things for you or this is as good as it gets.

See what Paul is doing? He is saying that if you are a Christian today and you have little or no peace, it may be because you are not thinking. Peace comes from a disciplined thinking out of the implications of what you believe. It comes from an intentional occupation of a vantage point. There is nothing more thrilling than climbing up to some high point on a mountain and then turning around and viewing from there all the terrain you have just traversed. Suddenly, you see the relationships—you see the creek you crossed, the foothills, the town from which you have journeyed. Your high vantage point gives you perspective, clarity, and a sense of beauty. Now this is what Paul is calling us to do. Think big and high. Realize who God is, what he has done, who you are in Christ, where history is going. Put your troubles in perspective by remembering Christ's troubles on your behalf, and all his promises to you, and what he is accomplishing.

Let me put it another way. There is a "stupid peace" and then there is a "smart peace." The stupid peace comes from refusing to think about your overall situation. If you go that way, you can pop a cork, sit under a tree or on the beach, and try not to think about the grand scheme of things. But Paul is saying that if you are a Christian, you can think about the big picture, and as you do, you are going to find peace. And if you are a Christian, and you have no peace at all, it may be that you are simply not thinking.

The early American theologian Jonathan Edwards was a Congregationalist preacher. The earliest extant sermon manuscript we have from him, composed at age eighteen, is entitled "Christian Happiness." Despite the youth of the author, its basic outline is striking. His simple point was that a Christian should be happy, "whatever his outward circumstances are."[385] Then he makes his case in three propositions, which I paraphrase. For Christians:

Their "bad things" will work out for good (Rom 8:28).

Their "good things"—adoption into God's family, justification in his sight, union with him—cannot be taken away (Rom 8:1).

Their best things—life in heaven, new heavens and the new earth, resurrection—are yet to come (Rev 22:1ff).

This sermon is simply an example of one young man doing what Paul is talking about. He is "reckoning," counting it all and adding it up and letting the glory of the gospel salvation sink in. Our bad things will turn out for good, our good things cannot be taken away, and the best is yet to come. "Think about such things" (Phil 4:8).

The Discipline of Thanking

If you first learn the discipline of thinking, then, second, there is the discipline of thanking. In Philippians 4:6, Paul says, "Don't be *anxious*, but make requests to God with *thanksgiving*." Thanksgiving is put over against anxiety. But look carefully—it is a little counterintuitive, isn't it? We would expect Paul to say first you make your requests to God and then, if you get your requests, you thank him for his answers. But that is not what Paul says. He says you thank him *as* you ask, before you know the response to your requests.

Why should I thank God ahead of time, as it were? It doesn't at first make sense. But if we think about it, we can see what Paul is getting at. Paul is essentially calling on us to trust God's sovereign rule of history and of our lives. He is telling us that we will never be content unless, as we make our heartfelt request, we also acknowledge that our lives are in his hands, and that he is wiser than we are. That is what you are doing when you thank him for what*ever* he is going to do with your request. This is of course the essence of those two crucial verses, one in the Old Testament and one in the New. "You meant it for evil, but God meant it for good" (Gen 50:20) and "all things work together for good for those who love God" (Rom 8:28). Romans 8 must not be read in a saccharine way. It does not say that every bad thing has a "silver lining" or that every terrible thing that can happen is somehow "actually a good thing if you learn to look at it properly." No, Paul says in Romans 8:28 that all things—even bad things—will ultimately *together* be overruled by God in such a way that the intended evil will, in the end, only accomplish the opposite of its designs—a greater good and glory than would otherwise have come to pass. Only God now has that eternal perspective and vantage point from which he can see all things working together for our good and for his glory—but eventually we will occupy that place and will see it too.

Now, we have covered this basic biblical teaching in a previous chapter. Because God is sovereign we are to trust him. But here Paul goes one step further. Because God is sovereign we are to thank him—we are to live thankfully because we know he is like this. We are to thank him beforehand, even as we make our requests. We are to thank him for whatever he sends to us, even if we don't understand it.

A vivid example of this for me was when, in my early twenties, I prayed for an entire year about a girl I was dating and wanted to marry, but she wanted out of the relationship. All year I prayed, "Lord, don't let her break up with me." Of course, in hindsight, it was the wrong girl. I actually did what I could to help God with the prayer, because one summer, near the end of the relationship, I got in a location that made it easier to see her. I was saying, "Lord, I am making this as easy as possible for you. I have asked you for this, and I have even taken the geographical distance away." But as I look back, God was saying, "Son, when a child of mine makes a request, I always give that person what he or she would have asked for if they knew everything I know."

Do you believe that? To the degree you believe that, you are going to have peace. And if you don't believe it, you won't have the peace you could otherwise have. Make your requests known with thanksgiving.

The Discipline of Reordering Our Loves

There is thinking, there is thanking, and, third, there is loving. In Philippians 4:8 Paul tells his readers to think first of "whatever is true, noble, right, and pure." These things are more traditional theological virtues that have to do with the mind and the will. But then he moves on and asks them to ponder "whatever is lovely, whatever is admirable—if anything is excellent or praiseworthy—think about such things." By definition, anything that is "lovely" is something that is not merely true but also attractive.[386] Here, I believe Paul is urging his readers not just to order the thoughts of their mind but to engage the affections of the heart. Paul is explaining how to get a spiritual ballast to keep you afloat in rough seas, how to keep your equilibrium in troubles and difficulties. And he says that in those times, it is not enough just to *think* the right things. It is also important to *love* the right things.

Here we must turn to St. Augustine, the great Christian thinker who lived in the third and fourth centuries. He was profoundly aware of *the* problem in Greek philosophy. In fact, Paul is referring to it. The great problem is: how can you live a life of contentment? The Greek word for that was *autarkeia*, and that is the very word Paul uses in verse 11. He says, "I have learned it, I have got the *autarkeia*." It meant to be independent of circumstances. It meant to always have this poise, this power, and not to be upset, devastated, melting down over anything.

The philosophers who worked hard on this—as we have seen in previous chapters—were the Stoics. The Stoics taught that the reason most people are not able to live contented, poised lives is that they love things too much. You should not love success too much, because even if you get it, you will always be anxious. You will never have peace because you will be afraid of losing it. Also, you shouldn't set your heart primarily on your family, because even if you get a good family, you will always be worried about it. You will always be anxious that something will go wrong with them. And if something does go wrong, you will be devastated.

The philosophers said the problem comes from loving things that you are not in control of. If you love something and something happens to it, you are lost. So therefore, they said, don't truly love anything but your own virtue. Why? Because your character is something you can control. You can't keep yourself successful. You can't keep your family alive forever. You can't control anything outside of your own heart. So set your heart only on your own virtue—you can determine to be courageous, have integrity, and be honest. The only thing that should and can make you content is the knowledge that you are being the person you choose to be and want to be. That is under your control, and nothing else is. So only if you make your own inner choices and character your happiness will you know tranquility.

But the Stoics were quite wrong, and particularly in their fundamental premise. It is wrong to think your virtue is under your control. Yes, if you set your heart on career success, you may be bitterly disappointed, but if instead you set your heart on being a noble, self-controlled person who always lives according to your principles, that is every bit as uncertain. You do *not* have control over that. You are a human being. You are frail. You are complex—an intricate combination of mind, will, heart, soul, and body. Your virtue can let you down just as much as anything else can. And if you fail, then—again—you have nothing. You are devastated.

Augustine rejected the Stoics approach as untenable. He argued instead that "only love of the immutable can bring tranquility."[387] The *immutable* is that which cannot change. Your virtue can and will change, as will your career, your family, your fortunes. The reason we don't have peace is we are loving *mutable* things, things that circumstances can take away from us.

But there is one thing that is immutable. It is God, his presence and his love. The only love that won't disappoint you is one that can't change, that can't be lost, that is not based on the ups and downs of life or of how well you live. It is something that not even death can take away from you. God's love is the only thing like that. Not only can your poor performance not block it, but even the worst possible circumstances in this life—sudden death—can only give you more of it! What is so certain and solid that even death can't make the slightest dent in it but only enhance it? The love and presence of God. The beauty of God. The face of God.

That is why Augustine could say this. In his *Confessions*, he says, "[God alone] is the place of peace that cannot be disturbed, and he will not hold himself from your love unless you withhold your love from him."[388]

Now, it is natural to respond to all this with a question. It goes like this: "Wait a minute. You are saying I have to love God. But I love a lot of things: I love material comforts; I love people; I love romance. Are you saying I have to love God and not these things?" No, you must *reorder* your loves. Your problem is not so much that you love your career or family too much, but that you love God too little in proportion to them. C. S. Lewis, following Augustine, writes:

> It is probably impossible to love any human being simply "too much." We may love him too much in proportion to our love for God; but it is the smallness of our love for God, not the greatness of our love for the many, that constitutes the inordinacy.[389]

That is the final way to get the calm, the tranquility, the peace. It is to love *him* supremely.

Relocating Your Glory

In Psalm 3, King David describes a dire situation in which he is surrounded by enemies. Things look so bad that his own people are whispering that God has abandoned him. How does David handle his loss of reputation among the people and the threat of his foes? David writes:

> Lord, how many are my foes!
> How many rise up against me!
> Many are saying of me,
> "God will not deliver him."
> But you, Lord, are a shield around me,
> my glory, the One who lifts my head high.
> I call out to the Lord,
> and he answers me from his holy mountain.
> I lie down and sleep;
> I wake again, because the Lord sustains me.
> I will not fear though tens of thousands
> assail me on every side (Psalm 3:1–6).

How does David get such peace that he can sleep peacefully with enemies massing on his borders? Verse 3 tells us. To lift up the head—to walk with "head held high"—even today is a metaphor for healthy pride, a clear conscience, and confidence. Despite his people's whispering about him, he is not weighed down by it. David says that God "lifts up his head," but how? The verse says, "But you, Lord, are . . . *my glory*." Derek Kidner writes: " 'My glory' is an expression to ponder: it indicates . . . the comparative unimportance of earthly esteem."[390] David realizes that he has tended to let his people's approval and praise be the cause of his self-esteem. He walked with "head held high" because of his acclaim and popularity. Now he asserts the theological truth that *God* is his only glory.

This is enormously important for learning how to process our suffering. When something is taken from us, our suffering is real and valid. But often, inside, we are disproportionately cast down because the suffering is shaking out of our grasp something that we allowed to become more than just a good thing to us. It had become too important spiritually and emotionally. We looked at it as our honor and glory—the reason we could walk with our head up. We may have said to others, "Jesus is my savior. His approval, and his opinion of me, and his service is all that matters." But functionally, we got our self-worth from something else. In suffering, these "something elses" get shaken. In David's case, most of his suffering was perfectly valid. To lose the love of your son and your people, and to be falsely accused, was searing pain. But he also realized that he had let popular opinion and "earthly esteem" become too important to him. He recommitted himself to finding God as his only glory—something that can be done only in prayer, through repentance and adoration. He reasserts that God's friendship and presence with him are the only things that really matter. And as he does this, we see him growing into buoyancy and courage.

It is possible to read verse 3 as a kind of adoration-based repentance. David is saying, "*But you* are a shield around me, O Lord—not any other thing! And *you* are my glory and the lifter of my head—not these others! Not my record nor political power nor even my son's love or my people's acclaim—only you!" That is praise, but it is grounded in repentance—and it is also repentance grounded in praise.

How does God actually become our glory? The only answer is: through a rediscovery of the gospel of free grace. If we hear the accusation in our heart: "God will not save *you;* you are unworthy!" the only answer is that God's salvation is not for the worthy but for the humble— those who admit they are not worthy. This is directly stated in verse 8— "From the Lord comes deliverance (salvation)." This is identical to the famous declaration of Jonah: *"Salvation is of the Lord"* (Jonah 2:9). We do not save ourselves—it is unmerited.

David had an intuitive grasp that he was saved by grace, but we have a far greater assurance than he had. If we read verse 3 in light of the cross, we can see it. In Christ, the Lord became very literally "our shield." A shield protects us by taking the blows that would have fallen upon us and destroyed us. It protects us through *substitution.* Jesus, of course, stood in our place and took the punishment we deserved. We know God won't forsake us, because he forsook Jesus for our sin. We know that in Christ we are "holy and blameless in his sight" (Col. 1:22), despite our spotty record. Christians, then, know that Christ is *literally* our glory and honor before the Father (1 John 2:1–2). If we have that, then we are not overthrown by accusation.

Here, then, is what we must do when we suffer. We should look around our lives to see if our suffering has not been unnecessarily intensified because there are some things that we have set our hearts and hopes upon too much. We must relocate our glory and reorder our loves. Suffering almost always shows you that some things you thought you couldn't live without, you *can* live without if you lean on God. And that brings freedom. This doesn't mean that if we loved God perfectly, we wouldn't suffer. No—because those who love God well do and should love all sorts of other good things in this life too. Jesus loved God perfectly but he was a Man of Sorrows, largely because he loved us so much. We should not take the Stoics' advice that we detach our hearts from things. We must love many things—and when these good things are taken away, it will hurt. And yet, if we cultivate within ourselves a deep rest in God, an existential grasp of his love for us, then we will find that suffering can sting and cause pain, but it can't uproot us, overthrow us. Because suffering can't touch our Main Thing—God, his love and his salvation.

Some years ago, I remember two young men at Redeemer who were actors. They both auditioned for the same role, and it was the biggest one for which they'd ever been considered. Both were professing Christians, but one, I believe, put all his emotional and spiritual hopes into having a successful acting career. He believed in Jesus, but it was clear that he could only enjoy life and feel good about himself if his career was going well. The other man was also a professing Christian, but after some disappointments, he had come to the place where he wanted as his main goal in life to please and honor the God who had saved him. He thought he could do that by being an actor.

They were both turned down—neither got the part. The first man was devastated, going into a time of depression and drug abuse. The other felt terrible at first, and wept. But not long afterward, he was fine, and saying, "I guess I was wrong. Looks like I can please and honor God better in some other career." See the difference? The second man held his acting career as a means to an end; the first man had made acting an end in itself. The circumstances of life couldn't touch the second man's main treasure in life, but it was able to sweep away the first man's treasure, and it was terrible for him. To be loved by God, to be known by God, is the ultimate treasure. And if you make it *your* ultimate treasure, then no "thief can break in and steal" it (Matt 6:19).

The Horrible, Beautiful Process

We have said suffering is like a furnace—like painful, searing heat that creates purity and beauty. And now we can see one of the ways it does this. Suffering puts its fingers on good things that have become too important to us. We must respond to suffering not ordinarily by jettisoning those loved things but by turning to God and loving him more, and by putting our roots down deeper into him. You will never really understand your heart when things are going well. It is only when things go badly that you can see it truly. And that's because it is only when suffering comes that you realize who is the true God and what are the false gods of your lives. Only the true God can go with you through that furnace and out to the other side. The other gods will abandon you in the furnace.

One hymn that expresses this process in a vivid way is one of John

Newton's *Olney Hymns* often entitled "These Inward Trials." In it, Newton speaks of "gourds," a reference to the gourd or plant that gave Jonah so much pleasure in Jonah 4, but which God blasted in order to show Jonah his misplaced priorities. In the hymn, they symbolize things that give us joy and pleasure but which are removed by trials to our grief. The hymn needs no comment—it speaks for itself.

> *I ask'd the Lord, that I might grow*
> *In faith, and love, and ev'ry grace,*
> *Might more of his salvation know,*
> *And seek more earnestly his face.*
> *I hop'd that in some favour'd hour,*
> *At once he'd answer my request:*
> *And by his love's constraining pow'r,*
> *Subdue my sins, and give me rest.*
>
> *Instead of this he made me feel*
> *The hidden evils of my heart;*
> *And let the angry pow'rs of hell*
> *Assault my soul in ev'ry part.*
>
> *Yea more, with his own hand he seem'd*
> *Intent to aggravate my woe;*
> *Cross'd all the fair designs I schem'd,*
> *Blasted my gourds, and laid me low.*
>
> *Lord, why is this, I trembling cry'd,*
> *Wilt thou pursue thy worm to death?*
> *"'Tis in this way," the Lord reply'd,*
> *"I answer pray'r for grace and faith.*
>
> *"These inward trials I employ,*
> *"From self and pride to set thee free;*
> *"And break thy schemes of earthly joy,*
> *"That thou mayst seek thy all in me."*

The Secret of Peace

Let's return to Philippians 4. How can we bring ourselves to love God more? "God" can be just an abstraction, even if you believe in him. How can we feel more love for God? Don't try to work directly on your emotions. That won't work. Instead, let your emotions flow naturally from what you are looking at. Notice what Paul says: The peace of God keeps your hearts and your minds not just in God but *in Christ Jesus* (v. 7). There it is. You can't just go home and try to love God in the abstract. You have to look at Jesus—at who he is and what he has done for you. It is not by gazing at God in general, but at the person and work of Christ in particular, that you will come to love the immutable and find tranquility. Look at what Jesus did for you—that is how to find God irresistibly beautiful.

There is a place in Isaiah 57 where it says, "The wicked are like the tossing sea, which cannot rest, whose waves cast up mire and mud. 'There is no peace,' says my God, 'for the wicked'" (v. 20–21). At first sight, that looks like just another of those Old Testament statements: God will smite the evildoers. But look again; this is talking about natural consequences. The Stoics had it right. If you live for and love anything more than God then your life is always going to be like a tossing sea. You will be restless, without peace. If you love anything more than God, you are always going to be in anxiety about it. God is saying, "The natural consequence of turning away from me—the natural consequence of not centering your whole life on me—is deep restlessness."

That is what we deserve. But 2 Corinthians 5:21 says, "God made Jesus sin who knew no sin that we might become the righteousness of God in him." That can't mean that God made Jesus actually sinful. It means that on the cross, he was treated as a sinner. He got what we deserve—and this is one of those things, this terrible loss of peace. Can't you see it? Do you see Jesus Christ walking to the crucifixion, saying, "I am just keeping my mind centered on God. I am content in whatever circumstance I am in"? No! Jesus didn't say that because he *wasn't*!

Jesus lost all of his peace. He cries out from the cross. In fact, we are told that he died with a cry. William Lane, commentator on the book of Mark, says,

> The cry of dereliction, that scream—crucified criminals ordinarily suffered complete exhaustion and for long periods were unconscious before they died. The stark realism of Mark's account describes a sudden, violent death. The cry of dereliction expresses unfathomable pain.[391]

On the cross Jesus got what we deserve, including this cosmic, profound pain and restlessness. He got what we deserve, 2 Corinthians 5:21 says, so we can get what he deserves. Jesus lost all of his peace so that you and I could have eternal peace. And looking at what he did and how he did it for you—that will get you through. That is what will make God lovely to you.

Let me show you how this works. Horatio Spafford was an American lawyer who lost everything he had in the Chicago fire of 1871. Only two years later, he sent his wife, Anna, and their four daughters on a ship across the Atlantic Ocean to England. The ship hit another ship and began to sink. As it was sinking, Anna got the four little girls together and prayed. The ship went under the water, and they all were scattered into the waves, and all four little girls drowned. Anna was found floating unconscious in the water by a rescue ship. They took her to England, and she cabled Horatio Spafford just two words: "saved alone."

When Spafford was on the ship on his way to England to bring his wife home, he began to write a hymn—"It is well with my soul . . . When peace, like a river . . ." Those are the words he wrote. Here is what I want you to think about: why would a man dealing with his grief, seeking the peace of God—the peace like a river—spend the entire hymn on Jesus and his work of salvation? And why would he bring up the subject of his own sin at such a time? He wrote:

> My sin, oh, though the bliss of this glorious thought!
> My sin, not in part but the whole,
> Is nailed to the cross, and I bear it no more.
> Praise the Lord, praise the Lord, O my soul.[392]

What has that got to do with his four little girls who are dead? Everything! Do you know why? When things go wrong, one of the ways you lose your peace is that you think maybe you are being punished. But look at the cross! All the punishment fell on Jesus. Another thing you may think is that maybe God doesn't care. But look at the cross! The Bible gives you a God that says, "I have lost a child too; but not involuntarily—voluntarily, on the cross, for your sake. So that I could bring you into my family."

In that hymn you can watch a man thinking, thanking, and loving himself into the peace of God. It worked for him under those circumstances. It worked for Paul under his circumstances. It will work for you.

SIXTEEN

Hoping

Then shall those powers, which work for grief,
Enter thy pay,
And day by day
Labour thy praise, and my relief;
With care and courage building me,
Till I reach heav'n, and much more, thee.

George Herbert, "Affliction IV"

Then I saw a new heaven and a new earth, for the first heaven
and the first earth had passed away, and there was no longer any
sea. I saw the Holy City, the new Jerusalem, coming down out of
heaven from God, prepared as a bride beautifully dressed for her
husband. And I heard a loud voice from the throne saying,
"Now the dwelling of God is with men, and he will live with
them. They will be his people, and God himself will be with them
and be their God. He will wipe every tear from their eyes. There
will be no more death or mourning or crying or pain, for the old
order of things has passed away" (Rev 21:1–5).

There is nothing more practical for sufferers than to have hope. The erosion or loss of hope is what makes suffering unbearable. And here at the end of the Bible is the ultimate hope—a material world in which all suffering is gone—"every tear wiped from our eyes." This is a life-transforming, living hope.

Who was John writing to in the book of Revelation? He was writing to people who were suffering terrible things. Verse 4 shows you the list. He was writing to people who were experiencing death and mourning and crying and pain. This book was written near the end of the first century when we know the Roman emperor Domitian was conducting large-scale persecutions of Christians. Some had their homes taken away and plundered, while some were sent into the arena to be torn to pieces by wild beasts as the crowds watched. Others were impaled on stakes and, while still alive, covered with pitch and lit afire. That is what the readers of this book were facing.

And what did John give them so they could face it all? John gave them the ultimate hope—a new heavens and a new earth that was coming. That is what he gave them to face it, and it is a simple fact of history that it worked. We know that the early Christians took their suffering with great poise and peace and they sang hymns as the beasts were tearing them apart and they forgave the people who were killing them. And so the more they were killed, the more the Christian movement grew. Why? Because when people watched Christians dying like that, they said, "These people have got something." Well, do you know what they had? They had this. It is a living hope.

Human beings are hope-shaped creatures. The way you live now is completely controlled by what you believe about your future. I was reading a story some years ago about two men who were captured and thrown into a dungeon. Just before they went into prison, one man discovered that his wife and child were dead, and the other learned that his wife and child were alive and waiting for him. In the first couple years of imprisonment the first man just wasted away, curled up and died. But the other man endured and stayed strong and walked out a free man ten years later. Notice that these two men experienced the very same circumstances but responded differently because, while they experienced the same present, they had their minds set on different futures. It was the future that determined how they handled the present.

John was quite right, then, to help suffering people by giving them hope. Do you believe that when you die, you rot? That life in this world is all the happiness you will ever get? Do you believe that someday the sun is going to die and all human civilization is going to be gone, and nobody will remember anything anyone has ever done? That's one way to imagine your future. But here's another. Do you believe in "new heavens and new earth"? Do you believe in a Judgment Day when every evil deed and injustice will be redressed? Do you believe you are headed for a future of endless joy? Those are two utterly different futures, and depending on which one you believe, you are going to handle your dungeons, your suffering, in two utterly different ways.

We said there is one historical proof of this principle—the way the early Christians took their horrendous trials and suffering. But there's another. In 1947 the African-American scholar Howard Thurman gave a lecture at Harvard University on the meaning of the Negro spiritual. He responded to one of the criticisms of these songs, namely, that they were too "otherworldly." And indeed they are filled with references to heaven and to Judgment Day and to the crowns and the thrones and the robes we will wear. The charge was that African-American slaves did not need all that. In fact, the talk of heaven may have made them docile and too resigned to their condition. But Howard Thurman responded,

> The facts make clear that [this sung faith] did serve to deepen the capacity of endurance and the absorption of suffering. . . . It taught a people how to ride high in life, to look squarely in the face those facts that argue most dramatically against all hope and to use those facts as raw material out of which they fashioned a hope that the environment, with all its cruelty could not crush. . . . This . . . enabled them to reject annihilation and to affirm a terrible right to live.[393]

Thurman argued that the slaves believed the Christian faith and therefore knew about the new heavens and new earth, and about Judgment Day. They knew that eventually all their desires would be fulfilled and that no perpetrator of injustice was going to get away with anything—that all wrongdoing would be put down. And that was a hope that no amount of oppression could extinguish. Why? Because their hope was not in the present but in the future. Some argued that it would have been better for the slaves to put their hope in some kind of concrete political action—but hopes in our own achievements can be dashed so that hopelessness engulfs us. But hope in the New Jerusalem can never be snuffed out because it is a certainty—it is based in God's action, not ours.

Now of course, there were many in Thurman's educated, secular audience who believed that while these things in the spirituals were wonderful symbols, you couldn't take such things literally. But Thurman argued, rightly, that if you can't take them literally, then they cannot be a real hope. He said:

> In the end to reject the literal truth is to deny life itself of its dignity and man the right or necessity of dimensional fulfillment. In such a [secular] view the present moment is all there is—man . . . becomes a prisoner in a tight world of momentary events—no more and no less. . . . For these slave singers such a view was completely unsatisfactory and it was therefore thoroughly and decisively rejected. And this is the miracle of their achievement causing them to take their place alongside the great creative religious thinkers of the human race. They made a worthless life, the life of chattel poverty . . . *worth living!* They yielded with abiding enthusiasm to a view of life which included all the events of their experience without exhausting themselves in those experiences. To them this quality of life was insistent fact because of that which deep within them, they discovered of God, and his far flung purposes. . . . To know him was to live a life worthy of the loftiest meaning of life. . . .[394]

Thurman is completely right to reject the "symbolic only" interpretation of the Bible's promises. Imagine you could go back in time and sit with the slaves and say, "Now, you know, I'm glad you get a lot out of your spirituals. But if you ever get the chance to go to a really good school, you will learn that this life is all there is. There really isn't any heaven that will make up for all the suffering here. And there isn't a

Judgment Day that will put all things right and address all injustices. But I still want you to live with hope and fearlessness." You can imagine some saying, "Let me get this straight. You tell me this life is all there is, and if we fail to achieve happiness here and now we never find it at all. And now knowing this, I am still supposed live with my head high under any circumstances? Give me my old hope back! It didn't depend strictly on my political fortunes."

None of us is likely to be thrown to lions and torn limb from limb as people cheer, and probably none of us will experience a life of servitude and slavery. We have things that are weighing us down, but nothing like lions and whips. So if this great hope helped these other people face their problems, shouldn't it help you and me with the ones we are facing now?

But how can we be sure this future is for us? The answer is—you can be sure if you believe in Jesus, who took what we deserve so we could have the heaven and the glory he deserved. Donald Grey Barnhouse, who was a pastor at Tenth Presbyterian Church in Philadelphia for many years, lost his wife when his daughter was still a child. Dr. Barnhouse was trying to help his little girl, and himself, process the loss of his wife and her mother. Once when they were driving, a huge moving van passed them. As it passed, the shadow of the truck swept over the car. The minister had a thought. He said something like this, "Would you rather be run over by a truck, or by its shadow?" His daughter replied, "By the shadow of course. That can't hurt us at all." Dr. Barnhouse replied, "Right. If the truck doesn't hit you, but only its shadow, then you are fine. Well, it was only the shadow of death that went over your mother. She's actually alive—more alive than we are. And that's because two thousand years ago, the real truck of death hit Jesus. And because death crushed Jesus, and we believe in him, now the only thing that can come over us is the shadow of death, and the shadow of death is but my entrance into glory."[395]

We sing that song "Christ the Lord Is Risen Today," and the last line of the last stanza is "made like him, like him we rise; ours the cross, the grave, the skies." What does that mean? It's almost like a taunt. It's like saying, "Come on, crosses, the lower you lay me, the higher you will raise me! Come on, grave, kill me and all you will do is make me better than before!" If the death of Jesus Christ happened for us and he bore our hopelessness so that now we can have hope—and if the resurrection of Jesus Christ happened—then even the worst things will turn into the best things, and the greatest are yet to come.

There have not been many times in my life when I felt "the peace that passes understanding." But there was one time for which I am very grateful, and it stemmed from this great Christian hope. It was just before for my cancer surgery. My thyroid was about to be removed, and after that, I faced a treatment with radioactive iodine to destroy any residual cancerous thyroid tissue in my body. Of course my whole family and I were shaken by it all, and deeply anxious. On the morning of my surgery, after I said my good-byes to my wife and sons, I was wheeled into a room to be prepped. And in the moments before they gave me the anesthetic, I prayed. To my surprise, I got a sudden, clear new perspective on everything. It seemed to me that the universe was an enormous realm of joy, mirth, and high beauty. Of course it was—didn't the Triune God make it to be filled with his own boundless joy, wisdom, love, and delight? And within this great globe of glory was only one little speck of darkness—our world—where there was temporarily pain and suffering. But it was only one speck, and soon that speck would fade away and everything would be light. And I thought, "It doesn't really matter how the surgery goes. Everything will be all right. Me—my wife, my children, my church—will all be all right." I went to sleep with a bright peace on my heart.

C. S. Lewis wrote:

> For if we take the Scripture seriously, if we believe that God will one day give us the Morning Star and cause us to put on the splendor of the sun, then we may surmise that both the ancient myths and the modern poetry, so false as history, may be very near the truth as prophecy. At present we are on the outside of the world, the wrong side of the door. We discern the freshness and purity of morning, but they do not make us fresh and pure. We cannot mingle with the splendors we see.

But all the leaves of the New Testament are rustling with the rumor that it will not always be so. Someday, God willing, we shall get in. When human souls have become as perfect in voluntary obedience as the inanimate creation is in its lifeless obedience, then they will put on its glory, or rather that greater glory of which Nature is only the first sketch. We are summoned to pass in through Nature, beyond her, into that splendor which she fitfully reflects.[396]

Epilogue

Let's summarize what we have learned. If we know the biblical theology of suffering and have our hearts and minds engaged by it, then when grief, pain, and loss come, we will not be surprised, and can respond in the various ways laid out in Scripture. Here they are organized into ten things we should do.

First, we must recognize the varieties of suffering. Some trials are largely brought on by wrong behavior. Some are largely due to betrayals and attacks by others. Then there are the more universal forms of loss that occur to all regardless of how they live, such as the death of a loved one, illnesses, financial reversals, or your own imminent death. A final kind of suffering could be called the horrendous—such as mass shootings in elementary schools. Of course, many actual cases of suffering combine several of these four types. Each kind of suffering brings somewhat different kinds of feelings—the first brings guilt and shame; the second, anger and resentment; the third, grief and fear; the fourth, confusion and perhaps anger at God. While all these forms of suffering share common themes—and are addressed in common ways—each also requires its own specific responses.

Second, you must recognize distinctions in temperament between yourself and other sufferers. You must be careful not to think that the way God helped some other sufferer through the fire will be exactly the way he will lead you. Simone Weil outlines the experience of affliction as consisting of isolation, self-absorption, condemnation, anger, and "complicity" with pain. A quick look at this list reveals that these factors will be stronger or weaker depending on a person's emotional temperament and spiritual maturity, and also depending on the causes behind the adversity. Make adjustments.

Third, there is *weeping*. It is crucial to be brutally honest with yourself and God about your pain and sorrow. Do not deny or try too much to control your feelings in the name of being faithful. Read the Psalms of lament or Job. God is very patient with us when we are desperate. Pour out your soul to him.

Fourth, there is *trusting*. Despite the invitation to pour out our hearts to God with emotional reality, we are also summoned to trust God's wisdom (since he is sovereign) and also to trust his love (since he has been through what you've been through). Despite your grief, you must eventually come to say, as Jesus did (after first honestly entreating, "Let this cup pass from me"), "Thy will be done." Wrestle until you can say that.

Fifth, we must be *praying*. Though Job did a lot of complaining and cursed the day he was born—he did it all in prayer. It was to God he complained; it was before God that he struggled. In suffering, you must read the Bible and pray and attend worship even though it is dry or painful. Simone Weil said, if you can't love God, you must *want* to love God, or at least ask him to help you love him.

Sixth, we must be disciplined in our *thinking*. You must meditate on the truth and gain the perspective that comes from remembering all God has done for you and is going to do. You should also do "self-communion." This is both listening to your heart and also reasoning and talking to your heart. It means saying, "Why are you cast down, *O my soul?* Forget not his benefits, his salvation" (Ps 42; Ps 103). This is not forcing yourself to feel in a certain way but rather directing your thoughts until your heart, sooner or later, is engaged. Much of the thinking and self-communing that we must do has to do with Christian hope. Heaven and the resurrection and the future-perfect world are particularly important to meditate on if you are dealing with death—your own or someone else's. But it is crucial in all suffering.

Seventh, we should be willing to do some *self-examining*. The biblical image of suffering as a "gymnasium" suggests this. We must exercise care here. This does not mean we should always be looking within ourselves for the cause of our suffering. Job's friends tried to do that, though Job's suffering did not occur because God was trying to correct him for something. Nevertheless, Job grew in grace and maturity, and every time of adversity is an opportunity to look at ourselves and ask—how do *I* need to grow? What weaknesses is this time of trouble revealing?

Eighth, we must be about *reordering our loves*. Suffering reveals that there are things we love too much, or we love God too little in proportion to them. Our suffering is often aggravated and doubled because we turned good things into ultimate things. Suffering will only make us better (rather than worse) if, during it, we teach ourselves to love God better than before. This happens by recognizing God's suffering for us in Jesus Christ, and by praying, thinking, and trusting that love into our souls.

Ninth, we should not shirk community. Simone Weil speaks about how isolating suffering can be. But the early Christian communities were famously good places to be a person in suffering. Christians "died well," the early church authors claimed, not because they were rugged individuals but because the church was a place of unparalleled sympathy and support. Gospel doctrine should make it impossible to grow many "miserable comforters" like Job's moralistic friends. And the Christian gospel accounts for and assigns meaning to the experience of suffering as secular society cannot. Find a Christian church where sufferers are loved and supported.

Tenth, some forms of suffering—particularly the first two among the four types listed above—require skill at receiving grace and forgiveness from God, and giving grace and forgiveness to others. When adversity reveals moral failures or sinful character flaws, it means we will have to learn how to repent and seek reconciliation with God and others. When our suffering is caused by betrayal and injustice, it is crucial to learn forgiveness. We must forgive the wrongdoers from the heart, laying aside vengefulness, if we will ever be able to pursue justice effectively.[397]

Doing all these things, as George Herbert writes, will first bring your "*joys to weep*" but then your "*griefs to sing.*"

Acknowledgments

As usual I want to thank the friends who every year make it possible in various ways for Kathy and me to get away for three weeks a year in order to write. Lynn Land, Tim and Mary Courtney Brooks, and Janice Worth go out of their way year after year to give us this uninterrupted time. I want to also thank the team of people who surround me in my work at Redeemer Presbyterian Church—Bruce Terrell, Craig Ellis, and Andi Brindley. They make me far more effective and efficient in my work than I would ever be alone, and they are one of the main reasons I still have the bandwidth to write while leading a large and great church. I also owe much to the people of the congregation in Hopewell, Virginia, where I ministered from the mid-1970s to mid-1980s. They were quite patient and supportive of a new, inexperienced pastor, and it was there that Kathy and I learned for the first time how to walk beside people who were facing grief, loss, death, and darkness.

Notes

INTRODUCTION—THE RUMBLE OF PANIC BENEATH EVERYTHING

1. Ernest Becker, *The Denial of Death* (Free Press, 1973), pp. 283–84.
2. We used the Revised Standard Version of this text in our wedding, though I added the word *come* as a way of emphasizing the fact that we were summoning each other into a life of "exalting the Lord together."
3. According to the World Health Organization, reported in *The Independent*, http://www.independent.co.uk/news/world/politics/un-report-uncovers-global-child-abuse-419700.html.
4. William Shakespeare, *Macbeth*, Act 4, Scene 3. Spoken by Macduff.
5. Becker, *Denial of Death*, pp. 283–84.
6. Ann Patchett, "Scared Senseless," *The New York Times Magazine*, October 20, 2002.
7. Reported by Philip Yancey in *Where Is God When It Hurts?* (Zondervan, 2002), p. 77.
8. Robert Andrews, *The Concise Columbia Dictionary of Quotations* (Columbia University Press, 1989), p. 125.
9. C. S. Lewis, *The Problem of Pain* (Harper, 2001), p. 94.
10. Ibid., p. 91.
11. "How Firm a Foundation," hymn by John Rippon, 1787.

CHAPTER 1—THE CULTURES OF SUFFERING

12. Max Scheler, "The Meaning of Suffering," in *On Feeling, Knowing, and Valuing: Selected Writings*, ed. H. J. Bershady (University of Chicago Press, 1992), p. 98.
13. This is the pioneering social theorist Max Weber, quoted in Christina Simko, "The Rhetorics of Suffering," *American Sociological Review* 7 (6), p. 882. See Weber, *The Sociology of Religion*, trans. Ephraim Fischoff (Beacon Press, 1963), pp. 138ff (chapter IX, "Theodicy, Salvation, and Rebirth").

[*325*]

14. Richard A. Shweder, Nancy C. Much, Manamohan Mahapatra, and Lawrence Park, "The 'Big Three' of Morality (Autonomy, Community, Divinity) and the 'Big Three' Explanations of Suffering," in *Why Do Men Barbecue?: Recipes for Cultural Psychology,* ed. Richard A. Shweder (Harvard University Press, 2003), p. 74.

15. Peter Berger, Brigitte Berger, and Hansfried Kellner, *The Homeless Mind: Modernization and Consciousness* (Vintage, 1974), p. 185. Berger, in this work and in *The Sacred Canopy: Elements of a Sociological Theory of Religion* (Anchor, 1967), follows Max Weber in using the word *theodicy* to describe this feature of every society or culture—namely, a way of bestowing meaning on suffering for sufferers. However, as originally coined by the philosopher Gottfried Leibniz, the term meant "justifying the ways of God in the wake of tragedy." *Theodicy* has traditionally meant a defense of God's reality against the argument that evil and suffering prove that God cannot exist. See Peter van Inwagen, *The Problem of Evil: The Gifford Lectures Delivered in the University of St Andrews in 2003* (Oxford University Press, 2006), pp. 6–7 and footnotes. I think the word is best used with Leibniz's original, more theological meaning, rather than as Berger deploys it.

16. Simko, "Rhetorics," p. 884.

17. Maureen Dowd, "Why, God?" *The New York Times,* December 25, 2012.

18. Ronald K. Rittgers, *The Reformation of Suffering: Pastoral Theology and Lay Piety in Late Medieval and Early Modern Germany* (Oxford University Press, 2012), p. 4.

19. Tom Shippey, *The Road to Middle-Earth* (Houghton Mifflin, 2003), p. 78.

20. Lewis, *The Problem of Pain,* p. 57.

21. Dr. Paul Brand and Philip Yancey, *The Gift of Pain* (Zondervan, 1997), p. 12.

22. See Berger, *The Sacred Canopy,* pp. 60–65.

23. Scheler, "The Meaning of Suffering," p. 98.

24. Berger, *The Sacred Canopy,* p. 62. Berger's discussion of "theodicies"—various cultural strategies for dealing with suffering—heavily relies on the typology of Max Weber.

25. See Berger, *Sacred Canopy,* pp. 73–76. Berger puts Calvinistic Christianity in this category and gives the category the unfortunate name *religious masochism.*

26. Weber, *Sociology of Religion,* pp. 144–5.

27. Ibid., p. 62.

28. Shweder, et al., *Why Do Men Barbecue?*, p. 125.
29. Richard Dawkins, *River Out of Eden: A Darwinian View of Life* (Basic Books, 1996), pp. 132–3.
30. Ibid., p. 96.
31. Richard Dawkins, *The God Delusion* (Houghton Mifflin, 2006), p. 360.
32. Shweder, et al., *Why Do Men Barbecue?*, p. 74.
33. Dawkins, *God Delusion*, p. 360.
34. This is the burden of Dawkins's TV program *Sex, Death and the Meaning of Life*, which was televised in October 2012. See the video at http://www .channel4.com/programmes/sex-death-and-the-meaning-of-life.
35. Schweder, et al., *Why Do Men Barbecue?*, p. 125.
36. Ibid.
37. James Davies, *The Importance of Suffering: The Value and Meaning of Emotional Discontent* (Routledge, 2012), p. 29.
38. Ibid., pp. 1–2.
39. Ibid., p. 2.
40. Ibid.
41. C. S. Lewis, *The Abolition of Man* (Harper, 2009), p. 77.
42. Charles Taylor, *A Secular Age* (Harvard University Press, 2007), pp. 373, 375.
43. http://www.bostonreview.net/books-ideas-mccoy-family-center-ethics -society-stanford-university/lives-moral-saints.
44. Scheler, "Meaning of Suffering," p. 110.
45. Ibid.
46. Ibid.
47. Ibid., p. 111.
48. Ibid.
49. Aleksandr Solzhenitsyn, *The Gulag Archipelago 1918–1956* (Harper & Row, 1974).
50. Ibid., p. 112.
51. Ibid., p. 113.

CHAPTER 2—THE VICTORY OF CHRISTIANITY

52. My paragraphs on ancient pagan consolation literature rely on Rittgers, *Reformation of Suffering,* chaps. 2–3, and Luc Ferry, *A Brief History of Thought: A Philosophical Guide to Living* (Harper, 2010), chaps. 1–3. See also Robert C. Gregg, *Consolation Philosophy: Greek and Christian Paideia in Basil and*

the Two Gregories (Philadelphia Patristic Foundation, 1975), chap. 1; and
John T. McNeill, *A History of the Cure of Souls* (Harper, 1951), chap. 2.

53. Rittgers, *Reformation of Suffering*, p. 39.
54. Ferry, *Brief History*, p. xiv.
55. Ibid.
56. Ibid., p. 4.
57. Ibid., p. 7.
58. Ibid., pp. 3–5.
59. Ibid., p. xiv.
60. See Ferry's helpful summary of Stoic philosophy in his *Brief History*, chap. 2, "The Greek Miracle." See also Rittgers, *Reformation of Suffering*, pp. 39–40.
61. Rittgers, *Reformation of Suffering*, p. 39.
62. Ferry, *Brief History*, p. 45.
63. Rittgers, *Reformation of Suffering*, p. 39.
64. Epictetus, *Discourses* III, 24, 84–88. Quoted in Ferry, *Brief History*, pp. 47–48.
65. Ibid., p. 48.
66. Ibid.
67. Ibid., p. 50.
68. Epictetus, *Discourses,* III, 24, 91–94, and Marcus Aurelius, *Meditations,* IV, 14. Quoted in Ferry, *Brief History*, p. 37.
69. Here is a summary of Cicero's advice to sufferers—a "cure of souls"—for sufferers in pain. First, they must be told that their pain should not be surprising to them, that many others have gone through the same experience, and that, in general, such losses and miseries are the lot of all people who live. Second, they must consider that it is "utter folly to be uselessly overcome by sorrow when one realizes that there is no possible advantage." (Cicero, *Tusculan Disputations,* III, 6, sect. 12, cited in Rittgers, *Reformation of Suffering*, p. 40.) Third, they should remember that time will have a healing effect on their pain, but that they could help accelerate that healing by the use of reason, by recognizing the transitory nature of things, and that all life is just a loan from nature that must be returned.
70. Henri Blocher does a good job of summarizing Eastern thought in this regard in his *Evil and the Cross: An Analytical Look at the Problem of Pain* (Kregel, 1994), pp. 15–17.

71. I realize that there are many who argue that Buddhism is not a form of pantheism but of atheism, and I know many atheists from Western cultures who have adopted Buddhist practices because they say it provides them a spirituality that does not require belief in God. But Buddhism is not truly atheistic in the Western sense. It believes very firmly in the supernatural and metaphysical; indeed, it believes the natural and the physical are illusions, and that everything is ultimately spirit. Many scholars have pointed out that Buddha did not want to overthrow but to reform the older religions of India. Henri Blocher quotes Ananda Coomaraswamy of Harvard, who wrote that the more one studies it, "the more difficult it becomes to distinguish Buddhism from Brahmanism." Blocher, *Evil and the Cross,* p. 17.

72. In addition to the Stoics, this approach to evil and suffering has been largely shared by Western philosophers such as Spinoza, Hegel, and mystics such as Meister Eckhart, as well as writers such as Ralph Waldo Emerson and Walt Whitman. And it characterizes much of what has been called "New Age" thought, as well as the views of Mary Baker Eddy, the founder of Christian Science. This is based on an understanding of God known as "pantheism." According to the *Stanford Dictionary of Philosophy*: "Pantheism . . . signifies the belief that every existing entity is only one Being; and that all other forms of reality are either modes (or appearances) of it or identical with it." http://plato.stanford.edu/entries/pantheism. At a popular level, the concept of an impersonal Divine Spirit that contains both good and evil has made its way into much science fiction. In the Star Wars movies, we have "The Force," the single life force binding all life together, containing a "dark side" as well as a good.

73. See Ferry, *Brief History,* pp. 43–49, for the close parallels between Buddhism and Greek Stoicism.

74. Plutarch, *A Letter of Condolence to Apollonius,* quoted in Rittgers, *Reformation of Suffering,* p. 43.

75. See Rittgers, *Reformation of Suffering*. This section and the next are heavily dependent on Rittgers's excellent and groundbreaking scholarship on this subject.

76. Cyprian, *On Mortality,* chap. 13. Cited in Rittgers, *Reformation of Suffering,* p. 45.

77. Ibid., p. 47.

78. Judith Perkins, *The Suffering Self: Pain and Narrative Representation in the Early Christian Era* (Routledge, 1995).

79. In Ferry, *Brief History*.

80. Ibid., p. 52.

81. Ambrose of Milan, *On the Death of Satyrus*. Quoted in Rittgers, *Reformation of Suffering*, pp. 43–44.

82. Ibid., p. 52.

83. Ibid., p. 52–53.

84. Ibid., p. 63.

85. Ibid., p. 46.

86. Ibid.

87. Ibid., p. 86.

88. Even Seneca, who believed in a God, believed God was subject to the dictates of fate. Fate in the Greco-Roman view is impersonal, its dispensations are completely inexplicable, there can be no appeal to fate for justice—that is a categorical mistake. Fate is completely fickle and random, even when it is poetically personified in the ancient writings. In Boethius's *Consolation of Philosophy*, he well expresses this view: "You are wrong if you think Fortune has changed towards you. Change is her normal behavior, her true nature. . . . You have discovered the changing face of the random goddess. . . . With domineering hand she moves the turning wheel [of chance], like currents in a treacherous bay swept to and from. No cries of misery she hears, no tears she heeds, but steely hearted laughs at groans her deeds have wrung." Boethius, *The Consolation of Philosophy*, translated with an introduction by Victor Watts (rev. ed.; Penguin, 1999), pp. 23–24.

89. Ibid., pp. 46–47.

90. Ibid., p. 47.

91. Ibid., p. 89.

92. Ibid., pp. 53, 90.

93. See Gregory the Great, *The Book of Pastoral Rule*, trans. George Demacopoulos (St Vladimir's Seminary Press, 2007), and the summary and discussion of this work in Thomas C. Oden, *Care of Souls in the Classic Tradition* (Fortress Press, 1984). For an overview of Gregory's *Moralia* and *Pastoral Rule*, see Rittgers, *Reformation of Suffering*, pp. 49–52.

94. Rittgers, *Reformation of Suffering*, p. 51.

95. Ibid., p. 53.

96. Ibid., p. 61.

97. Ibid., p. 62.

98. Ibid., p. 88.

99. Martin Luther, *Luther's Works*, Volume 29: *Lectures on Titus, Philemon, and Hebrews*, ed. Jaroslav Pelikan (Concordia, 1968), p. 189. Cited in Rittgers, *Reformation of Suffering*, pp. 103–104.

100. Rittgers, *Reformation of Suffering*, p. 95.

101. Martin Luther, *Luther's Works*, Volume 14: *Selected Psalms III*, ed. Jaroslav Pelikan (Concordia, 1968), p. 163. Cited in Rittgers, *Reformation of Suffering*, p. 101.

102. Rittgers, *Reformation of Suffering*, p. 112. See chap. 5, "Suffering and the Theology of the Cross," pp. 111–124.

103. Quoted in ibid., p. 112.

104. Ibid., p. 117.

105. Alister McGrath, *Luther's Theology of the Cross: Martin Luther's Theological Breakthrough* (Blackwell, 1990), p. 170.

106. Rittgers, *Reformation of Suffering*, p. 117. Luther went further than many Reformation theologians in arguing that God, even in his divine nature, experienced suffering. Luther held, of course, that God's divine nature cannot lose its omnipotence. God's divine nature cannot lose its omnipotence. And yet Luther "argued that in Christ, God had willed his deity to be united with human nature in such a way that the divine nature could be said to truly suffer." To some degree, Luther's statements reflect his particular view of the *communicatio idiomatum*—the way the attributes of Christ's divine and human nature relate to one another. In the Eucharistic controversies of the late 1520s, Luther insisted that the two natures can impart their properties to each other in a way that many Reformed theologians rejected. Nevertheless, the idea that the biblical God participates in and knows human suffering is a biblical teaching, and one that sets Christianity apart from other religions.

107. Ibid., p. 115.

108. Taylor, *Secular Age*, p. 25.

109. Ibid., p. 542.

110. I know that the order in which I am rolling out these phrases and concepts may lead to the impression that the immanent frame—the "buffered

world"—led to the "buffered self." Actually, Taylor believes the modern self preceded the modern world. His reasons are too complex to recount here.

111. Taylor, *Secular Age*. The first phrase in this sentence is taken from p. 38 and p. 581, respectively.

112. Ibid., p. 27.

113. Megan L. Wood, "When the New You Carries a Fresh Identity, Too," *The New York Times*, February 17, 2013.

114. Taylor, *Secular Age*, p. 232.

115. Ibid., p. 306.

116. Andrew Delbanco, *The Death of Satan: How Americans Have Lost the Sense of Evil* (Farrar, Straus, and Giroux, 1995), pp. 106–197.

117. Christian Smith, *Soul Searching: The Religious and Spiritual Lives of American Teenagers* (Oxford University Press, 2007).

118. Ferry, *Brief History*, pp. 3–5.

119. Susan Jacoby, "The Blessings of Atheism," *The New York Times*, January 5, 2013.

CHAPTER 3—THE CHALLENGE TO THE SECULAR

120. Henri Frédéric Amiel's words are cited in James Davies, *The Importance of Suffering: The Value and Meaning of Emotional Discontent* (Routledge, 2012), frontispiece.

121. Ibid., p. 75.

122. Samuel G. Freedman, "In a Crisis, Humanists Seem Absent," *The New York Times*, December 28, 2012.

123. Jacoby, "Blessings of Atheism."

124. Ibid.

125. As David L. Chappell argues in *A Stone of Hope*, it was not white, northern freethinkers and secularists who proposed civil disobedience, a key component in the strategy of the Civil Rights movement. It was the African American church and clergy with their more pessimistic view of sin and human nature. See Chappell, *A Stone of Hope: Prophetic Religion and the Death of Jim Crow* (University of North Carolina Press, 2007), chap. 2, "Recovering Optimists," and chap. 5, "The Civil Rights Movement as a Religious Revival." *The New York Times* said about the book that "it's impossible to read the book without doing some fundamental rethinking about the role religion can play in . . . public life."

126. Quoted in Steven D. Smith, *The Disenchantment of Secular Discourse* (Harvard University Press, 2010), p. 166.

127. Michael Sandel, *Justice: What's the Right Thing to Do?* (Farrar, Straus, and Giroux, 2010).

128. Comment on "Obama's Speech in Newtown," http://reason-being.com.

129. For a good statement of the essence of Frankl's thought, see Emily Esfahani Smith, "There's More to Life Than Being Happy," *The Atlantic*, January 9, 2013.

130. Victor Frankl, *Man's Search for Meaning* (Washington Square Press, 1984), p. 54.

131. Eleanor Barkhorn, "Why People Prayed for Boston on Twitter and Facebook, and Then Stopped," *The Atlantic*, April 20, 2013; available online at http://www.theatlantic.com/national/archive/2013/04/why-people-prayed-for-boston-on-twitter-and-facebook-and-then-stopped/275137.

132. Andrew Solomon, *Far from the Tree: Parents, Children, and the Search for Identity* (Scribner, 2012), p. 47.

133. Ibid., pp. 357–63.

134. Martha C. Nussbaum, *Women and Human Development: The Capabilities Approach* (Cambridge University Press, 2000), chap. one, "In Defense of Universal Values." Cited in Steven D. Smith, *Disenchantment*, p. 167. For more on why a secular account of human rights does not work, see both Smith's *Disenchantment* and Nicholas Wolterstorff, *Justice: Rights and Wrongs* (Princeton University Press, 2008), pp. 323–341.

135. Solomon, *Far from the Tree*, p. 147.

136. Ibid., p. 697.

137. Shweder, *Why Do Men Barbecue?*, p. 128.

138. John Gray, *Straw Dogs: Thoughts on Humans and Other Animals* (Farrar, Straus, and Giroux, 2003), p. 142.

139. Andrew Delbanco, *The Real American Dream: A Meditation on Hope* (Harvard University Press, 1999), pp. 1, 3.

140. Ibid., p. 5.

141. Quoted in Delbanco, *Real American Dream*, p. 109.

142. Ibid., pp. 96–97.

143. Ibid., pp. 102.

144. Ibid., p.103.

145. Robert Bellah et al, *Habits of the Heart: Individualism and Commitment in American Life* (University of California Press, 1985).

146. Wood, "New You."
147. William H. Willimon, *Pastor: The Theology and Practice of Ordained Ministry* (Abingdon, 2002), p. 99.
148. Ibid., pp. 98–99.
149. I recount the biblical story of Naaman and the prophet Elisha in detail in *Counterfeit Gods* (Dutton, 2009).
150. J. R. R. Tolkien, *The Lord of the Rings: The Fellowship of the Ring* (Houghton Mifflin, 2004), p. 50.

CHAPTER 4—THE PROBLEM OF EVIL

151. Albert Camus, *The Plague,* trans. Stuart Gilbert (Random House, 1991), p. 128.
152. David Hume, *Dialogues Concerning Natural Religion,* ed. Richard Popkin (Hackett Pub, 1980), p. 63.
153. See Peter Berger and Thomas Luckman, *The Social Construction of Reality: A Treatise in the Sociology of Knowledge* (Anchor, 1967); and see Berger, *A Rumor of Angels: Modern Society and the Rediscovery of the Supernatural* (Doubleday, 1969), pp. 40ff (chap. 2, "The Perspective of Sociology: Relativizing the Relativizers").
154. J. L. Mackie, "Evil and Omnipotence," *Mind* 64, no. 254 (April 1955), cited in Alvin Plantinga, *Warranted Christian Belief* (Oxford University Press, 2000), p. 460.
155. See Alvin Plantinga, *God, Freedom, and Evil* (Eerdmans, 1974) and *The Nature of Necessity* (Oxford University Press, 1974). The first place Plantinga gave a high-level treatment of the subject was in *God and Other Minds: A Study of the Rational Justification of Belief in God* (Cornell University Press, 1967; paperback ed. 1990), pp. 115–55 (chap. 5, "The Problem of Evil," and chap. 6, "The Free Will Defense").
156. Plantinga, *Warranted Christian Belief,* p. 461.
157. William P. Alston, "The Inductive Argument from Evil and the Human Cognitive Condition," *Philosophical Perspectives* 5 (1991): 30–67.
158. See Daniel Howard-Snyder, ed., *The Evidential Argument from Evil* (Indiana University Press, 1996). Alvin Plantinga interacts with probabilistic arguments set forth by William Rowe and Paul Draper, in his *Warranted Christian Belief,* pp. 465–81.
159. J. P. Moreland and William Lane Craig, *Philosophical Foundations for a*

Christian Worldview (Inter-Varsity Press, 2003), p. 552. This summarizes the cumulative arguments of Plantinga and his colleague.

160. Van Inwagen, *Problem of Evil*, p. 6.

161. John Hick, *Evil and the God of Love* (rev. ed.; Harper, 1978), pp. 255–56. For an example of this view in Irenaeus, see "Against Heresies," in *The Ante-Nicene Fathers*, eds. Alexander Roberts and James Donaldson (Hendrickson, 1994), vol. I, pp. 521–22.

162. A selection of Augustine's writings on evil and free will is found in A. I. Melden, ed., *Ethical Theories* (2nd ed.; Prentice-Hall, 1955).

163. Jean-Paul Sartre, *Being and Nothingness* (Philosophical Library, 1956), p. 367.

164. This is the view that evil is not a substance or thing but the "privation" of the good. The illustration of sight is often used to clarify the position. The inability of a tree to see is not evil, because sight is not part of the tree's nature. However, the inability of a human being to see with her eyes would be considered suffering or evil because visual sight is what human eyes are for. This view of evil as privation has been quite influential, put forth not just by Augustine and Aquinas but by many Protestant Reformed theologians and modern apologists like C. S. Lewis. While I think that, on the whole, it is a helpful way to think about evil, others point out the problems with at least some forms of this view—the view of Etienne Gilson, the Thomist theologian, that evil is basically "non-being." But is that all evil is? Doesn't the Bible depict it as a more active, aggressive force than that? Perhaps it is right to say that evil leads to weakening, disintegration, but to call evil just "slipping into non-being" seems far too thin a description. In the end, calling evil a corrupt condition rather than a created thing doesn't really answer the question why God allowed it. See John Frame's criticism of the evil-as-privation view in his essay "The Problem of Evil," in *Suffering and the Goodness of God*, eds. Christopher W. Morgan and Robert A. Peterson (Crossway, 2008), pp. 144–52. For a good summary of the view of evil-as-privation with citations of where this view was developed by Thomas Aquinas, see Jeremy A. Evans, *The Problem of Evil: The Challenge to Essential Christian Beliefs* (Broadman, 2013), pp. 1–2.

165. Van Inwagen, *Problem of Evil*, p. 90.

166. Ibid., pp. 85–86. Van Inwagen rejects the idea that the biblical story of the fall in Genesis—with Adam and Eve—could have happened literally. He says that "it contradicts what science has discovered about human evolution and

the history of the physical universe" (p. 84). But van Inwagen, a Christian, believes Genesis 1–3 was a representation "of actual events in human pre-history" (p. 85). The story van Inwagen tells is about God directing the course of evolution until there were perhaps "a few score" of primates, and God then "miraculously raised them to rationality . . . gave them gifts of language, abstract thought, and disinterested love—and, of course, the gift of free will . . . because free will is necessary for love" (p. 85). These original ancestors lived in a paradisiacal state, because they lived in the "harmony of perfect love" and "possessed . . . preternatural powers" that made them safe from disease, destructive natural events, aging, and death (p. 86). But in this story, these first human beings—created for a perfect world without suffering—turn away from God, rebelling against his rightful authority. "They abused the gift of free will and separated themselves from their union with God" (p. 86). The result is both moral and natural evil. Natural evil came because "they now faced destruction by the random forces of nature around them as a natural consequence of their rebellion." Moral evil came because "they formed the genetic substrate of what is called original or birth sin; an inborn tendency to do evil" (p. 87).

Van Inwagen argues that he does not need to prove his story to be true for it to serve its purpose. The argument against God from evil insists that there can't be any good reason why God would allow evil and suffering. That is its premise. Van Inwagen says, "I contend [only] that, given that the central character of the story, God, exists, the . . . story might well be true" (p. 90). But if the story gives a credible explanation of why God *might* allow evil and suffering—even if we can't be sure this is why God *does* allow it, that proves that the premise of the argument from evil—that there is no possible good reason for evil—is false.

Van Inwagen's story and argument is ingenious, and it allows people with Christian beliefs who believe in evolution to still use the Fall of humankind as an explanation for the existence of natural and moral evil. Nevertheless, while it has a lot of merit as a philosophical argument with skeptics, I do not believe this story fits in with the biblical accounts themselves. If there was no actual Adam and Eve, we can't explain why all human beings are equally sinful, nor how we reconcile what Paul says in Romans 5 and in 1 Corinthians 15 about Adam being a representative for the whole human race. For more on this subject, see chapter 8 and notes.

167. Ibid., p. 90.

168. For a comprehensive argument that "libertarian freedom" is not the biblical definition, see the classic essay "Human Freedom" by G. C. Berkouwer in his *Man: The Image of God* (Eerdmans, 1962), pp. 310–48.

169. For an excellent survey on the biblical material, see D. A. Carson, *How Long, O Lord?: Reflections on Suffering and Evil* (2nd ed.; Baker, 1990), pp. 177–203 (chap. 11, "The Mystery of Providence"). See also J. I. Packer, *Evangelism and the Sovereignty of God* (Inter-Varsity Press, 1961).

170. Alvin Plantinga gives the shorter version and Peter van Inwagen the "expanded" version of the free will theodicy. In both cases they claim that they are giving a *defense,* not a *theodicy.* Yet to me and to others, it seems that they are indeed offering the free will story as a theodicy, because they are using it to answer the question *why* God would allow evil and suffering.

171. C. S. Lewis, *The Problem of Pain* (Harper eBook, 2009); Richard Swinburne, *Providence and the Problem of Evil* (Oxford University Press, 1998).

172. See Donald A. Turner, "The Many-Universes Solution to the Problem of Evil," in Richard M. Gale and Alexander R. Pruss, eds., *The Existence of God,* Aschgate, 2003. pp. 143–59.

173. Ibid.

174. Alvin Plantinga, "Self-Profile," in *Alvin Plantinga,* eds. James E. Tomberlin and Peter van Inwagen (Reidel, 1985), p. 35.

175. The dialogue between the atheist and the theist over the problem of evil is found in van Inwagen, *Problem of Evil,* p. 64.

176. Ibid., p. 65.

177. It's helpful to notice that in offering this defense—not a full theodicy—against the argument from evil, the believer in God may (in showing the kinds of good reasons that God *may* have for allowing evil to continue) draw on some of the best thinking that has been offered in the traditional theodicies. Each theodicy offered cogent but not sufficient reasons that God allowed suffering.

178. Stated by Plantinga, *Warranted Christian Belief,* pp. 481–82.

179. Stephen John Wykstra, "Rowe's Noseeum Arguments from Evil," in *The Evidential Argument from Evil,* ed. Daniel Howard-Snyder (Indiana University Press, 1996), pp. 126–49.

180. Wykstra, "Rowe's Noseeum," p. 126.

181. Plantinga, *Warranted Christian Belief,* pp. 466–67.

182. The most prominent proponent of the evidential argument from evil is

William Rowe. See William L. Rowe, "The Problem of Evil and Some Varieties of Atheism," *American Philosophical Quarterly* 16 (1979): 335–41.

183. Ray Bradbury's short story *A Sound of Thunder* is available at http://www
.lasalle.edu/~didio/courses/hon462/hon462_assets/sound_of_thunder
.htm.

184. Moreland and Craig, *Philosophical Foundations*, p. 543.

185. Van Inwagen, *Problem of Evil*, p. 97.

186. Elie Wiesel, *Night* (Hill and Wang, 1960).

187. Ibid., pp. 43–44.

188. It is important to note that Elie Wiesel himself, though presenting the objection to God's existence and goodness so powerfully, did not ultimately abandon belief in God.

189. J. Christiaan Beker, *Suffering and Hope: The Biblical Vision and the Human Predicament* (Eerdmans, 1994). My information is taken from a preface, "The Story behind the Book," written by Ben C. Ollenburger.

190. Ibid., p. 16.

191. Blaise Pascal, *Pascal's Pensées* (Echo Library, p. 70), *Pensées*, 276, 277.

192. C. S. Lewis, *Mere Christianity* (Macmillan, 1960) p. 31.

193. C. S. Lewis, *Christian Reflections* (Eerdmans, 1967), p. 69.

194. Ibid., pp. 69–70.

195. Ibid., p. 70.

196. Ibid., pp. 69–70.

197. Alvin Plantinga, "A Christian Life Partly Lived," in *Philosophers Who Believe*, ed. Kelly James Clark (IVP, 1993), p. 73. See also Plantinga's letter to Peter van Inwagen. "I'm inclined to believe that there is a . . . problem of evil for atheists. . . . I believe there wouldn't be any such thing as right and wrong at all, and hence no such thing as evil, if theism were false. . . ," van Inwagen, *Problem of Evil*, p. 154, n14.

198. A. N. Wilson, "Why I Believe Again," *The New Statesman*, April 2, 2009.

199. Andrea Palpant Dilley, *Faith and Other Flat Tires: Searching for God on the Rough Road of Doubt* (Zondervan, 2012), pp. 224–25.

200. Dilley's comment appears in an interview with Micha Boyett at http://
www.patheos.com/blogs/michaboyett/2012/04/andrea-palpant-dilley
-doubt-flat-tires-and-the-goodness-of-god.

CHAPTER 5—THE CHALLENGE TO FAITH

201. Van Inwagen, *Problem of Evil*, p. 89.
202. NIV-1984 translation.
203. Alvin Plantinga, "Supralapsarianism, or 'O Felix Culpa,'" in *Christian Faith and the Problem of Evil*, ed. Peter van Inwagen (Eerdmans, 2004), p. 18. This article seems to take a more traditional Calvinistic approach to the problem of evil than Plantinga's more well known "Free Will Defense." See also van Inwagen's note that Calvinistic theodicies have promise, though he doesn't think they are yet strongly formulated enough; van Inwagen, *Problem of Evil*, p. 163, n9.
204. C. S. Lewis, *The Great Divorce* (Macmillan, 1946), p. 64.
205. J. R. R. Tolkien, "The Field of Cormallen," chapter in *The Lord of the Rings: The Return of the King* (various editions).
206. Berger, *Sacred Canopy*, p. 74.
207. Ibid., p. 75.
208. Ibid., pp. 76–77.
209. Ibid., p. 78.
210. John Dickson, *If I Were God I'd End All the Pain: Struggling with Evil, Suffering, and Faith* (Matthias Media, 2001), pp. 66–67.
211. Ann Voskamp, *One Thousand Gifts: A Dare to Live Fully Right Where You Are* (Zondervan, 2010), pp. 154–55.
212. Tolkien, *The Lord of the Rings*, p. 50.
213. John Gray, *The Silence of Animals: On Progress and Other Modern Myths* (Farrar, Straus, and Giroux, 2013), p. 79.

CHAPTER 6—THE SOVEREIGNTY OF GOD

214. C. S. Lewis, *George MacDonald: An Anthology* (Harper, 2001), p. 49.
215. Many will question the entire Genesis account as being out of accord with the overwhelming consensus of science, namely that life on earth evolved over the ages through a process of natural selection. That means that violence, suffering, and death were already existent (in massive amounts) before human beings ever appeared. As we saw earlier, Peter van Inwagen in *The Problem of Evil*, pp. 85–86, gives an account that is true "for all we know" in which, after guiding many years of evolution, God adopts a small number of hominids into full humanness—giving them the image of God and also creating a paradisiacal enclave in the world where they lived in the

"harmony of perfect love" and "possessed . . . preternatural powers" that made them safe from disease, destructive natural events, aging and death. But "they abused the gift of free will and separated themselves from their union with God" (p. 86). The result is that the natural evil—the suffering and death—out in the rest of the world engulfed them. "They now faced destruction by the random forces of nature around them as a natural consequence of their rebellion." Also, of course, for the first time the world saw moral evil, since now human nature was corrupted by sinful self-centeredness.

As I wrote earlier, I do not believe this story fits in with the rest of the Bible, let alone Genesis. If there was no actual Adam and Eve, then we can't explain why all human beings are equally sinful, nor how we reconcile what Paul says in Romans 5 and 1 Corinthians 15 about Adam being a representative for the whole human race. I believe there was a historical couple who turned from God and who brought natural and moral evil into the world and from whom all human beings are descended. Nevertheless, if you believe in a literal Adam and Eve and yet also believe that life came about on the earth through evolution, the same basic story of van Inwagen could serve you in a similar way. In this story, God adopts (or creates *de novo*) Adam and Eve and puts them in the Garden of Eden enclave. It was a paradise without suffering and death. This was the world God had created human beings for and also the kind of life that would have prevailed across the globe had Adam and Eve obeyed God. However, as soon as they fell, the surrounding world instead came upon them, and the natural evil of the world was enhanced by the addition of moral evil, making the world a very dark place. This story supports the basic biblical teaching that the suffering and evil of the world, as well as all moral evil and human death, are due to human sin.

216. See Walter C. Kaiser, "Eight Kinds of Suffering in the Old Testament," in *Suffering and Goodness,* eds. Morgan and Peterson, pp. 68–69. See also Klaus Koch, "Is There a Doctrine of Retribution in the Old Testament?" in *Theodicy in the Old Testament,* ed. James L. Crenshaw (Fortress, 1983), pp. 57–87.

217. Rittgers, *Reformation of Suffering,* p. 9.

218. Gerhard von Rad, *Wisdom in Israel* (SCM Press, 1972), pp. 144–76 (chap. 9, "The Self-Revelation of Creation").

219. Ibid., p. 310.

220. Graeme Goldsworthy, *The Goldsworthy Trilogy: Gospel and Wisdom* (Paternoster, 2000), pp. 428–58.

221. M. J. Lerner and D. T. Miller, "Just World Research and the Attribution Process: Looking Back and Ahead," *Psychological Bulletin* 85: 1030–1051. Cited in Jonathan Haidt, *The Happiness Hypothesis: Putting Ancient Wisdom and Philosophy to the Test of Modern Science* (Arrow Books, 2006), p. 146.

222. David Bentley Hart, *The Doors of the Sea: Where Was God in the Tsunami?* (Eerdmans, 2005), pp. 99, 101, 103–104. I should add that, in my opinion, Hart puts too much emphasis on this one strand of a biblical theology of suffering—suffering as injustice and as an enemy of God—and essentially turns away from the other biblical material about God's sovereignty over and purposes in suffering. In the book, Hart admits a sympathy for ancient Gnosticism, which did not believe that the high God could have had anything to do with evil and suffering, that it could not be part of his plan in any way. Hart may also be sympathetic to the position of Dostoevsky's character Ivan Karamazov, who rejects a God who might be using suffering in any way to bring about a "greater good." Karamazov shows the self-righteousness of the modern inhabitant of the "immanent frame" who is sure ahead of time that on Judgment Day, God could not reveal any insight or wisdom that Karamazov has not already thought of. It is important to hold this truth—that suffering is something God hates—together with the teaching that God is sovereign over it. If we refuse to believe that God's suffering and evil are ever part of God's plan, we not only turn our back on a fair amount of biblical teaching (as we will see), but we also are left without the comfort that God is somehow working in actual experiences and incidents of evil. Nor will we have much incentive to think that God might be teaching us something so that we can grow through it.

223. B. B. Warfield, "The Emotional Life of Our Lord," in *The Person and Work of Christ*, ed. Samuel G. Craig (P&R, 1950), p. 115.

224. Ibid., pp. 116–17.

225. Rittgers, *Reformation of Suffering*, p. 9.

226. Ibid., p. 261.

227. The view that humanity's free will is compatible with God's absolute determination of history is one that is especially associated with Reformed theology. For an alternate view, see Roger Olson, *Arminian Theology: Myths and Realities* (Inter-Varsity Press, 2006). Philosophers such as Peter van

Inwagen also argue that free will is incompatible with determinism. Two at-length descriptions of the view I am putting forth here are D. A. Carson, *Divine Sovereignty and Human Responsibility: Biblical Perspectives in Tension* (John Knox, 1981), and Packer, *Evangelism.*

228. There are almost innumerable passages that teach God's absolute control over all things that happen in history (cf. Gen 14:8; Prov 21:1; Matt 10:29; Rom 9:20ff.) as well as which teach that every human being is responsible for their choices and actions (cf. Matt 25; Rom 2:1–16; Rev 20:11–13).

229. In a classic passage, J. I. Packer characterizes the relationship of divine sovereignty to human responsibility as an "antinomy," which he defines as "the appearance of contradiction . . . an *apparent* incompatibility between two apparent truths." An antinomy exists when two principles stand side by side, seemingly irreconcilable, yet both undeniable. He then offers the example of light—which sometimes behaves as waves, sometimes as particles. While it is not clear *how* it can behave in both ways (since, classically understood, a wave is not a particle and vice versa), nevertheless it does. In the same way, according to the Bible, God *must* be sovereign or much of history is meaningless, happening for no good purpose; also we *must* be responsible, or so much of what we do with our lives is meaningless. The Bible teaches both. Packer is at pains to say this contradiction is not real, only apparent, because of our limitations as observers. See Packer, *Evangelism,* pp. 18–19.

230. Carson, *How Long, O Lord?*, p. 189.

231. Ibid.

232. This verse says that God is the ultimate source of everything in the world that is good. Literally, it says "every good giving and perfect gift comes down . . ." J. B. Adamson sums up the verse's teaching as: "All human good comes from the perfect Father of the universe." J. B. Adamson, *The Epistle of James*. The New International Commentary on the New Testament (Eerdmans, 1976), p. 74.

CHAPTER 7—THE SUFFERING OF GOD

233. Dan G. McCartney, *Why Does It Have to Hurt?: The Meaning of Christian Suffering* (P&R, 1998), p. 56. Emphasis mine.

234. Derek Kidner, *Genesis: An Introduction and Commentary* (Inter-Varsity Press, 1967), p. 86.

235. J. Alec Motyer, *The Message of Exodus: The Days of our Pilgrimage* (Inter-Varsity Press, 2005), p. 69.

236. Carson, *How Long, O Lord?*, p. 166.

237. See F. L. Cross and E. A. Livingstone, eds., *The Oxford Dictionary of the Christian Church* (Oxford University Press, 1974), p. 694. Cited in Carson, *How Long, O Lord?*, p. 164.

238. Kidner, *Genesis*, p. 86. Emphasis mine.

239. Carson, *How Long, O Lord?*, p. 159.

240. McCartney, *Why Does It Hurt?*, pp. 57, 59.

241. R. M. M'Cheyne, *Sermons of the Rev. Robert Murray M'Cheyne* (Banner of Truth, 1961), pp. 47–49.

242. McCartney, *Why Does It Hurt?*, p. 60.

243. See Douglas John Hall, *God and Human Suffering: An Exercise in the Theology of the Cross* (Augsburg, 1986). See also Warren McWilliams, *The Passion of God: Divine Suffering in Contemporary Protestant Theology* (Mercer University Press, 1985).

244. Rittgers, *Reformation of Suffering*, p. 261.

245. Ibid.

246. Albert Camus, *The Rebel* (Vintage, 1956), p. 34. Quoted in Berger, *Sacred Canopy*, p. 77.

247. Albert Camus, *Essais* (Gallimard, 1965), p. 444.

248. Berger, *Sacred Canopy*, p. 77.

249. Louis Berkhof, *Systematic Theology* (new ed. in 2 vols.; Eerdmans, 1996), p. 729.

250. Ibid.

251. Christopher J. H. Wright, *The God I Don't Understand: Reflections on Tough Questions of Faith* (Zondervan, 2008), p. 64.

252. Ibid., p. 67.

253. Henri Blocher, *Evil and the Cross*, p. 131.

254. These two views of evil are sometimes called the "Boethian" and "Manichean" views, named after Boethius, *The Consolation of Philosophy*, and the ancient Manichees. Tom Shippey, in *The Road to Middle Earth*, provides a fascinating look at how Tolkien's work *The Lord of the Rings* depicts evil as "both-and." It is both an inner lack and a real power in the universe. Shippey shows that sometimes the Ring in the narrative acts as a psychic magnifier of what is twisted and wrong inside the wearer, but other times it is depicted of having a malevolent power of its own. In my view, this "both-

and" fits the Bible's view of evil as well. See Shippey, *The Road to Middle Earth* (Mariner Books, 2003), pp. 138ff.

255. John Calvin, Introduction to Olievatan's translation of the New Testament.

256. Ibid., p. 132.

257. Ibid., pp. 131–32.

258. Ibid., p. 132.

259. Fyodor Dostoevsky, *The Brothers Karamazov*, chapter 34. The character who says these words, Ivan Karamazov, rejects even this possibility, but that does not mean that Dostoevsky himself does not believe this eloquent statement. I think it should also be stated that Dostoevsky does not say here it will be possible to justify the evil itself. Evil may be used by God to bring about even greater good than if it had not occurred, but it nonetheless remains evil, and therefore inexcusable and unjustifiable in itself.

CHAPTER 8—THE REASON FOR SUFFERING

260. Haidt, *Happiness Hypothesis*, p. 136.

261. Ibid.

262. Ibid., p. 137.

263. Ibid., p. 138.

264. Ibid.

265. Ibid., p. 140.

266. Robert A. Emmons, *The Psychology of Ultimate Concerns: Motivation and Spirituality in Personality* (Guilford, 1999), and "Personal Goals, Life Meaning, and Virtue," in *Flourishing: Positive Psychology and the Life Well Lived,* eds. Corey L. M. Keyes and Jonathan Haidt (APA, 2003), pp. 105–28. Cited in Haidt, *Happiness Hypothesis*, p. 143.

267. Haidt, *Happiness Hypothesis*, p. 145.

268. Ibid.

269. Ibid., p. 141.

270. C. S. Lewis, *Reflections on the Psalms* (Harcourt, 1958), p. 90.

271. Ibid., p. 92.

272. J. R. R. Tolkien, *The Letters of J. R. R. Tolkien,* ed. Humphrey Carpenter (1981), letter #121. Quoted at http://tolkien.cro.net/rings/sauron.html.

273. Jonathan Edwards, *The Miscellanies* [entry nos. a–z, aa–zz, 1–500], *The Works of Jonathan Edwards*, Volume 13. Edited by Thomas A. Schafer (New Haven: Yale University Press, 1994), no. 448, p. 495.

274. Elisabeth Elliot, *No Graven Image* (Avon Books, 1966).
275. Ibid., p. 158.
276. Ibid., p. 164.
277. Ibid., p. 165.
278. Ibid., p. 174.
279. Ibid., p. 175.
280. Ibid.
281. Elisabeth Elliot, *These Strange Ashes* (Harper, 1975), p. 109.
282. Ibid., pp. 130–32.
283. The account of this is found in Elisabeth Elliot, *Through the Gates of Splendor* (2nd ed.; Hendrickson, 2010).
284. Ibid., p. 268.
285. Elisabeth Elliot, "The Glory of God's Will," in *Declare His Glory among the Nations,* ed. David Howard (Inter-Varsity Press, 1977), p. 133.
286. Rittgers, *Reformation of Suffering,* p. 47.
287. Cindy Stauffer, "Film Depicting Nickel Mines Shootings Questioned," Lancaster Online, http://lancasteronline.com/article/local/249326_Film-depicting-Nickel-Mines-shootings-questioned.html.
288. Donald B. Kraybill, Steven M. Nolt, and David L. Weaver-Zercher, *Amish Grace: How Forgiveness Transcended Tragedy* (Jossey-Bass, 2010).
289. Ibid., p. 183.
290. Ibid., p. 176–77.
291. Ibid., p. 181.
292. This story, and much of what Joni learned in the first years after her accident, are told in a fine book on suffering, Joni Eareckson Tada and Steve Estes, *A Step Further* (Zondervan, 1978). The chapter on Denise Walters is "When Nobody's Watching," pp. 56–62.
293. Ibid., p. 59.
294. Ibid., p. 61.
295. Ibid., p. 62.

CHAPTER 9—LEARNING TO WALK

296. Quoted in Haidt, *Happiness Hypothesis,* p. 152.
297. Lewis, *Mere Christianity,* p. 134 (chap. 10, "Hope").
298. Davies, *Importance of Suffering,* p. 133.
299. Ibid., p. 130.

300. Ibid. Emphasis is the author's.

301. Ibid., p. 131.

302. Ibid., pp. 133–34.

303. Haidt, *Happiness Hypothesis*, p. 146.

304. Ibid., pp. 146–47.

305. John Newton, *The Letters of John Newton* (Banner of Truth, 1960), p. 180.

306. Quoted in C. S. Lewis, "Epigraph," *The Problem of Pain* (HarperOne, 2001), p. viii.

307. See D. Martin Lloyd-Jones, *Spiritual Depression: Its Causes and Cure* (Eerdmans, 1965), pp. 247–59 (chap. 18, "In God's Gymnasium").

308. Michael Horton, *A Place for Weakness* (Zondervan, 2006), p. 19.

309. Simone Weil, *Waiting for God* (Harper, 2009), p. 70.

310. Plantinga, *God, Freedom, and Evil*, pp. 63–64.

311. John S. Feinberg, "A Journey in Suffering: Personal Reflections on the Religious Problem of Evil," in *Suffering and Goodness*, eds. Morgan and Peterson, p. 214.

312. Ibid., p. 215.

313. Ibid., p. 217.

314. Ibid., p. 218.

315. Ibid., p. 219.

316. Ibid.

317. Carson, *How Long, O Lord?*, pp. 18, 20.

318. Ibid., p. 20.

CHAPTER 10—THE VARIETIES OF SUFFERING

319. I am aware that Jonah and David were not New Testament believers in Jesus Christ, and so Paul's claims about believers "in Christ" cannot be applied directly to them. The comparison of the status of Old Testament Jewish believers and New Testament Christians is a complex subject. But for our purposes, we need to ask ourselves if we as believers today are punished for our sins by God in suffering. The best answer—which does justice to what the Bible says—is that, strictly speaking, we are not being given the just penalty for our sins. Jesus took that. But can God bring bad things into our lives as "corrective discipline" the way a parent brings painful consequences into a child's life to teach him or her to obey? The Bible says yes, he does.

320. Weil, *Waiting for God*, pp. 67ff.

321. Ibid., pp. 68, 70.

322. Ibid., p. 68.

323. Solomon, *Far From the Tree*.

324. Weil, *Waiting for God*, p. 69.

325. J. R. R. Tolkien, *The Lord of the Rings: The Two Towers* (Houghton Mifflin, 2004), p. 914.

326. Ibid., p. 70.

327. Ibid.

328. Ibid., p. 71.

329. D. A. Carson, *For the Love of God: A Daily Companion for Discovering the Treasures of God's Word*, vol. 2 (Crossway, 1999), February 17 reading. Free online at http://s3.amazonaws.com/tgc-documents/carson/1999_for_the_love_of_God.pdf.

330. Feinberg, "Journey in Suffering," p. 222.

331. Ibid., pp. 223–24.

332. Ibid., p. 224.

333. John Feinberg relates that one of his students and his wife had an infant who died. Someone said to them, in all sincerity, "You know, it's probably a good thing your son died. . . . Maybe he would have been a drug addict. . . . God knows these things in advance and he was probably saving you from those problems." Feinberg, "Journey in Suffering," p. 221.

Chapter 11—Walking

334. While Matthew Bridges is given credit for most of the hymn "Crown Him with Many Crowns" from his work *The Passion of Jesus*, 1852, the verse quoted, verse 3, is attributed to Godfrey Thring, *Hymns and Sacred Lyrics*, 1874. Public domain.

335. Karen H. Jobes, *1 Peter*, Baker Exegetical Commentary on the New Testament (Baker, 2005), p. 94.

336. J. Alec Motyer, *The Prophecy of Isaiah: An Introduction and Commentary* (Inter-Varsity Press, 1993), p. 331.

337. "Twelve of the forty-one New Testament occurrences of the verb [to suffer] come in this brief letter, together with four of the sixteen occurrences of the noun form. . . . These figures indicate clearly that suffering is a major theme in 1 Peter." I. Howard Marshall, *1 Peter*, The IVP New Testament Commentary Series (Inter-Varsity Press, 1991), p. 89n.

338. Frederick W. Danker and Walter Bauer, *A Greek-English Lexicon of the New Testament and Other Early Christian Literature* (3rd ed.; University of Chicago Press, 2000), p. 793.

339. Marshall, *1 Peter*, p. 42.

340. Peter's statement that gold "perishes even though refined by fire" does not mean he believes that fire can destroy gold. It can melt it but not destroy it. Most commentators believe Peter is here contrasting gold with faith. He is "simply drawing a contrast between faith and gold as respectively lasting and not lasting into the next world." Marshall, *1 Peter,* p. 41n.

341. Many commentators see the story of Daniel 3 to be a "midrash" or commentary on Isaiah 43:2. See John E. Goldingay, *Daniel,* Word Biblical Commentary, vol. 30 (Word, 1998), p. 68.

342. J. Alec Motyer, *The Message of Exodus: The Bible Speaks Today* (Inter-Varsity Press, 2005), p. 51.

343. Iain M. Duguid, *Daniel,* Reformed Expository Commentary (P&R, 2008), p. 58.

CHAPTER 12—WEEPING

344. Tremper Longman III, *How to Read the Psalms* (Inter-Varsity Press, 1988), p. 26.

345. Rittgers, *Reformation of Suffering,* p. 258.

346. Richard Sibbes, *The Bruised Reed and Smoking Flax,* in *Works,* vol. 1 (Banner of Truth, 2001).

347. Joseph Bayly, *The View from a Hearse* (Cook, 1969), pp. 40–41.

348. Derek Kidner, *Psalms 73–150: A Commentary on Books III–V of the Psalms* (Inter-Varsity Press, 1973), p. 316.

349. Martin Marty, *A Cry of Absence: Reflections for the Winter of the Heart* (Harper, 1983), p. 68.

350. Derek Kidner, *Psalms 1–72: A Commentary on Books I–II of the Psalms* (Inter-Varsity Press, 1973), p. 157. This comment comes at the end of his commentary on Psalm 39, the other psalm in the Psalter that also ends without an expression of hope.

351. Tolkien, *The Lord of the Rings,* Houghton Mifflin, one volume edition, 1994, p. 913.

352. Kidner, *Psalms 73–150,* p. 317.

353. Quoted in Elisabeth Elliot, *Keep a Quiet Heart* (Servant, 1995), p. 73.

354. Michael Wilcock, *The Message of Psalms 73–150: Songs for the People of God* (Inter-Varsity Press, 2001), p. 65.

355. Commentators have noted a certain ambiguity in Peter's verbs—they can be taken as both present indicatives as well as present imperatives. This is why the translators convey the verb tenses with some difficulty—"*You may have had to suffer grief.*" Many see the ambiguity as deliberate and skillful. It means that those who are already simultaneously rejoicing and grieving can read Peter as commending them, and those who are not yet doing this can read Peter as directing and urging them to do so. See Marshall, *1 Peter*, p. 93.

356. Lloyd-Jones, *Spiritual Depression*, pp. 220–21.

CHAPTER 13—TRUSTING

357. Quoted in Preface to *These Strange Ashes* (Revell, 1982), p. 7.

358. Kidner, *Genesis*, p. 199.

359. Ibid., p. 205.

360. Elliot, "Glory of God's Will," p. 130.

361. Kidner, *Genesis*, p. 181.

362. Newton, *Letters*, pp. 179–80.

363. Kidner, *Genesis*, p. 207.

CHAPTER 14—PRAYING

364. Quoted in Peter Kreeft, *Three Philosophies of Life* (Ignatius Press, 1989), p. 61, "Job: Life as Suffering."

365. Ibid.

366. "Job stands far above its nearest competitors, in the coherence of its sustained treatment of the theme of human misery, in the scope of its many-sided examination of the problem . . . in the heights of its lyrical poetry, in its dramatic impact, and in the intellectual integrity with which it faces the 'unintelligible burden' of human existence. In all this Job stands alone. Nothing . . . has risen to the same heights. Comparison only serves to enhance the solitary greatness of the book of Job." Francis I. Anderson, *Job: An Introduction and Commentary* (Inter-Varsity Press, 1976), p. 32.

367. Anderson, *Job*, p. 123.

368. Ibid., p. 124.

369. Ibid., p. 125.
370. Gerald H. Wilson, *Job*, New International Biblical Commentary (Hendrickson, 2007), p. 422.
371. Anderson, *Job*, p. 270, n2, quoted from George Bernard Shaw's *The Adventures of the Black Girl in Her Search for God*, 1932, pp. 12, 19.
372. Wilson, *Job*, p. 423.
373. Anderson, *Job*, p. 270, n1.
374. Ibid., p. 287.
375. Ibid., pp. 287–88. See also Thomas Nagel's review of John Gray's book *The Silence of Animals* in *The New York Times Book Review*. Gray charges that western secular society believes it can rid the world of evil through human self-improvement, without God, but that many such grandiose schemes have led to greater evil. Nagel admits that "It is true that we are faced with a secular version of the problem of evil: how can we expect beings capable of behaving so badly to design and sustain a system that will lead them to be good? Gray is right that some of the attempted solutions to this problem have been catastrophic. . . ." Thomas Nagel, "Pecking Order," *The New York Times Book Review*, July 7, 2013, p. 10.
376. Elisabeth Elliot, "Epilogue II," in *Through the Gates of Splendor* (40th Anniversary ed.; Tyndale, 1996), p. 267.
377. Lloyd-Jones, *Spiritual Depression*, pp. 20–21.
378. John White, *The Masks of Melancholy: A Christian Physician Looks at Depression & Suicide* (1982). Quote from audio.
379. Anderson, *Job*, p. 267.
380. Wilson, *Job*, p. 455.
381. Anderson, *Job*, p. 73.

CHAPTER 15—THINKING, THANKING, LOVING

382. Quoted in C. S. Lewis, "Epigraph," *The Problem of Pain* (HarperOne, 2001), p. viii.
383. "But what Paul says here is much less clear than the English translations would lead one to believe. The impression given is that he is calling on them one final time to 'give their minds' to nobler things. That may be true in one sense, but the language and grammar suggest something slightly different. The verb ordinarily means to 'reckon' in the sense of 'take into account,' rather than simply to 'think about.' This suggests that Paul is telling

them not so much to 'think high thoughts' as to 'take into account' the good they have long known from their own past, as long as it is conformable to Christ." G. D. Fee *Paul's Letter to the Philippians*. The New International Commentary on the New Testament (Eerdmans, 1995), pp. 415–16.

384. There are innumerable examples that could be given of the bleakness of the secular view of things. Charles Darwin wrote: "A [person] who has no assured and ever present belief in the existence of a personal God or of future existence with retribution and reward, can have for his rule of life, as far as I can see, only to follow those impulses and instincts which are the strongest or which seem to him the best ones" (Charles Darwin, *Evolutionary Writings*, edited by James A. Secord, p. 396. See books.google.com.). Oliver Wendell Holmes Jr., the great Supreme Court Justice, and a formidable intellectual in the early twentieth century, once wrote this in his personal correspondence to a friend: "There is no reason for attributing to a man a significance different in kind from that which belongs to a baboon or a grain of sand. . . . The world has produced the rattlesnake as well as me; but I kill it if I get a chance . . . and the only reason is because it is congruous to the world I want, the world everyone is trying to make according to one's own power." (Paraphrased from Oliver Wendell Holmes Jr., *The Essential Holmes*, edited and with an introduction by Richard A. Posner, pp. 108, 114. See books.google.com.) Historian Carl L. Becker famously said that, from a strictly scientific viewpoint, human beings must be viewed as "little more than a chance deposit on the surface of the world, carelessly thrown up between two ice ages by the same forces that rust iron and ripen corn." (Quoted in Steven D. Smith, *Disenchantment*, p. 179.) British philosopher John N. Gray writes scathingly about the modern secular myth that human beings have any unique value or meaning in life, or that there is any hope that we are getting better or that history is going somewhere. Human beings have no more value than animals or plants. "Human uniqueness is a myth inherited from religion, which humanists have recycled into science," he writes. "Evolution has no end-point or direction, so if the development of society is an evolutionary process it is one that is going nowhere." Gray, *The Silence of Animals*, p. 78.

385. Jonathan Edwards, "Christian Happiness," in *Works of Jonathan Edwards: Sermons and Discourses 1720–1723*, vol. 10, ed. Wilson H. Kimnach (Yale University Press, 1992), p. 297.

386. This word has to do primarily with what people consider "lovable," in the sense of having a friendly disposition toward. The NJB catches the sense well by translating, "everything that we love." Fee, *Paul's Letter to the Philippians,* p. 418.
387. How Augustine overthrew the "Eudaimonism"—the idea that the highest source of happiness is in one's virtue—is told in chapters 7 and 8 of Wolterstorff, *Justice.* The phrase "Only Love of the Immutable Can Bring Tranquility" is a summary of Augustine's teaching used as a heading for chapter 8, p. 180.
388. Saint Augustine, *Confessions,* Book IV, 11.
389. C. S. Lewis, *The Four Loves* (Harcourt, 1988), p. 122.
390. Kidner, *Psalms 1–72,* p. 55.
391. See William L. Lane, *The Gospel of Mark,* The New International Commentary on the New Testament (Eerdmans, 1974), pp. 573–74.
392. Horatio Spafford, "It Is Well with My Soul," 1873 hymn.

Chapter 16—Hoping

393. Howard Thurman, *A Strange Freedom: The Best of Howard Thurman on Religious Experience and Public Life,* eds. Walter Earl Fluker and Catherine Tumber (Beacon Press, 1998), p. 71.
394. Ibid., p. 79.
395. There are numerous versions of this story, each somewhat different. See a typical one at http://www.family-times.net/illustration/Troubled/200318.
396. C. S. Lewis, "The Weight of Glory." Found at https://docs.google.com/viewer?url=http%3A%2F%2Fwww.verber.com%2Fmark%2Fxian%2Fweight-of-glory.pdf, p. 8.

Epilogue

397. In this book we concentrated on those strategies—trusting, self-communing, reordering loves, etc.—that all varieties of suffering require. We did not, however, look at two spiritual skills that are, in some cases, very necessary. The first skill is receiving forgiveness from God through repentance and reconciliation with him. Often suffering reveals our own personal failures and we are filled with shame. It is critical to relieve that guilt and shame by receiving grace from God. On the other hand, we often need the skill of granting

forgiveness to others. Many instances of adversity come from betrayals by others. In those cases, the danger is not to be eaten with guilt but with anger. It is critical to relieve anger by giving grace, but forgiving. In this volume, we did not treat either of these practices. Other books that can help are the following. J. R. W. Stott, *Confess Your Sins: The Way of Reconciliation* (Westminster, 1965); Dan Hamilton, *Forgiveness* (Inter-Varsity Press, 1980); Judith Gundry-Volf and Miroslav Volf, *A Spacious Heart: Essays on Identity and Belonging* (Trinity Press, 1997). And see Timothy Keller and Kathy Keller, *The Meaning of Marriage: Facing the Complexities of Commitment with the Wisdom of God* (Dutton, 2011), pp. 159–69.

About the Author

Timothy Keller was born and raised in Pennsylvania and educated at Bucknell University, Gordon-Conwell Theological Seminary, and Westminster Theological Seminary. He was first a pastor in Hopewell, Virginia. In 1989 he started Redeemer Presbyterian Church in New York City, with his wife, Kathy, and their three sons. Today, Redeemer has more than five thousand regular Sunday attendees and has helped to start more than two hundred and fifty new churches around the world. Also the author of *Every Good Endeavor*, *The Meaning of Marriage*, *Generous Justice*, *Counterfeit Gods*, *The Prodigal God*, *Jesus the King*, and *The Reason for God*, Timothy Keller lives in New York City with his family.

REDEEMER

The Redeemer imprint is dedicated to books that address pressing spiritual and social issues of the day in a way that speaks to both the core Christian audience and to seekers and skeptics alike. The mission for the Redeemer imprint is to bring the power of the Christian gospel to every part of life. The name comes from Redeemer Presbyterian Church in New York City, which Tim Keller started in 1989 with his wife, Kathy, and their three sons. Redeemer has begun a movement of contextualized urban ministry, thoughtful preaching, and church planting across America and throughout major world cities.